POINTS OF VIEW

POINTS OF VIEW

A. W. MOORE

CLARENDON PRESS · OXFORD
1997

Oxford University Press, Great Clarendon Street, Oxford OX2 6DP

Oxford New York
Athens Auckland Bangkok Bogota Bombay
Buenos Aires Calcutta Cape Town Dar es Salaam
Delhi Florence Hong Kong Istanbul Karachi
Kuala Lumpur Madras Madrid Melbourne
Mexico City Nairobi Paris Singapore
Taipei Tokyo Toronto
and associated companies in
Berlin Ibadan

Oxford is a trade mark of Oxford University Press

Published in the United States by
Oxford University Press Inc., New York

British Library Cataloguing in Publication Data
Data available

Library of Congress Cataloging-in-Publication Data
Data available

ISBN 0–19–823692–1

1 3 5 7 9 10 8 6 4 2

Typeset by Invisible Ink
Printed in Great Britain
on acid-free paper by
Biddles Ltd, Guildford and King's Lynn

For Christine

PREFACE

I SHOULD like to thank the Principal and Fellows of St. Hugh's College Oxford and the General Board of Oxford University for granting me leave of absence for the academic year 1994–5, during which I carried out the bulk of the work on this book. In the second term of that year I held a Visiting Fellowship at the Australian National University. I should like to thank all those responsible for making my stay there so enjoyable and so productive. Many other people have helped me, more or less directly, with the writing of this book. Peter Momtchiloff, Philosophy Editor at Oxford University Press, has provided enthusiastic support. Angela Blackburn, who produced and copy-edited the book, has improved the text in all sorts of ways. Pamela Anderson, Uri Henig, Mark Sacks, Leslie Stevenson, Peter Sullivan, Alan Thomas, Bernard Williams, Felizitas Zigan, and two anonymous referees for Oxford University Press have all either commented on earlier drafts of the book, prompting important changes, or had a significant influence of some other kind on the book. Especial thanks are due to Naomi Eilan, Carolyn Price, and Garrett Thomson, all three of whom have been a source of invaluable encouragement and detailed critical advice. Philip Turetzky's influence on my philosophical thinking remains greater than that of anyone else, though ironically he has some of the deepest reservations about my ideas, especially about what he would call the "romantic vitalism" of the last three chapters. It will not surprise me if, in time, I have these reservations too.

A. W. Moore

CONTENTS

The nature of the monad is representative, and consequently nothing can limit it to representing a part of things only, although it is true that its representation is confused as regards the detail of the whole universe and can only be distinct as regards a small part of things; that is to say as regards those which are either the nearest or the largest in relation to each of the monads; otherwise each monad would be a divinity. It is not in the object, but in the modification of the knowledge of the object, that monads are limited. In a confused way they all go towards the infinite, towards the whole; but they are limited and distinguished from one another by the degrees of their distinct perceptions.

(G. W. Leibniz)

Man reckons with immortality, and forgets to reckon with death.

(Milan Kundera)

And the Lord God said, Behold, the man is become as one of us, to know good and evil: and now, lest he put forth his hand, and take also of the tree of life, and eat, and live for ever: Therefore the Lord God sent him forth from the garden of Eden, to till the ground from whence he was taken.

(Genesis 3: 22–3)

ANALYTICAL TABLE OF CONTENTS

CHAPTER ONE: *"Are absolute representations possible?" This question, which is a question about the possibility of detached thought about the world, grounds the whole enquiry. A "representation" is anything that is either true or false. An "absolute" representation is a representation that is not from any point of view. A "perspectival" representation—the complementary notion—is a representation that is from some point of view. These ideas are defined in terms of the ways in which representations can be integrated with one another.*

CHAPTER TWO: *What makes the question significant is its bearing on a range of traditional philosophical concerns: the limits of objectivity; the ambitions of science; relativism; the way in which our thoughts relate to reality; and our aspiration to transcend our own finitude.*

CHAPTER THREE: *There is an illusion associated with the question, which must be dispelled before the question can be properly addressed. The illusion is that there are perspectival features of reality which figure in perspectival facts; and that what makes (some) true perspectival representations true is the obtaining of such facts. This is incoherent. The absolute/perspectival distinction applies exclusively to representations, not to what is represented.*

CHAPTER FOUR: *The answer to the question is yes. This is established by "the Basic Argument", an embellishment of an argument due to Williams. The Basic Argument has as one of its premises "the Basic Assumption". This is an assumption which involves a cluster of interrelated ideas about the unity, substantiality, and autonomy of reality, and which is expressed as follows: 'Representations are representations of what is there anyway.'*

CHAPTER FIVE: *Many arguments have been advanced for answering the question negatively. Most of these can be countered—but not those in which the Basic Assumption is rejected. In their case, we seem to reach an*

impasse. However, there is a view which affords the prospect of a reconcil-
iation. This view is a species of "transcendental idealism", according to
which all our representations are from a "transcendent" point of view. It
affords the prospect of reconciliation by distinguishing between levels. At a
transcendent level, the Basic Assumption is rejected and the question is
answered negatively. At a non-transcendent level, the Basic Assumption is
retained and the question is answered affirmatively (in accord with the
Basic Argument). If the Basic Argument is not simply to be repudiated,
then considerations in favour of answering the question negatively even-
tually become considerations in favour of this radical view; radical,
because at the level at which the question is answered negatively, our rep-
resentations are soaked in perspective of a deep and extraordinary kind.

CHAPTER SIX: *Both Kant and, in his later work, Wittgenstein (the*
latter in spite of himself) indicate the possibility of such a response to the
Basic Argument. However, transcendental idealism is incoherent.
Specifically, it is self-stultifying. It does not provide an alternative to unre-
generate endorsement of the Basic Argument after all.

CHAPTER SEVEN: *But it does retain its appeal, even when it has been*
exposed. This creates a need for diagnosis. Transcendental idealists them-
selves may say that there is nothing wrong with the doctrine itself, but only
with the attempt to state it; that transcendental idealism is inexpressibly
true. This too, however, is incoherent. A related but importantly different
proposal, deriving from Wittgenstein's earlier work, is this. While we can-
not coherently state that transcendental idealism is true, we are shown
that it is, where 'A is shown that x' is defined as '(i) A has ineffable know-
ledge, and (ii) when an attempt is made to put that knowledge into words,
the result is: x'. Provided that we can make sense of (i) and (ii), this pro-
posal has the threefold merit of: avoiding self-stultification; being compat-
ible with the incoherence of transcendental idealism; and providing an
account of transcendental idealism's appeal.

CHAPTER EIGHT: *We can make sense of (i). Ineffable knowledge is a*
kind of practical knowledge, distinguished by the fact that it has nothing
to answer to. Prime examples of ineffable knowledge are certain states of
understanding.

CHAPTER NINE: *We can make sense of (ii). This requires a critique of*
nonsense, since what replaces 'x' in the schema must be nonsense. Because

our ineffable knowledge is a mark of our finitude, and because we have a shared aspiration to transcend our finitude, we have a shared temptation to put our ineffable knowledge into words. This in turn gives us a shared sense of when a piece of nonsense is "apt" to replace 'x' in the schema, where "aptness" is a quasi-aesthetic attribute, such as might occur in poetics. This, finally, is enough for instances of the schema to be true or false. In particular, both the following instances are true: 'We are shown that all our representations are from a transcendent point of view', 'We are shown that transcendental idealism is true.'

INTERLUDE

CHAPTER TEN: *Once these ideas are in place, further examples of things we are shown are forthcoming. These concern: the nature and identity of persons; the narrative unity of an individual life; scepticism; the subject matter of mathematics (or more specifically, of set theory); and the doctrine that Dummett calls anti-realism.*

CHAPTER ELEVEN: *Three principles underlie these ideas: first, that we are finite; secondly, that we are conscious of ourselves as finite; and thirdly, that we aspire to be infinite. The third of these also explains the value of certain things. That is, it explains their value for us. These things are not of value tout court. Nothing is. However, another thing we are shown is that they are of value tout court. Our aspiration to be infinite, precisely in determining that these things are of value for us, leads to our being shown this. (It also leads to our being shown that value tout court has an absoluteness that locates it at the transcendent level.) The question arises, finally, what value our aspiration to be infinite itself has. Exploration of this question indicates ways in which our ineffable knowledge stands in relation to God.*

BIBLIOGRAPHIES: Each chapter concludes with a short annotated bibliography of further relevant reading. These bibliographies do not include material already covered by the footnotes for their respective chapters. All items referred to in the bibliographies and footnotes are assembled in the main bibliography at the end of the book, together with publication details.

GLOSSARY: I have found it necessary to introduce my own terminology at various points in the book. Definitions of the terms I use most frequently are given in a glossary at the end.

CHAPTER ONE

Some of our descriptions of the world are more local, or perspectival, or anthropocentric, than others . . . I can say of the moon that it is a body of a certain shape with irregularities on its surface some of which, when illuminated by the sun, reflect more light than others. I can say that when so illuminated, it looks like a man's face. I can say that it looks like your Uncle Henry, indeed . . . that it looks amusingly, or strangely, or evocatively like him. These are all human descriptions of the same thing, but the understandings they call upon are increasingly parochial. On a larger scale, when Pascal said of the spaces of the universe that they were immense, that they were silent, and that they were terrifying, he spoke from an increasingly local perspective.

(Bernard Williams)

Introduction.

§ 1: The general idea of a point of view is introduced, through a range of examples.

§ 2: The idea of a representation is introduced. It is with respect to representations that the distinction is drawn between being from a point of view (being perspectival) and being from no point of view (being absolute).

§ 3: Three definitions of what this distinction comes to are considered. The first is rejected. The second is endorsed, but then set aside on the grounds that it relies on a notion of self-consciousness that is not yet clear enough for the definition to be suitable for our purposes. The third definition is adopted, though with the caveat that it will, in Chapter Five, be seen to involve a circularity. (By then, we shall be in a position to accept the circularity with equanimity.)

§ 4: Some related concepts are introduced, and an argument for the impossibility of absolute representations is sketched.

IS IT ever possible to think about the world with complete detachment?

I shall argue in Chapter Four that it is. Before that, I want to use this chapter to clarify the question, Chapter Two to consider its importance, and Chapter Three to dispel a certain illusion associated with it.

It is one of the great philosophical questions. Even so, I am not posing it merely for its own sake. Answering the question, or attempting to answer it, is as much a means for me as an end. In Chapter Five onwards, as I work through various objections to my position and clarify what I say in the first four chapters, I shall turn increasingly to other issues.

1

We often try to think as objectively as possible about the world around us, and to express ourselves accordingly. Whether we are musing in general terms about what kind of world it is, or assessing a particular situation, we try to ensure that what we think and what we say are not coloured by our own feelings, concerns, or special involvement with our subject matter. Such detachment is even sometimes required of us, for example if we are compiling an official report or giving evidence in a court of law. Someone might deliberately refrain from describing an event as amusing, say, because such a description would be an expression of his or her own particular sense of humour.

Science acts as a paradigm here. What a scientific theory is supposed to be is, precisely, a completely objective account of what the world is like and how it works. This is why many people regard science with a kind of reverence. They think that it contains pure, unadulterated truth.

Not that we always aim at objectivity. Sometimes it would be quite inappropriate to do so. If you are writing a poem or a love letter, or rallying support for a political cause, you may express yourself in a way that betrays your deepest commitments, aspirations, and values. You need not hold back from describing a state of affairs as amusing, or intolerable, just because such a description is conditioned by your attitude to it. On the contrary, you may describe it in that way precisely in order to convey that attitude. Your description may reveal, and may be intended to reveal, as much about you as about what you are describing.

Does this mean that you are not (really) trying to express the truth? It is tempting to think that it must mean that. It is tempting to think that truth and objectivity are the same thing, or at least inseparable, so that if you are not trying to say objectively how things are, then you are not really trying to say how they are at all. An extreme version of this view is that the only authentic way of saying how things are is in scientific terms, and that science is the sole repository of truth.

But this view is quite unwarranted. A perfectly legitimate and very important way of saying how things are is from a particular point of deep involvement or engagement with them, in a way that it is not objective. Much of our understanding of the world, and of our own position in it, is informed by how it appears from such points of involvement—as beautiful, dreadful, bewildering, or frightening, say. Our understanding of death, for example, is not purely biological. It is conditioned by our own mortality, our own point of involvement with death. Each of us will die, each of us is affected by the deaths of others, and each of us understands death from that perspective. When it comes to giving voice to such understanding, the relevant paradigm will not be the scientific formula but the song, the prayer, the requiem.

There are ways of expressing the truth that are not objective, then. My opening question about detachment is not a question about whether it is possible to attain the truth. It is a question that arises granted that possibility. It is a question about whether it is possible to attain a certain kind of truth.

To see more clearly what is at stake here we need to broaden the discussion. Objectivity is merely one example of the kind of detachment that concerns me. There are many ways in which our thinking about the world can depend on how and where we are situated.

Suppose somebody says, 'It is snowing,' and somebody else says, 'It has stopped snowing.' There need be no conflict. They may be speaking in different places. It is possible that what each of them says is true. This unremarkable fact illustrates the way in which the content of a true judgement can depend quite literally on its location. To grasp that content it is not enough to know what *type* of judgement it is, by which I mean, in this case, it is not enough to understand the English sentence that has been used. One must also know *where* the judgement has been made. I say 'where', and I talk about a literal sense of location, but in fact even this banal example illustrates how location can also be relevant in a metaphorical (non-spatial) sense. For it matters also *when* the judgement is made, in other words what its temporal location is. Someone can comment truly, 'It is snowing,' and, without moving but simply by waiting long enough, comment, again truly, 'It has stopped snowing.' There are other obvious ways of extending the metaphorical reach of the term 'location'. You may say, 'This box is light enough to lift,' while I say, referring to the same box, 'It is too heavy to lift.' Again there is no conflict. Each of us may have spoken truly, you for your part and I for mine.

It is when the idea of a location is allowed to extend yet further that we confront the concept of objectivity. An *objective* judgement is a judgement whose content does not depend on what I have been calling a 'point of involvement'. Points of involvement are locations, in this extended sense. (But not all locations are points of involvement. Merely spatial or temporal locations are not. Objectivity, as I said, is only one example of the kind of detachment that concerns me.) What it comes to is this. An objective judgement is a judgement whose content does not depend, peculiarly, on any of the concerns, interests, or values of whoever makes it, including any that are shared presuppositions of the context.

Once we have the more banal examples of location-dependence in mind, we can see more easily, perhaps, why 'objective truth' is not a pleonasm. Imagine a judgement of beauty made in a particular historical and cultural context. For instance, imagine a judgement about a child's physical beauty made in a sixteenth-century European setting, or a judgement about the beauty of a piece of classical Chinese music made by some suitable initiate. There is no reason why such a judgement should not be true. Whoever makes it may be revealing insight which others lack. This insight may have been achieved as a result of careful training, or special sensitivity, or both. The person may even be able to amplify on the judgement in such a way as to awaken similar sensitivity in others, directing their attention to pertinent features of the child or piece of music in question so that they too can see that the judgement is true. Even so, the judgement is not objective. Its content is conditioned by the relevant backcloth of shared cultural interests and sensibilities. There may be no possibility, at a later time or in a different culture, of making a judgement to the same effect about the same child or the same piece of music; certainly not in the same way and with the same claim to truth. The original judgement is from a position of (cultural) involvement with what is being judged.

For another example, imagine someone's lament that her marriage has become a burden. We can suppose that she is justified in saying this even though the marriage has not become a burden for her husband. For him it has opened up possibilities without which he could now scarcely function. There is truth in his wife's lament, in part, because of the point of involvement from which it is made.

The idea of a location can be extended in other directions too. Simple colour ascriptions provide one important example, according to a well-known argument. The argument runs as follows. Consider colour-blindness. Some observers can make colour discriminations that others cannot. The latter are said to be deficient in this respect. But we can imagine something analogous where there is no question of deficiency. Suppose, for instance, that there are aliens who are so physiologically constituted that a particular substance looks red to them though it looks green to all normal-sighted human beings: the substance affects their visual apparatus differently from ours, though they otherwise make the same discriminations as we do. Imagine now that one of these aliens classifies the substance as red while one of us classifies it as green. There need no more be a conflict than in the case where one person remarks, 'It is snowing,' and another remarks, 'It has stopped snowing,' or indeed in the case where an alien says that our sun is thousands of light-years away and one of us says that it is approximately 93 million miles away. Both classifications may be correct, the one because of its alien location, the other because of its human location. And although this talk of aliens is science fiction, the very fact that it is intelligible means that our ordinary ascriptions of colour must already be conditioned by their location. For how could whether or not they are depend on whether or not such aliens do in fact exist? Thus when I say, 'Grass is green,' I am producing a correct account of how things are from that same human perspective.

—*"But surely colour concepts are more responsive to independent checks than this argument allows. Suppose we measure the relevant wave-*

*lengths. And suppose that these are in line with the alien classification. Do
we not then count as deficient? Are we not forced to say that the substance,
though it looks green to us because of some physiological quirk, is really
red?"*——

Perhaps we are forced to say this. Even so, the argument serves
to remind us of how our colour concepts are responsive, at some
fundamental level, to the look of things. Ordinary uses of 'green'
may not involve a suppressed relativization ('green for humans').
But beings whose visual apparatus differed radically from ours, or
who had no visual apparatus at all, would be unable to grasp our
colour concepts. Even if they could measure wavelengths, and even
if they could tell, indirectly, that something was green, they would
still not understand this in the way that we do. They might well not
be able to see the point of our classifications. To that extent our use
of colour concepts is dependent on its location. There is still a sense
in which, when I say, 'Grass is green,' I am producing a correct
account of how things are from a human perspective.

Once the idea of a location has been extended like this, we may
wonder whether *all* the concepts we use in characterizing the world
are location-dependent, perhaps in similar ways, perhaps in ways
that would unsettle us, perhaps even in ways that we are incapable
of recognizing. This possibility is brought closer by the fact that,
even when the idea of a location is comparatively restricted, loca-
tion-*dependence* can take unexpected forms. For instance, frames of
reference, as understood in relativity theory, are locations of a spatio-temporal kind, but it took the genius of Einstein to recognize
that judgements of simultaneity depend on them: events that are
simultaneous relative to one frame of reference may not be simultaneous relative to another. It ought at least to be clearer now how
much force there is in my opening question about detachment.
Detachment, we now see, does not come cheaply.

I shall draw this part of the discussion to a close by invoking the
idea of a *point of view*. By a point of view I shall mean a location in
the broadest possible sense. Hence points of view include points in
space, points in time, frames of reference, historical and cultural
contexts, different roles in personal relationships, points of involvement of other kinds, and the sensory apparatuses of different
species. My question, in these terms, is whether there can be
thought about the world that is not from any point of view.

2

At this stage in the discussion there are two principal problems. First, now that the idea of a location is being stretched to its limit in the idea of a point of view, something needs to be said to keep it in check. Otherwise the question will vacuously receive the answer no. (Sidgwick once talked about "the point of view of the Universe".[1] Clearly there cannot be any coherent thought which is not at least from *that*.) The sheer range of examples given is part of this first problem. The second problem is that the idea of location-dependence, that is, the idea of what it is for something to be *from* a point of view, is still not sufficiently clear.

Let us call that which is from a point of view 'perspectival', and that which is from no point of view 'absolute'. If we can give a satisfactory account of what it is for something to be perspectival (or absolute—it does not matter which), then we shall have solved both problems at once.

The 'something' in that last sentence indicates our first task: to specify the domain over which the two terms 'perspectival' and 'absolute' are defined. So far I have been vague about this. I have treated thought, understanding, theories, judgements, expressions of the truth, and other things as if they were candidates for being perspectival or absolute. These do, however, have something in common. This common element can be encapsulated in the idea of a *representation*. By a representation I shall mean anything which has content—that things are thus and so—and which, because of its content, is true or false. Whenever we think about how things are, or say how they are, or reveal that we take them to be a certain way, whether we do so verbally, pictorially, inwardly to ourselves, or simply through the way in which we behave, then we can be said to have produced a representation. It is representations that are perspectival or absolute.

This idea of a representation raises huge philosophical problems. Much ink has been spilled in an effort to say when something qualifies as true or false. A lot of the attention has settled on statements which satisfy the relevant grammatical criteria—they involve the use of declarative sentences—but which are suspect on other grounds. Examples are: mathematical statements ('No square

---

[1] Henry Sidgwick, *The Methods of Ethics*, pp. 382 and 420.

number is twice another'); self-ascriptions of pain ('That hurts!');
and, most notably, evaluations, including expressions of moral conviction ('She has a right to do whatever she likes with her own
money'). The first of these have been likened to rule-specifications
for a game; the second, to interjections; the third, to cheers or jeers,
or, quite differently, imperatives. In each case talk of truth or falsity
may be inappropriate. At any rate there is a major philosophical difficulty, or family of difficulties, about what counts as a representation.

I shall simply bypass these difficulties. I want to take the idea of
a representation as given. The issues that concern me arise once
that idea is in play. Some of what I go on to say may be of use to
anyone who wants to come back to these difficulties. But for now, I
shall say no more about what counts as a representation other than
to mention two things that I am taking for granted. First, the content of any representation can also be the content of some belief.
That is, given any representation that things are thus and so, it is
possible to *think* that things are thus and so. (This I take to be both
platitudinous and important. It is a useful tool for anyone wanting
to show why some apparent representation is not really such.)
Secondly—the assumption that guided the early part of this chapter—a representation need not be objective. In other words, a representation can be from a point of involvement. From now on I
shall call any representation that is from a point of involvement
'subjective'.

This is a point of terminology worth dwelling on. The term
'subjective' is often used to characterize that which is disqualified
from being a representation on the grounds that it is evaluative. My
usage is quite different. On my usage, the term applies *only* to representations. Being subjective is one particular way of being perspectival.[2]

There is one other point of terminology before I proceed. This
concerns the phrase 'point of view' itself. This phrase is often used
to signify a kind of screening mechanism. To adopt a point of view,
in this sense, is to attend only to certain limited aspects of whatever one is dealing with, those which are relevant to the concerns and

[2] For future reference I have included a diagram at the end of the glossary to illustrate the
relationship between the objective/subjective distinction and the absolute/perspectival distinction.

interests that define one's point of view, and to disregard all the rest. This is certainly related to my conception, but it is important for my purposes not to take anything about the relationship for granted. In particular, I presuppose no connection between the perspectival and the incomplete, or again between the absolute and the complete. If a complete perspectival representation of reality is impossible, as it would trivially be on this alternative conception, and as indeed the various resonances of the word 'partial' encourage us to think, then even so, in my terms, this is something to be argued for.

3

What, then, is it for a representation to be perspectival?

Some of the examples above may have engendered an oversimplified model. On that model a state of affairs in which someone stands in a certain relation to some part of reality can be represented from the point of view of that person as a state of affairs in which that part of reality has some corresponding feature. Thus, for example, a state of affairs in which an astronaut is within fifty miles of the moon can be represented, from the point of view of that astronaut, as a state of affairs in which the moon is less than fifty miles away.

This model only fits cases which involve a suppressed relativization. Arguably, it does not fit the colour case. Certainly it would not fit the case of any representation which was so soaked in perspective that the very things to which it made reference existed only from that point of view. (I will give examples of such representations in Chapter Ten. On some extreme theories, they include representations that make reference to physical objects. Physical objects are said to exist only from the point of view of human, or animal, experience. The underlying reality is said to be neither spatial nor temporal. We shall encounter such theories in Chapter Six.) Still, the model indicates a promising way forward.

There are two notions associated with the idea of a representation which have great intuitive appeal and of which I have already made free use: the notion of the *content* of a representation, and the notion of its *type*. The model above helps to illustrate both these notions. Suppose that the astronaut, in the case described, says, 'The moon is less than fifty miles away,' while somebody else, referring to him, says, 'He is now within fifty miles of the moon.' Then they have produced two representations with the same content, but of different types. Conversely, suppose that the astronaut says, 'The moon is less than fifty miles away,' while somebody else, on the surface of the earth, utters the same sentence. Then they have produced two representations of the same type, but with different contents (one true, the other false). It is precisely because of perspectival representations that the notions of content and type cut across each other in this way. The content of a perspectival representation depends not only on its type, but also on the point of view from which it is produced. It is tempting, now, to work this into a definition: a perspectival representation is a representation whose type can be shared by other representations which do not share its content. Equivalently: an absolute representation is a representation such that any other representation of the same type must have the same content.

However, there are two major obstacles to resting with this definition. The first obstacle is that the notions of content and type are themselves in need of clarification. The little that I have just said should have sufficed to tap their intuitive appeal, but it does not provide a secure basis for discussion. For one thing, it is unnerving to have made such significant play with the workings of language. Not all representations are linguistic.

One very natural account of the two notions runs as follows. The *content* of a representation is how things must be if it is true. The *type* of a representation is the role it must play in the psychology of whoever produces it, if he or she (or it) *thinks* the representation is true, that is if the representation expresses a belief of whoever produces it. Thus when the astronaut says, 'The moon is less than fifty miles away,' the content of his representation is that he is, at that time, within fifty miles of the moon. The type of his representation determines how he is disposed to act if the representation is an expression of what he thinks; for instance, and very roughly, if he is trying to land on the moon, then he is disposed to carry out the procedures that are necessary, or that he takes to be necessary, for landing on the moon from a distance of less than fifty miles. (Compare: the person who says, referring to him, 'He is now within fifty miles of the moon,' has said something with the same conditions of truth, but is disposed to act in a different way; a crackpot on earth who says, believing it, 'The moon is less than fifty miles away,' is disposed to act in the same way, but has said something with different conditions of truth.) Corresponding to the content and the type of any representation are two levels at which it can be understood. To understand the representation at one level one must know its content. This will help in ascertaining whether or not it is true. To understand the representation at the other level one must know its type. This will help in explaining the behaviour of whoever produced it, if he or she thinks it is true.

This seems to me to be perfectly acceptable as far as it goes. But it does not go far. "Ways things must be" and "ways of being disposed to act" must themselves be individuated; and individuating them is every bit as difficult, and raises essentially the same problems, as saying what the content and the type of a representation are. A full account of these matters would have to expound the grounds on which representations are produced, the conclusions which are drawn from them, the conceptual abilities which are involved in their production, and the principles which determine what they are about. It would have to constitute a significant chapter in both the philosophy of psychology and the philosophy of language.

At this point I shall do precisely what I did when it came to saying what a representation is. I shall simply proceed as if such an account were to hand. As before, this means gliding over an area of great philosophical difficulty, in which much important work has been done and in which there is still much to do. My excuse is once again that I am interested in issues that arise at a later stage.

There remains the second obstacle to the proposed definition. On that definition, to repeat, a perspectival representation is a representation whose type does not determine its content. But we have to reckon with the possibility of a kind of representation which I shall call "radically perspectival". A radically perspectival representation would be a representation which was from a point of view such that there could not be another representation of the same type that was not also from that point of view. This would be because even to operate with those concepts would already be to see things from that point of view. Examples would include representations of the kind for which I insisted the model above would be inadequate, that is representations that made reference to things whose very existence could only be acknowledged from that point of view (physical objects, on the extreme theories). Other possible examples would be subjective representations involving concepts such as *chivalry* or *dignity*, concepts whose application is arguably unintelligible except against a specific background of shared sensibilities and values. Suppose now that ρ is some radically perspectival representation. And suppose that ρ is not from any point of view other than that which makes it radically perspectival. By definition, any other representation of the same type would have to be from the same point of view. Hence it would have to have the same content. On the proposed definition, then, ρ would count as absolute.

The definition could be amended. We could say: a perspectival representation is a representation whose type does not determine its content *unless* that type is such that it cannot be shared by a representation from any other point of view. From any other point of view, though? The problem with this, at least as a definition, is that it invokes the very ideas that we are trying to explicate.

We do best to look for a different kind of definition, though we can continue to work with the notions of content and type. One thing that is liable to be significant is the endorsement of representations. To *endorse* a representation is to produce another representation with the same content. To endorse a representation *by simple repetition* is to endorse it by producing another representation of the same type. An absolute representation can always be endorsed by simple repetition. A perspectival representation, on the other hand, sometimes cannot be. Suppose, for example, that I wish to endorse an assertion I made yesterday of the sentence, 'It is humid today.' I have no alternative but to produce a representation of some other type ('It was humid yesterday').

This seems immediately to furnish us with a new definition. But it does not. Consider the 'always' and the 'sometimes' in the last paragraph. These are effectively quantifiers ranging over points of view. An absolute representation is a representation such that, for any point of view, it is possible to endorse the representation by producing another representation of the same type at that point of view (where incidentally the idea of producing a representation *at* a point of view presents an additional complexity). As before, then, essential use has been made of the very ideas that we are trying to explicate. Can we avoid this? We can, in two ways. (The two ways are related.)

The first way is to focus on a particular kind of endorsement, that which is fully self-conscious. By full self-consciousness here I have in mind something both distinctive and demanding. Self-consciousness is what enables me to see my own representations *as* my own representations. It is what I need if I am not only to know something but to know that I know it. (This is a very sketchy account of an idea that will be of crucial importance, and will receive further clarification, in later chapters.) In the case of an absolute representation, fully self-conscious endorsement can be achieved by simple repetition. In the case of a perspectival representation, on the other hand, full self-consciousness demands more. It demands reference to the relevant point of view. For it must allow for an understanding of how the original representation, if true, coheres with true representations from other points of view. The astronaut, if he is to provide a fully self-conscious endorsement of his own true report, 'The moon is less than fifty miles away,' must do so in such a way that he can see how it coheres with true assertions, made on the surface of the earth, of the sentence, 'The moon is nearly a quarter of a million miles away.' He may continue to think in perspectival terms: 'The moon is less than fifty miles away from *me*.' But since somebody on the surface of the earth can equally think, 'The moon is nearly a quarter of a million miles away from *me*,' the astronaut must supplement this with a conception of himself as one item among others, occupying a particular position in space. Eventually he must produce a representation in which the original element of perspective is superseded. Here, then, is a way of drawing the distinction between the perspectival and the absolute. A perspectival representation is a representation which cannot (and an absolute representation, a representation which can) be fully self-consciously endorsed by simple repetition.

Although I think this definition is correct, I readily concede that this idea of full self-consciousness is not yet clear enough for such a definition to be suitable for our purposes. We do better to turn to the second way of avoiding the specified circularity. We shall see in Chapter Five that this involves its own rather different circularity, but by then we shall be in a position to accept the circularity with equanimity. What we need to focus on is the joint endorsement of two representations, or, as I shall say, their integration. To *integrate* two representations is to produce a third representation whose content is the product of theirs, in other words a representation which is true if and only if they are both true. To integrate two representations *by simple addition* is to integrate them by producing a representation which is the conjunction of two representations of the same types as theirs. (Simple addition is the "two representation" counterpart of simple repetition.) In order to integrate two perspectival representations by simple addition it would be necessary to produce a third representation from all the same points of view as each. This would not always be possible. Some points of view are "incompatible", by which I mean that no representation could be produced from both of them. Points widely separated in time are an example. Thus suppose I say one day, 'It is humid today.' And suppose, some sixth months later, I say, 'It is snowing.' I could not then integrate these two representations by saying, 'It is humid today and it is snowing.' I should have to do something more circuitous, such as make explicit reference to the two dates concerned. Representations from incompatible points of view cannot be integrated by simple addition, then. Moreover, given any point of view, there are bound to be others incompatible with it: we have to insist on this if we are to stop the idea of a point of view from expanding into triviality. (Recall Sidgwick's "point of view of the Universe".) It follows that, given any perspectival representation, it is bound to be possible to produce a representation with which it cannot be integrated by simple addition. Not so in the case of an absolute representation. Here is the definition we seek then. A perspectival representation is a representation such that there is some possible representation with which it cannot be integrated by simple addition. An absolute representation is a representation which can be integrated by simple addition with any possible representation.

My opening question, in these terms, is this. Are absolute representations possible?

4

Now that the question has been clarified in this way, we may have lost sense of its significance. To activate that sense is the main task of Chapter Two. Before I bring this chapter to a close, however, I want to focus on a few concepts which the last part of the discussion has brought to light; and then I want to say a little more about why the question does not obviously receive the answer yes.

It may be that some perspectival representations can be endorsed *only* by simple repetition—or at least, only by producing a representation from the same point of view. (Producing a representation from the same point of view does not preclude, for example, introducing a new element of perspective.) For instance, it *may* be that only from the point of view of beings with the relevant visual apparatus is it possible to have a thought with precisely the same content as the thoughts which you or I have whenever we think that grass is green. Call any such representation "inherently perspectival". It is instructive to compare this idea of inherent perspective with the earlier idea of radical perspective. A radically perspectival representation is a representation which is from a point of view that must be shared by any other representation of the same type. An inherently perspectival representation is a representation which is from a point of view that must be shared by any other representation with the same *content*. But the connections between the two kinds of representations do not stop there. If there *are* any inherently perspectival representations, then they are also likely to be radically perspectival, and vice versa. This is because any distinctive conceptual tools that serve to define a point of view are likely to be reflected in the content of a representation if and only if they are also reflected in its type. (I shall say a little more about this, and give some examples, in Chapter Three.)

However that may be, I claim that even if it is possible to endorse a certain representation only by adopting the same point of view, still it must be possible, even without adopting that point of view, to tell a story sufficiently long and complex to have the content of the representation as part of its own. In other words, it must be possible to tell a story that has the representation as a consequence. I leave open the question of how strong a notion of consequence this is. I certainly do not want to insist on the conceptual impossibility of the story's being true without the representation's also being true. All I require is that there should be *some* non-trivial notion of consequence for which my claim holds, for instance something that depends on a notion of supervenience.[3] Thus, for example, aliens without the relevant visual apparatus might nevertheless be able to

---

[3] See e.g. David Charles, 'Supervenience, Composition, and Physicalism'.

tell a sufficiently long and complex story about pigment, wavelengths, retinas, and the rest to capture what we mean in calling
grass green. Let us say that one representation *weakly entails* another when the former has the latter as·a consequence in this sense.
And let us say that a representation has been *indirectly* endorsed
when another representation has been produced which weakly
entails it. (So endorsement is a special case of indirect endorsement.) Then my claim is this: even if there are inherently perspectival representations, that is to say, representations which can be
endorsed only by adopting the same point of view, there is none
which can be *indirectly* endorsed only by adopting the same point of
view.

In an entirely parallel way, I claim that, even if there are some
pairs of representations which cannot be integrated, there is none
which cannot be *indirectly* integrated. (By indirect integration I
mean the "two representation" counterpart of indirect endorsement: for two representations to be indirectly integrated is for a
third representation to be produced that weakly entails each of
them.) I claim, furthermore, that given any pair of true representations, their indirect integration can be achieved by producing a representation which is in turn true.[4] This is our first glimpse of something that I shall later parade as a fundamental principle about the
unity of reality.

All the unsubstantiated claims that I have made in the last two
paragraphs are controversial, require elaboration, and will be dealt
with at greater length in later chapters. But it is useful to have got
the relevant concepts into focus at an early stage. Moreover, they
give us another angle on absolute representations. Consider any
finite set of representations. If what I have been claiming is correct,
a single representation can be produced which weakly entails every
one of them. This single representation can be obtained by a series
of indirect integrations, of the first representation with the second,
of the result of this indirect integration with the third, of the result
of *this* indirect integration with the fourth, and so on. It is entirely
possible that no part of what results will bear any resemblance to
any of the original representations. Indeed it is possible that no part
of what results *can* bear any resemblance to any of the original rep-

---

[4] Cf. Wiggins on what he calls the fifth mark of truth, in David Wiggins, 'Truth, and
Truth as Predicated of Moral Judgements', pp. 148 and 152.

resentations—unless they include representations that are absolute. Absolute representations can always be kept in reserve until the end of the process and then tagged on by simple addition. An absolute representation is always of a type fit to appear at the end-stage of any multiple integration of this kind.

—*"Very well, why are there not clear examples in mathematics? If I say, '2 + 2 = 4,' have I not produced an absolute representation whose content can be straightforwardly added to the content of any story by simply appending another representation of the same type?"*—

Well, remember that mathematical statements were among the problematical cases cited earlier when we considered what counts as a representation. In saying, '2 + 2 = 4,' you may not have produced a representation at all. But suppose we waive that worry. Perhaps your representation is from the point of view of people who count and do arithmetic in a certain way. Perhaps, if there were people, or aliens, who counted differently, one of them could say, '2 + 2 = 4,' and be in error.

—*"That is beside the point. Of course there could be people for whom the actual string of symbols '2 + 2 = 4' meant something false. They might use '4' as we use '3': one of them might assert, '2 + 2 = 4,' and mean that 2 + 2 = 3. But a merely linguistic difference of this kind would prove nothing. Such a representation would not be of the same type as mine."*—

What is that type, though? What is a "merely linguistic" difference? Is mathematical reality as separate from the use of mathematical symbols as you are suggesting? Is there a clear distinction between saying that, for certain people, '2 + 2 = 4' means something false, and saying that, from their point of view, 2 + 2 ≠ 4?

I ask these questions rhetorically. They are among the most fundamental in the philosophy of mathematics. Indeed they are among the most fundamental in philosophy. The point, for now, is that we are still far from being able to look at any representation and see straight away that it is absolute. Identifying elements of perspective can be both heady and disconcerting. It can also be extraordinarily difficult. The sheer variety of points of view already put us in mind of this. Nothing in the subsequent discussion has alleviated the difficulty.

The answer to my opening question is not obviously yes. Some may think it is obviously no. They may think that there is a simple argument to show, not just that any representation must be perspectival, but that any representation must be radically perspectival.

The argument runs as follows. Any representation must involve its own distinctive battery of conceptual apparatus, with its own distinctive systems of classification and organization. To operate these is already to see things in one way rather than another. It is already to see things from a particular point of view.

We shall come back to this argument in Chapter Five. Our first priority, however, is to get a better understanding of what hangs on such arguments. I shall now try to say some more about what does.

FURTHER READING

A precursor to this book is my 'Points of View': I should like to thank the editor and publisher of *Philosophical Quarterly* for permission to re-use material from this article. (I do however depart from some of the claims made there, and in other previously published work.)

The question raised in this chapter is particularly associated with Bernard Williams: see especially *Descartes*, pp. 64–5, 239, 245–9, and 301–3; and *Ethics and the Limits of Philosophy*, pp. 138–40. See also, for discussion of Williams's views, the material cited in the further reading for Chapter Four. The question raised is also associated with Thomas Nagel: see 'Subjective and Objective'; and, in much greater depth, *The View From Nowhere*. Also relevant to the question, and to the tools used in this chapter for clarifying it, are: Fred D'Agostino, 'Transcendence and Conversation: Two Concepts of Objectivity'; Miranda Fricker, 'Perspectival Realism: Towards a Pluralist Theory of Knowledge'; Geoffrey V. Klempner, *Naïve Metaphysics*; Colin McGinn, *The Subjective View*; D. H. Mellor, 'I and Now'; John Perry, *The Problem of the Essential Indexical and Other Essays*; John Perry and Simon Blackburn, 'Thoughts Without Representation'; Amartya Sen, 'Positional Objectivity'; and Galen Strawson, *The Secret Connexion*, Appendix B.

For somewhat different approaches to the idea of a point of view (more in keeping with what I described in the main text as the idea of a point of view as a screening mechanism) see Robert Brandom, 'Points of View and Practical Reasoning'; Antti Hautamäki, 'Points of View and Their Logical Analysis'; and Jon Moline, 'On Points of View'.

On the question of what counts as a representation, which I passed over, see Brad Hooker (ed.), *Truth in Ethics*; Paul Horwich, *Truth*; and Crispin Wright, *Truth and Objectivity*.

On the issues associated with the notions of content and type, which I also passed over, see Jon Barwise and John Perry, *Situations and Attitudes*; Michael Dummett, 'More About Thoughts'; Gareth Evans, *The Varieties of Reference*; David Lewis, 'Attitudes *De Dicto* and *De Se*'; and John Perry, *The Problem of the Essential Indexical and Other Essays*.

CHAPTER TWO

First she placed her fingertips to a spot between her breasts, as if she wanted to point to the very centre of what is known as the self. Then she flung her arms forward, as if she wanted to transport that self somewhere far away, to the horizon, to infinity. The gesture of longing for immortality knows only two points in space: the self here, the horizon far in the distance; only two concepts: the absolute that is the self, and the absolute that is the world.

(Milan Kundera)

§ 1: What is the significance of the question whether absolute representations are possible? Various reasons are given, in this chapter, for thinking that a negative answer to the question would be disquieting. First, some general remarks are made about why absoluteness is, or might be, a desideratum of certain enquiries.

§ 2: The bearing of a negative answer on the limits of objectivity is considered.

§ 3: Absoluteness is argued to be a desideratum of the natural sciences, or at any rate of physics.

§ 4: Problems about disagreement and relativism are considered. Certain difficulties are identified that would be the more severe if absoluteness were unattainable.

§ 5: Absoluteness is shown to lie at the limit of an ideal of rational reflective self-understanding.

§ 6: Some final comments are made about the threat that a negative answer would pose for our idea of reality. These comments presage the argument that will eventually be given for an affirmative answer.

1

ANY enquiry, in so far as it has pretensions to comprehensiveness, demands a certain transcendence of perspective. This is one conclusion that we can already draw. Comprehensiveness is a feature of representations. It comes in degrees. And it is of two kinds. The first kind is comprehensiveness of *coverage*. This is roughly a matter of how large the content of the representation is: "how much it says". (A representation to the effect that Jupiter and Saturn both have moons has larger content than a representation to the effect merely that Jupiter does.) Comprehensiveness of coverage is, so to speak, the *telos* of integration. And integration is bound sometimes to involve loss of perspective, as we saw in the last chapter. The more extensive the integration, the more extensive the likely loss. The second kind of comprehensiveness is comprehensiveness of *appeal*. This is roughly a matter of how large the range of enquir-ers is who can assimilate the representation. Assimilation here is basically what I have been calling endorsement by simple repeti-tion. So increased comprehensiveness of appeal will likewise require loss of perspective.

But when is an enquiry likely to have pretensions to either kind of comprehensiveness?

Comprehensiveness of coverage is likely to be sought whenever the aim of the enquiry is to synthesize various things that are known into a single representation—a theory—in order to produce a systematic overview of a given area. Such is the aim of scientific enquiries. The comprehensiveness in such cases is sought as an end in itself, not merely as a means. (But it is not a supreme end. There are competing goods. For instance, one scientific theory might have greater content than another yet have less explanatory power or be less manageable.)

Comprehensiveness of coverage is also sometimes sought as a means to the end of rational and reflective understanding of one-self, or more particularly of oneself in relation to others. This con-nects with the brief comments about self-conscious endorsement in the previous chapter. It also connects with what I signalled as a fundamental principle about the unity of reality. The principle, which I shall henceforth refer to as the Fundamental Principle, is this. Given any pair of true representations, it is possible to produce a true representation that weakly entails each of them (in the sense of weak entailment introduced in the previous chapter). This can scarcely be proved. It is after all fundamental. But here are some comments that may serve to motivate it. The truth of any true rep-resentation is determined by how the world is—by how reality is.

There is only one world. This is what I mean when I talk about the unity of reality. So given any pair of true representations, that one world—reality—must be how both of them represent it as being. But if that is how reality is, then it must be possible to produce a true representation to that effect. Embellishing somewhat: given any pair of true representations, there must be a way of understanding not only how each of them can be true, but how *both* of them can be true. To see now how this connects with the goal of rational reflective self-understanding, suppose that I wish to endorse my own representations, perhaps along with the representations of others. And suppose that I wish to do so in a way that is fully and rationally reflective. Then I shall not be satisfied except in so far as I am satisfied that these representations conform to the Fundamental Principle. Piecemeal endorsement will not be good enough. Integration is called for, or at least indirect integration, the more extensive the better. In other words, I shall be aiming for a certain comprehensiveness of coverage.

When is an enquiry likely to have pretensions to comprehensiveness of appeal?

Comprehensiveness of appeal, like comprehensiveness of coverage, is a goal of science. Partly this is because of a presupposition of scientific enquiry that I shall amplify later in this chapter, namely that there is, as far as scientific enquiry is concerned, no privileged point of view: no point of view is particularly apt for the statement of scientific laws. Partly it is because scientific enquiry shares with other kinds of enquiry the further goal of common understanding. Common understanding occurs when independent enquirers not only reach agreement with one another but also attain a shared conception of things which, granted success in mutual translation, facilitates their seeing that they have reached agreement and aids further concerted enquiry. For this they need to produce accounts that are not only alike in content, but also alike in type.

These highly schematic remarks, which develop some of the equally schematic remarks made at the end of the last chapter, already suggest that absoluteness is a desideratum of certain enquiries. This gives significant fillip to the question whether absolute representations are possible. But two caveats should be entered to prevent the question from assuming too great an importance too soon. First, absoluteness is certainly not a desideratum of all enquiries. This is something that I tried to emphasize at the beginning of the previous chapter. There are plenty of circumstances in which we actively seek a high degree of perspective, indeed a high degree of subjectivity, in our representations. If I am trying to understand some petty fear that is currently debilitating me, then I shall be relatively immune to the demands of comprehensiveness. My aim is to understand something very specific, from a very specific point of involvement with it. Secondly, even given an enquiry for which absoluteness is a desideratum, the question whether absolute representations are possible in no way puts the enquiry on trial. If they are possible, then one aim of the enquiry will be to produce them; and independent participants in the enquiry might be expected to converge on one type of account. But even if they are not possible, the desideratum might still be a reasonable one. The aim will then be, through successive excisions of elements of perspective, to get closer and closer to absoluteness, even though it is impossible to get so close that there is no room for improvement. Absoluteness will then be what Kant might have called a regulative ideal.[1]

What I have said so far in this chapter presents, in outline, one of its main threads. As I follow this thread I shall try to do three things. First, I shall try to say more about how, how far, and in what sense, absoluteness is a desideratum of any enquiry—if indeed it ever is. So far all I have done is make a suggestion: that absoluteness is a desideratum wherever there is an aspiration to comprehensiveness. The second thing I shall try to do is to substantiate this suggestion. Finally, I shall try to make the discussion less schematic. I shall begin by returning to an idea that dominated the early part of Chapter One, the idea of objectivity.

2

The objective/subjective distinction is a distinction of degree. There is no harm in calling a representation simply objective, or simply subjective; nor in construing 'objective' and 'subjective' as contradictories over the domain of representations, as we have

---

[1] Immanuel Kant, *Critique of Pure Reason*, A567–71/B595–9.

been doing. But what determines whether a representation is objective or subjective, namely whether or not it is from a point of involvement, admits of various sorts of gradation. Thus one representation may be from many different points of involvement, another from not so many. One representation may be from a point of involvement that is harder to surmount than another. One representation may be from a point of deeper involvement than another. Now all of these have analogues in the case of the absolute/perspectival distinction, which is likewise, in *that* sense, a distinction of degree. None of them, in itself, threatens the presumption that there is a clear cut-off point between being from *no* point of involvement and being from at least one, any more than their analogues threaten the presumption that there is a clear cut-off point between being from no point of view (absolute) and being from at least one (perspectival). However, the objective/subjective distinction is further afflicted by an inherent vagueness that has no analogue in the case of the absolute/perspectival distinction: the vagueness that attaches to the very idea of a point of involvement. My talk of concerns, interests, and values in Chapter One did not constitute, and was not intended to constitute, a precise tool for prising apart subjectivity from other kinds of perspective. So here is another sort of gradation. One representation may be from a point of view that more definitely *counts* as a point of involvement.

Granted these different sorts of gradation, there is a question about the degree of objectivity to which we can aspire in any given context. Writing a treatise on microphysical structure and falling in love might be two extremes. For reasons that I shall try to make clear, this question can be vital. Whether absolute representations are possible bears on it.

It does not bear on it directly. Even if absoluteness is never attainable, complete objectivity may be. For by definition, absoluteness is harder to attain than objectivity. But the latter question bears on the former indirectly. For if absolute representations are not possible, then there must be some reason why; and this reason may well turn out to set limits on how objective we can be. Thus one embellishment of the argument sketched right at the end of the last chapter would have it that any set of concepts is inevitably an expression of certain needs, interests, concerns, and values. The argument would then show not only that any representation must be perspectival, but that any representation must be to some degree subjective. A similar but more modest argument would show that any representation specifically with a certain kind of content must be subjective; or that there are special impediments to producing a representation with a certain kind of content beyond a certain level of objectivity. Thus, for example, there might be special impediments to thinking about certain emotional investments that we have made from anything other than our own points of involvement with them.

Would this matter?

Yes. Consider what accrues when we attain greater objectivity and stop viewing situations just from our own points of involvement. We begin to see why the situations look the way they do from those points of involvement. It becomes easier for us to imagine viewing the situations from the points of involvement of others. It is consequently easier for us to accept that the situations look different from there, without this indicating error or misunderstanding on anybody's part. So too it is easier for us to acknowledge that we can express these differences without disagreeing with one another. And quite generally, it is easier for us to understand and empathize with other people. Attaining such objectivity gives us a less narrow, less tainted, and less distorted conception of things. It gives us (paradoxically) a greater sense of perspective.

Not that such objectivity, in itself, makes us any the more altruistic. Empathy is not the same as sympathy. Indeed there are many ways in which such objectivity can animate a selfish unconcern for the welfare of others. Some vices actually require it—calculated cruelty and envy, for example. (This is one way in which these differ from callousness and greed.) Nevertheless, the value and importance of cultivating such objectivity are clear. So yes; certainly it would matter if there were special impediments in the way of our doing so, or even worse, if it were sometimes impossible to do so.

But this is not a plea for complete objectivity. In order to identify with other people,[2] we must learn to rise above our own points of involvement; but not above every point of involvement; not above a *human* point of involvement. Consider: I, along with many others, owe my very existence to the Second World War. Now it would be a psychopathic failure of objectivity if, just on that

[2] Strictly I should say 'other human beings' here: I shall come back to this distinction in Chapter Ten.

account, I were unable to grieve over the War. But equally, it would be a psychopathic failure of *subj*ectivity if, at the other extreme, I were unable to grieve over the War because I had so little sense of the human perspective that I came to see the War as a meaningless blip on the screen of eternity.[3]

Once again we are reminded that 'more objective' does not mean 'better'. The degree of objectivity that is desirable in our representations is heavily dependent on context. Nor does each context demand just one degree of objectivity. After all, I could scarcely view anything from a human point of involvement unless I also viewed it, or something suitably similar to it, from a human's point of involvement: my own. In most contexts, that is to say in most situations and for most purposes, what counts as an appropriate understanding of the situation will be something that combines representations of varying degrees of objectivity, each sustaining and informing the others.

It is not just that subjective representations have their place. All the most important representations that directly engage us are subjective. This is a modification of a principle which will assume importance at the end of the book, and which I shall refer to as the Engagement Principle. The Engagement Principle is this: *all* the representations that directly engage us are perspectival. Already I can give a simple illustration. Consider Mr Meanour. Suffering from amnesia after a car crash, he reads in the newspaper that Mr Meanour is wanted by the police. The news has no effect on him. Later he discovers that *he* is Mr Meanour. At once he takes steps to avoid arrest. He has come to view the situation in an appropriately perspectival way, from his own position within it. This illustrates how, given the perspectival character of our basic aims, projects, and wishes—Mr Meanour's concern is that *he* should not be arrested—only representations that are correspondingly perspectival, albeit usually in a way that is much more subtle than this, can have any immediate influence on our actions. (I shall amplify on this in Chapter Eleven.)

---

[3] Cf. David Hume, *A Treatise of Human Nature*, pp. 581–2; and David Hume, *Enquiry Concerning the Principles of Morals*, pp. 272–3. Consider also in this connection Mao Zedong's remarkable claim, quoted by Jung Chang, *Wild Swans*, p. 293: 'Even if the United States . . . blew [the earth] to pieces . . . [this] would still be an insignificant matter as far as the universe as a whole is concerned.'

How does the question of the possibility of absolute representations fare now? Initially the question looked important because of
its bearing on the question of how objective we can be. Now we
seem to have reached the conclusion that objectivity beyond a certain level is of dubious interest to us anyway. If it transpired that we
humans could not but view things from a human point of involvement, and *a fortiori* that we could not view things absolutely, nothing that has been said so far would make this disturbing.

But we must think again about the interplay of representations.
What is true of the representations that directly engage us need not
be true of the representations that (to echo the phrase I used above)
sustain and inform them. Mr Meanour comes to the realization that
he is wanted by the police by first discovering that Mr Meanour is
wanted by the police. The representation that directly engages him
is from his own point of view. The one that supports it is not. There
is still plenty of scope for concluding that we sometimes do well to
look at things completely objectively. In fact there is scope for concluding that we sometimes do well to look at things absolutely.

This conclusion has been drawn time and again throughout the
history of human enquiry. Often it has been linked to a belief in
God. The idea has been that we do well, sometimes, to look at
things from God's point of view—which means (oxymoronically)
from no point of view at all, since God *has* no point of view: God
is not *in* the world. In more narrowly philosophical contexts the
conclusion has been drawn alongside certain very general considerations about rationality. Certain Kantians have held that the most
basic questions about how we ought to live have answers dictated
purely by reason, and that it is inappropriate to address them from
any particular vantage-point. (This arguably excludes Kant himself,
whose own view might be better expressed by saying that we
should address such questions from the vantage-point of rational
beings. I shall discuss some of the complications that arise here in
Chapter Eleven.) Others have held views that are structurally similar to the Kantian view, but with reason replaced by abstract principles of impartiality or by some maximizing principle of utility.
Others again have argued that, just as there is a distinctively human
conception of things which can act as a corrective to a narrowly
self-centred conception not by annulling it but by making *sense* of
it, so too there is an absolute conception which makes sense of the
distinctively human conception by revealing our place in the wider

scheme of things. To hold any of these views is to acknowledge the value and importance of looking at things absolutely.

Not one of these views is viable, however, unless absolute representations are possible. So given the attraction, power, and historical significance of such views, the question of the possibility of absolute representations assumes, after all, a certain urgency.

3

The representations that nowadays have the most compelling claim to the title of absoluteness are those of the natural sciences, paradigmatically physics. Some would say that it is a defining characteristic of these sciences that their practitioners should aim for absoluteness. Certainly many scientists have in fact aimed for absoluteness. Not that they have been alone in this. Plenty of philosophers have had the ambition to produce absolute representations too, as witness the views outlined above concerning God and rationality, traditional focal points of philosophical enquiry. But it is in the natural sciences, and especially in physics, that the ambition has looked most realistic. Indeed it can lay claim to being systematically built into the very methods and principles of enquiry that are used there. For while some scientists seek absoluteness simply for its own sake, most who seek it do so also as a criterion of truth. Their primary aim is to discover laws, laws that govern the workings of nature. And it is a deep prejudice of scientific enquiry that such laws, by their very essence, are best couched absolutely. This is the point I made earlier when talking about comprehensiveness of appeal. Put somewhat differently, the prejudice is this. With regard to its basic workings, the physical world (nature) looks the same from every point of view. There are no privileged positions in the world from which its natural laws are peculiarly perspicuous, or peculiarly evident, or peculiarly simple.

In describing this as a prejudice I am using the term in its original and non-pejorative sense. I mean that it is a prejudgement, a judgement made in advance of, and designed to guide, the quest for an understanding of nature. I do not mean that nothing could convince those who hold it that they should give it up. Nor, for that matter, am I claiming that it is a prejudice of each and every scientist. Some may already think that there are reasons for giving it up. But the prejudice has undeniably had a vital role to play in scientific development. A beautiful example of what I have in mind can be found in the history of relativity theory. Newton's first law of mechanics states that a body continues in a state of rest or of uniform motion in a straight line unless it is compelled to change that state by forces acting upon it.[4] This statement of the law turns out to be perspectival. It is from the point of view of an *inertial frame*. The earth, for example, is not an inertial frame. A representation of the same type from the point of view of the earth (where this means taking the earth as frame of reference and hence as not moving) would not be true. From this point of view the sun describes something approximating to a colossal circle every twenty-four hours, even though there are no relevant forces acting upon it. This is precisely the sort of case in which physicists will look for some more fundamental law. What they seek is a law whose crispest statement is not similarly perspectival. To quote Einstein, "no person whose mode of thought is logical can rest satisfied with [Newton's law] . . . How does it come about that certain [frames of reference] . . . are given priority over other [frames of reference] . . .? *What is the reason for this preference?*"[5] Einstein himself looked for a more general law whereby the offending element of perspective could be eliminated, and this was a main impetus in the formulation of his general theory of relativity.

These remarks have been concerned with comprehensiveness of appeal. There is also comprehensiveness of coverage. Many people think that precisely what distinguishes physics from all other enquiries is its title to the claim of comprehensive coverage. And they think that it earns this title in a very distinctive way: its subject matter just is that minimal range of states, whatever they may be, whose redistribution constitutes anything's happening. (Among philosophers, this view of physics is particularly associated with Quine.)[6] Certainly, in seeking the laws that relate physical states, physicists are aiming for maximum content. The more extensive the laws they discover—the more of what goes on they are able to

[4] Isaac Newton, *Mathematical Principles of Natural Philosophy*, Bk. I, Law I.

[5] Albert Einstein, *Relativity*, pp. 71–2, his emphasis. Cf. also pp. 11, 61, and 99.

[6] See e.g. W. V. Quine, 'Facts of the Matter'. See also the passage excerpted at the head of Chapter Four, from Quine, 'Goodman's *Ways of Worldmaking*', p. 98.

account for—the better. And, for reasons that I indicated earlier, such an aspiration to comprehensiveness of coverage has a tendency to dispel perspective; that is, to conduce absoluteness.

At any rate there is now a presumption in favour of seeing absoluteness as a desideratum of physics, and to a lesser extent of the other natural sciences, in the sense defined, and subject to the qualifications given. This may or may not be a distinguishing feature of the natural sciences. Those who think it is are liable to fasten on it as a polarizing difference between the scientific and the ethical (in so far as the ethical admits of truth and falsity at all). But there are those, as we have seen, who think that absoluteness has its place in ethics as well. Indeed there are those who think that there is something ethical corresponding to what I called the prejudice of scientific enquiry: that, with regard to its basic workings, the moral world, just like the physical world, looks the same from any point of view. This means, for example, that no-one should adopt a moral principle that sanctions doing whatever it would be harmless for one person to do. For some things that it would be harmless for one person to do it would be catastrophic for everyone to do. Not everyone could adopt a principle of this type, then. In other words, principles of this type could not be true from everyone's point of view. They could be true only from the points of view of a privileged few—precisely what is ruled out.

Those, incidentally, who think that ethical representations must be absolute, and *a fortiori* those who think that they can be, are still at liberty to embrace the Engagement Principle (the principle that the representations which directly engage us are all perspectival). They are at liberty, in fact, to embrace the modification of that principle considered earlier, that the representations which directly engage us are, in the most important cases, subjective. The point, once again, is that there can be interplay between representations. Absolute representations can be applied. By the same token, those who think that ethical representations must be perspectival, perhaps because they accept the Engagement Principle and they think that ethical representations must directly engage us, can still acknowledge the value and importance of looking at things absolutely. This is the mast to which I would want to nail my own colours. (See further Chapter Eleven.)

However that may be, the aspiration to absoluteness in the natural sciences finally quashes any suggestion that absoluteness is of no interest to us. It also gives the question of the possibility of absolute representations further urgency. It poses no threat to the Engagement Principle, for the reason just indicated. The huge and sometimes importunate impact of science on our lives can be seen as a mediated impact, brought about by the application of science. But it does mean that whether or not absolute representations are possible is crucial to our idea of the scientific enterprise.

4

It is also crucial to our idea of disagreement.

Disagreement, platitudinously, occurs in a variety of contexts and takes a variety of forms. To be able to identify, understand, and explain disagreement, and in particular to be able to tell the difference between real and apparent disagreement, is important both practically and theoretically. It is important for deciding how, if at all, to oppose those with whom we disagree. It is important for locating error, including error in our own views, which is in turn important for understanding what knowledge is and how to increase it. It is important in connection with our idea of reality. Reality is what representations answer to. If we are to have a suitably robust sense of what this means, then we can reasonably expect two things: first, that we shall tend to agree, in the long run, about what reality is like; and secondly, if the first expectation is not to be hollow, that we shall be able to *recognize* when we agree. It is important, lastly, for overcoming the frustrations of merely apparent disagreement. Often we think one thing, others seem to think the opposite, and there is an impasse in all attempts at resolution. If we can see that there is only apparent disagreement here, it will be clear that resolution is not to the point: perhaps we are right and they are right too.

Whether absolute representations are possible has a bearing on our chances of being able to get the measure of disagreement in this way. The chances are lower if absolute representations are not possible. (I claim no more than this. In what follows I shall indicate a difficulty that besets perspective. But it does not beset perspective in *all* its guises. In particular, it does not beset what I referred to in Chapter One as radical perspective, where the type of a representation already determines the point of view from which the representation is produced.)

The point is this. Perspectival representations have an in-built tendency to create merely apparent disagreement. Whenever two people produce representations such that the type of one is the negation of the type of the other, then it is bound to look, if only to some minimal extent, as if they are disagreeing with each other—even if the representations are from different points of view and there is no disagreement at all. Sometimes the appearance of disagreement is very minimal indeed. It may require a special exercise of the intellect to recognize it. Thus if one person says, 'I am English,' and another person says, 'I am not English,' then of course they are not disagreeing with each other (though even in this case, the appearance of disagreement is enough to have obvious comic potential). At other times, however, the appearance of disagreement is much more compelling. Consider two observers moving rapidly relative to each other, one of whom describes two events as simultaneous and the other of whom describes the same two events as non-simultaneous. Or consider the alien who, in the story in Chapter One, says that the specified substance is red while one of us says that it is not red. In this case it is still an unresolved matter how deep the appearance of disagreement does go. Even very simple elements of perspective can trouble the unwary. Small children placed opposite each other sometimes think they disagree about whether something is on the left or right. As long as we are dealing with perspectival representations, or as long, at least, as we do not know that we are not, then it can take hard work to recognize genuine disagreement.

That hard work even sometimes compounds itself. Here is a simple example. One person says that the earth is stationary. Another says that it is rotating. Their representations look incompatible. In fact, however, both are true. The speakers have adopted different frames of reference. Only after considerable effort do they come to appreciate this. But the result is that the focus of their apparent disagreement shifts elsewhere. The issue now, they think, is which frame of reference is more *convenient*. They fail to recognize that convenience, no less than motion, is dependent on a point of view—a point of view defined largely by interests. If absolute representations are impossible, then this sort of thing is set to happen indefinitely. We have no guarantee that a merely apparent disagreement will not persist in seeming real, or that it will not at least give way to some other apparent disagreement, no less illusory. If we were dealing with absolute representations, on the other hand, or at least if we knew that we were, then none of these difficulties would arise.

Nor, for that matter, would we be tempted in the other direction, of postulating perspective to dismiss as merely apparent what are in fact genuine disagreements. This temptation is particularly strong with respect to what may loosely be called issues of right and wrong (for example, whether capitalism is evil; whether it is wrong to eat meat; whether it is important to avoid splitting infinitives; whether this is a good time for a particular couple to have a baby). It is notoriously difficult to resolve apparent disagreements about these issues. So it is very tempting, in any given case, to try to appeal to perspective as a way of showing that the disagreement is merely apparent and that there is no need for a resolution. Thus relativism.

To be sure, as long as we are not knowingly dealing with absolute representations, then we do well to bear such relativism in mind. But we also do well to bear in mind at least four hazards that we confront whenever we try to invoke such relativism to dissolve an apparent disagreement in this way. First, it is by no means always obvious, indeed it can be a matter of deep philosophical perplexity, whether we are dealing with representations in the first place. (What counts as a representation, you will recall, was one of the issues that I glided over in Chapter One.) If we are not dealing with representations, then relativism of the sort described is beside the point. And it is entirely possible that we are not. Disagreement is multifarious. Some disagreements, for all their apparent discursiveness, are little more than trials of power. Truth and falsity do not come into it. The second hazard is that, even if we are dealing with representations, it is easy to make facile assumptions about what kind of perspective they involve. The temptation is usually to find an element of perspective in some directly suppressed relativization, as in the example of the earth. But in issues of right and wrong the temptation should nearly always be resisted. Nearly always it leads to something absurdly over-simplistic, as witness the frequent glib use of phrases such as 'true from a woman's point of view', 'all right for you because you are not a Catholic', 'perfectly justified in time of war'. The third hazard is that, even when there is a suppressed relativization, it is certainly not guaranteed that noticing it will make the appearance of disagreement go away. More likely, in fact, is that the disputants will seem to disagree about the newly acknowledged relata. In other words, they will be in the same kind of position as the disputants in the example of the earth. Thus if you and I appear to disagree about whether some practice is acceptable, then we shall almost certainly appear to disagree about whether any mores are acceptable that make it such. The fourth hazard is that, even when such relativism can be successfully invoked and the appearance of disagreement can be allayed, this will not automatically settle all questions about what to *do*. After all, the procedure may simply reveal that each disputant has been talking indirectly about his or her considered preference. (Think about the couple trying to decide whether this is a good time to have a baby.) There remains the question of whose preference is to be satisfied.

Wherever we find ourselves reckoning with perspective, relativism is sure to be lurking. Of all "isms" it is surely the most treacherous. The four hazards just mentioned are but a tiny indication of that. Relativism has its place, certainly. But it also has a tendency to encroach. Part of the importance of the question whether absolute representations are possible has to do with the importance of keeping relativism at bay.

5

In Chapter One I claimed that a perspectival representation can never be fully self-consciously endorsed by simple repetition. At the beginning of this chapter I picked up on this idea when talking about rational reflective self-understanding. The conclusion that I tried to motivate was this. In so far as we seek not only to represent the world as being thus and so, but also to make sense of ourselves as so representing it, we seek to transcend perspective. At the limit we seek absoluteness. For our goal is to locate our own representations, to explain them, and to show how they can all be representations of one and the same world, in accordance with the Fundamental Principle. At the limit our goal is to attain a self-understanding that applies even to itself. But it cannot apply to itself—it cannot transcend its own perspective—unless it has none. Whether absolute representations are possible, then, has a direct bearing on whether we can achieve our goal. If we cannot, then (to use the Kantian phrase once again) our goal is a regulative ideal.

Let us reflect further on how explanation fits in here. To explain a representation (by which I mean, to explain its occurrence, not its content) is sometimes to vindicate it. More precisely, it is to vindicate it when the explanation weakly entails the representation, or in other words when giving the explanation means indirectly endorsing the representation. A simple example would be an explanation of my conviction that my spectacles are in the other room which, by going into suitable detail about my having seen them there, my subsequently remembering that I saw them there, and my being able to rule out anything's having happened to them since, entails that my spectacles are indeed in the other room. Now, let us say that an explanation of a representation is *interpretative* if it includes an explanation of why the producer of the representation accepts it. And let us say that one explanation is *superior to* another if it better conforms to a paradigm involving maximum reflection and minimum perspective. Let us say, finally, that a representation's *best* explanation is a true interpretative explanation of it which is superior to any other true interpretative explanation of it. (Two comments on these definitions are in order. First, it is entirely possible that the producer of a representation does not accept it. For instance, the production of the representation may be a lie. There is no harm in allowing the definitions to extend to such cases, though those are clearly not the cases that give the definitions their point. Secondly, the definition of superiority, while it can be regarded simply as a piece of linguistic legislation, is not meant to be totally unmotivated: it connects with the earlier discussion of science.) Given these definitions, a false representation cannot be vindicated by its best explanation. Nor can many true representations. For instance, someone may accurately foretell a disaster by thinking that it is written in the tea-leaves. But it is a desideratum, when producing a representation that one takes to be true, to produce one whose best explanation does vindicate it, much as it is a desideratum, when forming an opinion about something, to acquire knowledge rather than to guess. Or so I claim. (I do not deny that it is a desideratum that can be overridden.) This is not uncontroversial. There is a view which recognizes exceptions. According to this

view, some types of representation preclude their instances being
vindicated by their best explanations, even when those instances are
true, which means that it is never a desideratum, when producing
a representation of one of these types, to produce a representation
whose best explanation vindicates it. The representations in question are subjective representations, or radically perspectival representations, whose best explanations are of a historical, sociological,
or anthropological kind, so far removed from the relevant points of
view that no part of them can provide endorsement of the representations. An example would be someone's thinking (perhaps correctly) that she has been impolite. The best explanation of this, on
the view in question, does not entail anything about her impoliteness. This is not to deny that other perfectly adequate explanations
of the representation do entail that she has been impolite, but the
best explanation, on the view in question, is more detached: it incorporates some story about how use of the culture-bound *concept* of
impoliteness enables her and others to live in a particular social
world, just one of the many social worlds in which it is possible to
live.[7] I think that this is to underestimate how indirect an indirect
endorsement can be, or else to exaggerate how "good" an explanation's best explanation can be. Whenever a representation's best
explanation does not vindicate it, it casts doubt on it—however
mildly, however briefly, and however easily the doubt can be overcome. For, at least as far as this explanation goes, there is nothing in
the actual production of the representation to provide any reason
to endorse it.[8] That is why I claim that it is a desideratum, when
producing a representation that one takes to be true, to produce
one whose best explanation vindicates it. And I claim that it is all
the more of a desideratum, when trying to arrive at rational reflective self-understanding, to produce representations whose best
explanations vindicate them. For if, in explaining our own views,
we call them into question, then only something irrational, unre-
flective, or unselfconscious is liable to sustain those views. On the
other hand, if, in explaining our own views, we *vindicate* them,
then, in that very process, we strengthen our grip on the views, and

    [7] Cf. Bernard Williams, *Ethics and the Limits of Philosophy*, ch. 8, though he may want to
distance himself from some aspects of the view being presented.
    [8] Williams, ibid., notes the unsettling effect that reflective explanations can have: see e.g.
p. 148.

thus move one step closer to that reflective ideal in which explanation and vindication come together.

This too, however, is an ideal with absoluteness at its limit. At that limit, any representation on which the rational reflective self-understanding is focused is part of its own best explanation: the world's being represented as thus and so is already part of a full explanatory understanding of how the world comes to be represented as thus and so. And this, given the paradigm of explanation involved, requires that the representation be absolute. Once again, then, we have an ideal whose status depends on whether absolute representations are possible. If they are not, then it is an unrealizable regulative ideal.

I shall return to these ideas throughout the book. They will be particularly important towards the end. Here they constitute our first glimpse of what I think is the main reason for the significance of the question whether absolute representations are possible, though I shall defer discussion of this to the final chapters. For now, I shall simply state what I have in mind. The kind of self-understanding that we have just been envisaging is an ideal. It is the kind of self-understanding that an infinite or divine being might have. (I say this without prejudice as to whether the notion of such a being makes sense.) The main reason for the significance of the question whether absolute representations are possible is this. There is, in each of us, a craving for infinitude.

6

That brings us almost to the end of this chapter. I hope I have done something to show why the question I have posed is worth addressing, though as I have already indicated, my own interest in it is somewhat removed from any intrinsic importance that attaches to it and will not properly emerge until after I have tried to answer it. In that respect this chapter is at something of a tangent to the rest of the book. In other respects too we should be wary of exaggerating the bearing of this chapter on what is to come. I have been largely concerned with showing how disquieting a negative answer to the question would be. But if I am right about that, it by no means follows that an affirmative answer to the question would offer corresponding reassurances. The affirmative answer that I shall eventually give will contain great scope for disappointment. Thus I shall not be offering solace to those who think that ethical representations can be absolute. Nor shall I be doing anything to show that we can ever *knowingly* produce absolute representations. The various advantages which I have said would accrue from our knowing that we were dealing with absolute representations (but which might not accrue from our merely dealing with them) may, for all I shall argue, have to remain a pipe dream. In particular, the menace of relativism, against which the possibility of absolute representations could in any case offer only limited protection, may not be much mitigated. Other ways in which my answer is disappointing will be obvious after I have given it.

There is, however, one further reason why the question is important, which will, by contrast, turn out to give my answer considerable impact. I shall close this chapter by sketching it. It connects with something I said earlier when talking about the relationship between disagreement and our idea of reality. Reality, I said, is what representations answer to. In other words, it is reality that determines whether representations are true or false. This does not mean that we can put our representations to one side and then look at reality directly to see whether or not they are true. We can only assess our representations in the light of some definite *conception* of reality, and this must itself be a matter of how we represent it. In other words, we are only ever able to assess some of our representations in the light of others. Even so, no representation is true unless reality makes it so.

This, and the various other claims that relate to it, are truisms, more or less enforced by the very meaning of the terms 'representation', 'true', 'reality'. But there is a question—a basic question—about how much of substance underpins the truisms; how far, for example, our concept of reality is a concept *of* anything, rather than mere linguistic fluff. We have a sense that there is something very substantial underpinning the truisms. In saying that representations answer to reality, we mean precisely that there *is* something, reality, to which representations answer, something which is how all true representations represent it as being. To adapt a phrase made famous by Williams, we mean that representations are representations of what is there *anyway*.[9] Hence the Fundamental Principle:

---

[9] Bernard Williams, *Descartes*, p. 64.

given any pair of true representations, reality must be how each of them represents it as being, and this is in turn one of the ways it can be truly represented as being. But suppose now that it is impossible to form a determinate conception of this reality that is not just one more set of perspectival representations. How then are we to maintain any sense that our concept of reality *is* more than linguistic fluff? Unless we can be sure that there is some privileged account of what reality is like, how can we be sure that there is ultimately anything other than the representations, and the various techniques of indirect integration that are severally applied to them? If our idea of reality as something substantial is to be sustained, then it seems it must be possible to form a conception of reality that undergirds these techniques and whose own integration with other conceptions is secured without such techniques, a conception, in other words, that is absolute. Thus the final twist to the question whether absolute representations are possible.

——*"But surely our idea of reality as something substantial is to be sustained. Can these reflections not be used to show that the answer to the question is yes, in other words that absolute representations are possible?"*——

The argument for their possibility that I shall eventually present, in Chapter Four, will in fact be a variation on this theme. Its main premiss will be that representations are representations of what is there anyway. But there are many philosophers who would reject this premiss and who are prepared to surrender their idea of reality as something substantial. I think they are wrong. And I think that at least one common source of their error is a seductive misunderstanding about what it takes for a perspectival representation to be true. I shall attempt in the next chapter to put paid to this misunderstanding. That, I think, will put us in a good position to address the main question.

FURTHER READING

Of general relevance to this chapter are Robert Brandom, 'Points of View and Practical Reasoning'; and Fred D'Agostino, 'Transcendence and Conversation: Two Concepts of Objectivity'.

On regulative ideals, see Dorothy Emmett, *The Role of the Unrealisable*.

On the role and importance of objectivity in ethics (in the sense of 'objectivity' appropriated in this book), see Immanuel Kant, *Groundwork of the Metaphysic of Morals*; Thomas Nagel, *The Possibility of Altruism*; Thomas Nagel, *Equality and Partiality*; Derek Parfit, *Reasons and Persons*; John Rawls, *A Theory of Justice*; and David Wiggins, *Needs, Values, Truth*, especially Essay II, 'Universalizability, Impartiality, Truth'. Wiggins's book also contains a good deal that bears on the ideal discussed in this chapter in which vindication and explanation come together.

On the scientific prejudice that there are no privileged points of view, see John Lucas, *Space, Time, and Causality*.

On relativism, see Gilbert Harman, 'Moral Relativism Defended'; Bernard Williams, *Morality*, ch. 3; and Bernard Williams, *Ethics and the Limits of Philosophy*, ch. 9.

CHAPTER THREE

In taking [how things are from *A*'s point of view], and putting it into
the world as something we can conceive of as there, we are in effect
trying to abstract from *how it is for A*, the *how it is* and leave it as a
fact on its own, which however has the mysterious property that it
is available only to *A*.

(Bernard Williams)

Introduction.

*§ 1: A temptation is identified, with the help of four examples. The temptation is
to think that perspective is a characteristic not only of representations but also of
what is represented.*

§ 2: Remarks are made about how to resist the temptation.

§ 3: An account is given of what is wrong with succumbing to the temptation.

*§ 4: An explanation is given for why the temptation exists. There are all sorts of
reasons for thinking that there must be perspectival facts, but none of these reasons is unanswerable.*

*§ 5: Some final brief comments are made about the bearing of this chapter on the
main question, whether absolute representations are possible.*

WHAT makes a true representation true? The way the world is;
nothing more, nothing less. There is, however, a temptation to
qualify this answer in the case of (some) perspectival representations. My aim in this chapter is to combat the temptation. More
specifically my aim is fourfold: to say what the temptation is; to
show how it can be resisted; to say what is wrong with succumbing
to it; and to explain why we feel it.

1

What is the temptation?

Here straight away I face a difficulty. The temptation is a temptation to say something confused and incoherent. The clearer I make my characterization of it, the less clear I shall make its enticement. I will therefore content myself, for the time being, with something sketchy, relying heavily on examples.

In broad terms the temptation is to think the following (the Specious View, as I shall call it).

> *The Specious View*: Perspective is a characteristic not only of representations but also of what is represented. There are perspectival features of reality, which figure in perspectival facts. Perspectival facts are like any other facts in that for them to obtain is for the world to be a certain way. But they are unlike other facts in that their obtaining is itself relative to a point of view. The perspectival facts that obtain from one point of view are different from those that obtain from another. What makes (some) true perspectival representations true is, precisely, the obtaining of perspectival facts.

I shall present four cases by way of illustration. The temptation will be seen at its strongest in the first case. It will get successively weaker in the remaining three cases. By the fourth it will be so weak as to point to its own means of resistance.

> *Case 1*: Alison, pointing to a green apple, says, 'This apple is green.' Her representation is both true and perspectival. It is from the point of view of creatures with a certain visual apparatus. Even if there is no question of relativization here, so that, in particular, there is no question of the apple's not being green from an alien point of view, nor indeed of its not being green from a feline point of view, still a representation of the same type could not be produced from the point of view of beings that did not have that visual apparatus. Lacking the apparatus would mean lacking the relevant concepts. In calling the apple green, Alison is drawing attention to how the apple looks to beings suitably endowed and suitably situated. Now, imagine a long scientific story concerning wavelengths and the rest, which says everything that can be said, scientifically, about what is

involved in the apple's being green, and which can be grasped even by beings that are *not* so endowed. Is that the whole story? In other words, does it weakly entail Alison's representation (in the sense of weak entailment which I introduced in Chapter One)? Or in other words again, is telling the scientific story a way of indirectly endorsing Alison's representation? The temptation is to answer no. For the scientific story seems (literally) colourless. That is, it seems to miss out how the apple actually *looks*. This is the very feature that ensures the truth of Alison's representation. It seems that in order (even) to indirectly endorse her representation, one must produce a representation from the same point of view. And this in turn suggests that only from that point of view *is* how the apple looks, that is to say its greenness, a feature of reality; elsewhere, the difference between the apple's being green and its not being green cannot amount to anything. The position, then, is this. Alison's representation is made true by the fact that the apple is green. That much is trivial, and not in dispute. The temptation is to add: the fact that the apple is green is a perspectival fact, obtaining only from her sensory point of view.

Case 2: Bill is suffering in a dentist's chair. As soon as there is an opportunity to speak he says, 'That drilling is painful.' This is another true, perspectival representation. It is from his own point of view. (I am assuming, contra a suggestion made in Chapter One, that what we have here is indeed a representation.) The temptation this time is to think that the representation is true in virtue of a feature of reality that exists for Bill and for Bill alone: the drilling's painfulness. Imagine the dentist giving an impersonal account of what is going on, rather like the scientific account envisaged in Case 1. She describes how the drill bores Bill's teeth and strikes a nerve and how his eyes begin to water. She may even add, in her aloof, third-personal way, that he is suffering. Yet still her account seems to miss out the very thing that is captured by Bill's original representation. The features to which she refers are there for him and her alike. Not so, it seems, the actual painfulness, to which she is happily denied access. The temptation, then, is to think that Bill's representation is made true by a perspectival fact, the fact that the drilling is painful, which obtains only from his point of view.

Case 3: Colin is speaking at the start of a football match. He says, 'The match is beginning.' His representation is true and perspectival. It is from a particular temporal point of view. The temptation this time is to think that it is true in virtue of a feature of reality that is there only at the start of the match, namely its beginning. Its beginning is not the same as its beginning at 3 p.m. on Saturday, 6 November 1971, even though that is the time (let us say) at which Colin is speaking. The latter is a feature that the match never loses. It will always be true that the match was beginning at 3 p.m. on Saturday, 6 November 1971. Its *simply* beginning, on the other hand, is there only from the relevant temporal point of view, just as the apple's greenness and the drilling's painfulness were there only from the relevant points of view. As before, then, the temptation is to think that Colin's representation is made true by a perspectival fact, the fact that the match is beginning, which obtains only from his then temporal point of view.

Case 4: Dorothy sees a box on her left and says, 'The box is there on the left.' Again her representation is both true and perspectival. It is from her spatial point of view. Here the temptation's grip is so slight as to be virtually negligible. It is the temptation to think that her representation is true in virtue of a feature of reality that is there from where she is situated but not from other positions, namely the box's being on the left. For reasons like those spelt out in Case 3, this is not the same as the box's being on the left of anyone or anything in particular. The temptation, then, is to think that Dorothy's representation is made true by a perspectival fact, the fact that the box is there on the left, which obtains only from her spatial point of view.

2

How can the temptation be resisted?

Case 4 is revealing precisely because the temptation has such a weak grip there. After a moment's reflection it has no grip at all. Dorothy's representation is true simply in virtue of the relevant spatial relation between her and the box. The representation is made true by the non-perspectival fact that the box is on the left *of her*. There are no features of reality involved in this fact that are not there from other points of view. The way to resist the temptation is to keep this case in mind as a kind of exemplar and to treat all other cases analogously.

Thus in Case 1 the apparently colourless scientific story *is* the whole story. The apple is green, certainly. Alison correctly represents it as such. But I am able to say that because I am able to represent it from the same sensory point of view. I have indirectly endorsed Alison's representation. But I could have done so just as well by telling the scientific story. There is nothing that is only there from her sensory point of view. The fact that the apple is green is not a perspectival fact.

In Case 2 Bill's plaint is true, not because of some painfulness which exists from his point of view but not from anybody else's. It is true because the drilling has a certain effect *on him*. It hurts him. The fact that it hurts him, a fact which the dentist is equally able to convey, is not a perspectival fact.

In Case 3 what Colin says is true, not because the match is, in some free-floating sense, beginning, but rather because it is beginning at 3 p.m. on Saturday, 6 November 1971, the time at which he is speaking. The fact that it is beginning then—the fact that it is beginning *then*, mind—is not a perspectival fact.

Nor is it an absolute fact. 'Absolute' and 'perspectival' simply do not apply to facts. They apply at the level of what represents, not at the level of what is represented.

3

What is wrong with succumbing to the temptation?

The Specious View is incoherent. This incoherence lies in an irresoluble tension concerning whether the obtaining of perspectival facts is relative to a point of view or not.

On the one hand the Specious View requires that the obtaining of perspectival facts should indeed be relative to a point of view. (This requirement was explicitly included in the characterization of the view given above.) Otherwise inconsistency beckons. Reconsider Case 4. And suppose that Dorothy's brother, directly

opposite her, says, 'The box is not on the left.' Both her representation and his are true. But if what makes hers true is the simple
obtaining of a perspectival fact, that the box is on the left, and if
what makes his true is the simple obtaining of another perspectival
fact, that the box is *not* on the left, then the box both is, and is not,
on the left—a blatant contradiction. To avoid this contradiction
(without simply joining forces with the opposition and acquiescing
in the box's being on the left of her and on the right of him) one
must say that there are different worlds constituted by facts obtaining from different points of view, the box's "leftness" being a feature
of some worlds but not of others. This, admittedly, has little appeal.
The temptation in Case 4 is very weak. But the same sort of thing
is going on in cases where the temptation is strong. Even in these
cases the pressure to say that there are different worlds (and thereby to deny the unity of reality) arises from a hazy sense that one
world cannot accommodate all the different perspectival facts that
are supposed to obtain. It cannot. Unless one acknowledges that the
obtaining of these facts is relative to a point of view, one always,
ultimately, lapses into incoherence.

   On the other hand the Specious View requires that the obtaining
of perspectival facts should *not* be relative to a point of view. It
requires that perspectival facts should simply obtain, and, as with
other facts, that their obtaining should consist in the world's being
a certain way. Otherwise it is just a terminological variant on its
rival. Reconsider Case 3. And suppose that the perspectival fact here
does not obtain *simpliciter*, but only from the relevant temporal
point of view. What this means is that it is not a fact, *simpliciter*, that
the match is beginning; rather it is a fact, from that point of view,
that the match is beginning. In other words it is a fact, at that time,
that the match is beginning. But if this means anything at all, then
I do not see what else it can mean but that it is a fact that the match
is beginning at that time, which is precisely what those who are
opposed to the Specious View think is the correct thing to say.
There no longer seems to be anything, at the level of the facts, with
an unassailable claim to the title of perspective.

   Eventually the Specious View must break apart. Its advocates are
often dimly aware that there is this tension. Typically, and rather
uneasily, they say that perspectival facts and perspectival features of
reality are only "accessible", or only "available", or only "there"
even, from particular points of view, despite being otherwise per-

fectly regular. To be sure, there are good, homespun ways of making sense of the claim that a particular fact or a particular feature of reality is only accessible from a particular point of view: only at the start of the match can the kick-off be directly witnessed, for instance. But when the claim occurs as part of the Specious View, it is intended with more metaphysical bite than that. Accessibility is intended in a minimal way. The accessibility of a fact is meant to be nothing other than its very facthood. And this means that the claim that a fact is accessible only from a particular point of view cannot but flout any pretensions that the fact has to "regularity".

Another way to look at the matter is this. The temptation is fundamentally a temptation to align content with type, in other words to think that what makes a true representation true depends solely on what type of representation it is. A perspectival fact is a fact determined by a particular type of perspectival representation. This is why, when trying to specify a perspectival fact, one affects to produce a representation of the relevant type but without anchorage to any point of view. One says, for example, that what makes Dorothy's representation true is the fact that the box is there on the left (not on the left of her, just there on the left). And then one prevaricates about whether this fact obtains *simpliciter* or only relative to a point of view. It is impossible, ultimately, to maintain any show of intelligibility here. Content simply cannot in general be aligned with type. Sooner or later, having succumbed to temptation, one must fall foul of this basic datum.

—*"But are you not fighting a straw man? The idea of being on the left, in some free-floating sense, is easily ridiculed, which is why the temptation to talk in such terms is so weak. However, there are some true perspectival representations for which content can be aligned with type, and type with content, namely those which, in your terminology, are both radically perspectival and inherently perspectival. (Or at least, content and type for these representations can be aligned modulo additional elements of perspective, a qualification that I shall take for granted in what follows.) Suppose we say that these representations are made true by perspectival facts—meaning that they are made true by facts determined solely by the representations' types. This time we can make good sense of the idea. Such facts are like any others, in that for them to obtain is for the world to be a certain way: there is no need for relativization. But unlike before, this does not generate an inconsistency, because there is no longer any prospect of our producing two representations of the same type with different truth values: it was when we could do this, or some variant on this, that talking in these terms saddled us with incompatible perspectival facts. On the other hand, there is a non-homespun, metaphysically ambitious sense in which such facts are only accessible from particular points of view: namely, they can only be represented from particular points of view, something which follows immediately from the way in which they have been identified.*

—"This is the kind of idea, extended mutatis mutandis *to perspectival features of reality, that finds expression in Nagel's book* The View From Nowhere.[1] *Again and again in this book Nagel comes back to the thought that there are features of reality that cannot be grasped or, as a result of that, represented except from particular points of view. One of his (less serious) examples is how scrambled eggs taste to a cockroach. We non-cockroaches can know that scrambled eggs taste some way to a cockroach. But we cannot know how they taste. That is something that cannot be known except from a suitably orthopterous point of view. Another of Nagel's examples, developed in an earlier work, is what it is like to be a bat.[2] This likewise, he argues, is something that cannot be known except from the point of view of a bat. So too, representations that make direct reference to these things—how scrambled eggs taste to a cockroach, what it is like to be a bat, and suchlike—cannot be produced except from the relevant points of view. Now, what is the objection to adopting a Nagelian stance and saying that such representations are made true by perspectival facts involving perspectival features of reality?"—*

None. That is, there is no objection to *saying* that. You may, if you wish, apply the term 'perspectival' to the facts that make these representations true, and to the features of reality peculiarly involved in such facts. I am not going to quibble about labels. But I do deny that these facts are categorially distinct from facts of any other kind. And I deny that labelling them 'perspectival' in this way constitutes any kind of defence of the Specious View, even a defence limited to representations of a certain kind. This is not the use of 'perspectival' to which I have been taking exception. The fact that content can be aligned with type in the case of certain perspectival representations—just as it can, of course, in the case of absolute representations, if there are any such things—means that in their case one is allowed to say some of the things that one would say if one succumbed to temptation. It remains the case that

[1] Thomas Nagel, *The View From Nowhere.*
[2] Thomas Nagel, 'What is it Like to be a Bat?'

succumbing to temptation means adopting a view that is irremediably incoherent. As regards your earlier suggestion that only straw men succumb, I think there is plenty of evidence to the contrary, some of which I present in the further reading at the end of this chapter. But I would not care much if I were wrong about that. The temptation still exists, and it is a revealing exercise to combat it.

—*"What do you mean by denying that certain facts are "categorially distinct" from others?"*—

I mean essentially this: that they constitute a single world. Somewhat more prosaically, I mean that logical relations obtain between their corresponding representations. In particular, I insist that the representations made true by the facts which you wish to label 'perspectival' are weakly entailed by other representations. This is why I claimed, in Chapter One, that even an inherently perspectival representation, if such there be, can be indirectly endorsed without adopting its point of view. In much the same vein, I claim that a sufficiently long scientific story could weakly entail a representation from the point of view of a cockroach about what something tasted like—just as a sufficiently long scientific story could weakly entail Alison's representation in Case 1. If part of your intent in applying the term 'perspectival' to certain facts is to deny such claims, then we do disagree.

—*"But what is your justification for making these claims? Are they meant to follow from the unity of reality?"*—

The unity of reality is the nub of the matter. It is acting as a fundamental premiss here. These claims are embellishments of it. I do not profess to be able to supply them with a full justification. (I shall have to more to say about this in later chapters.) But roughly, the idea is this. Let ρ be an inherently perspectival representation. And let π be a point of view, other than that which makes ρ inherently perspectival, from which ρ can be recognized as a representation. Then ρ can be indirectly endorsed from π. For, given that all representations are representations of the same world, to recognize something as a representation is to recognize that there is some way the world could be that would make it true. And this comes to nothing without the wherewithal, in principle, to indicate such a way.[3] But to indicate such a way is indirectly to endorse the representation.

[3] A related idea is to be found in Donald Davidson, 'On the Very Idea of a Conceptual Scheme'; and Ludwig Wittgenstein, *Philosophical Investigations*, §§ 206–7.

There are echoes of the Fundamental Principle here. Indirect integration of two representations is itself indirect endorsement of each of them. So we can indirectly endorse ρ, without adopting its point of view, by indirectly integrating it with a representation from some other, incompatible point of view and ensuring that the result is either from this other point of view or else from neither.

—*"But it may not be possible to ensure that. Or worse, we may not even be able to find a representation from another point of view. This will be the case if ρ is from a point of view that is in some sense inescapable for us— if, say, it is the point of view of a common element of inherent and radical perspective in all our representations. Indeed, will not your earlier assumption concerning ρ, namely that it can be recognized as a representation from some point of view other than that which makes it inherently perspectival, also fail in that case? For the very concept of a representation, being one of our concepts, will not then be available at any other point of view."*—

This is an extremely important objection. I shall try to rebut it in Chapters Five and Six. Meanwhile I hope to have said enough to indicate what is wrong with the Specious View. In order to forestall any confusion I shall keep resolutely to my own avowed use of the terms 'perspectival' and 'absolute'. On that use they apply only to representations.

To take stock, then: the position that I am advocating is this. One and the same reality is represented from different points of view in different ways. Tuesday's rain is represented on Monday by saying, 'It will rain tomorrow.' It is represented on Wednesday by saying, 'It rained yesterday.' The shift from one point of view to another is not a transfer to a different world. It is a move within the same world. The world is constituted by the facts. These simply obtain. There is no question of a fact's obtaining from one point of view but not from another. There is only a question of its being represented in one way from one point of view, and in another from another. A perspectival representation of things is not a representation of perspectival things.

4

Why does the temptation exist?

Although I have not yet committed myself to this, I certainly believe that there are inherently perspectival representations. They include the Nagelian examples: representations concerning how scrambled eggs taste to a cockroach, what it is like to be a bat, and suchlike. They also include many subjective representations. A subjective representation often has a content whose conceptual structure reflects a particular outlook on life. (Consider, for instance, a representation to the effect that certain behaviour is *blasphemous*.) To capture that content one would need to have the relevant concepts. To have the relevant concepts one would need to see the point of applying them. To see the point of applying them one would need to share the beliefs, concerns, or values that help to define that particular outlook. To share those beliefs, concerns, or values would already be to have adopted the point of view from which the representation was originally produced.[4]

The perspective in all these cases is radical as well as inherent. (Consider again the representation involving the concept of blasphemy. If having that concept means adopting the point of view from which the representation has been produced, then there could not be a representation of the same type that was not also from that point of view—which is the defining characteristic of radical perspective. I suggested in Chapter One that it is common to find these two kinds of perspective together. This helps to show why.) There are some representations, then, that are both inherently perspectival and radically perspectival. And, as we have seen, these can help to sustain the temptation. In their case, type and content effectively come together. In particular it is impossible, from other than the given point of view, to carve out the same chunk of conceptual space. This impossibility is easily confused with the impossibility of carving out a chunk of the same conceptual space. It is easy to think that what brings type and content together in such a case is the only thing that could bring them together in a case of any other kind, namely that the point of view carries its own space with it; or, to switch the metaphor in a way that brings out more clearly my opposition to this conception, that adopting the point of view means moving over to a different world.

But the temptation is not confined to representations of this kind. It can be strong even where a representation is neither inher-

[4] Cf. Bernard Williams, *Ethics and the Limits of Philosophy*, pp. 141–2, with further references. Cf. also John McDowell, 'Non-Cognitivism and Rule-Following', pp. 144–5.

ently perspectival nor radically perspectival. In fact it is strong
wherever a perspectival representation seems peculiarly appropriate for picking out its content. ('Appropriate' here is schematic. In
different contexts it has different connotations, for instance of per-
spicuity, immediacy, direct involvement, and the like. The important point is that type and content should once again be brought
into a specially close relationship.) Consider Bill. The content of his
representation is that the drilling hurts him. His own perspectival
representation seems to get to the heart of the matter. For in considering this content we cannot help imagining the situation from
Bill's point of view, where the difference between the drilling's hurting him and its not hurting him is especially acute. The temptation
is to think that what we are imagining are the different ways that
things could be in Bill's world; and that what makes his representation true is how things actually are in that world. We confuse his
unique access to the situation with access to a situation that is
uniquely his.[5]

—"*But in a sense his is a different world. Other people may be able to
tell from Bill's behaviour that he is in pain. They may also be able to imagine the pain. But only Bill can feel it. The pain is only really a feature of
reality for him.*"—

There may be a sense in which the pain is only a feature of reality "for" Bill. Bill's involvement in this state of affairs is certainly
special. But the *facts* that obtain here are facts such as this: *the
drilling hurts Bill.* These provide no warrant for a multi-world conception. In so far as the fact that the drilling hurts Bill helps to constitute a world, then it helps to constitute *the* world, neither more
nor less.

—"*You say this because you too have felt pain and can imagine what
the fact is like from Bill's point of view. In thinking about this fact you
import Bill's world into your thinking. It is a separate world for all that.
And we only have a proper conception of Bill's pain in so far as we think
how things are in that world. There are many things, or many kinds of
thing, that cannot be properly conceived except in terms of what they are
like from a particular point of view. Pain is just one example. Colour is
another. Whether or not Alison's representation can be indirectly endorsed
by telling a long scientific story, there is no knowing what it is for an apple*

---

[5] Cf. Bernard Williams, *Descartes*, pp. 295–6, part of which is quoted at the head of this
chapter.

to be green except in terms of what this is like from a particular sensory point of view. Temporal relations are another good example. There is no knowing what it is for one event to precede another except in terms of what this is like from a temporal point of view, a point of view, say, from which the former event is in the past and the latter event is in the present. True, the temporal case is somewhat different from the others in that no one temporal point of view is privileged. In the temporal case we are dealing with things that cannot be understood except in terms of what they are like from some suitable point of view or other. From different points of view they are different. For instance, the two events just considered will be respectively in the present and in the future from another temporal point of view. In the temporal case, then, there are many different temporal worlds, in which the same events recur. Their temporal features change from one world to another. But that is just as it should be. Change is of the essence of time. The crucial point is that a being which was completely outside time, and which could not think about events in terms of their impingement on different temporal points of view, could have no conception of past, present, or future—and hence, since past, present, and future constitute time, could have no conception of time at all. None of this seems explicable if all features of reality are part of the same (unchanging) world."—

Once again, I can agree with a lot of this. I can agree that if one does not know what something is like from a particular point of view, then one's conception of that thing is limited. But this is because one lacks knowledge concerning the thing's standing in this world: knowledge of its relation to the relevant point of view. Again, I can agree that events change from one temporal point of view to another—in the sense, for example, that an event which is present at 3 p.m. on Saturday, 6 November 1971 is past at 5 p.m. on the same day. But these again are facts that are easily accommodated within a single world. If you mean more than this, and in particular if you mean something that requires past, present, and future to be unrelativized free-floating features of reality, then I can make no sense of what you are saying.

I could make sense of something that required past, present, and future to be unrelativized free-floating features of a certain way of *representing* reality. The beginning of a football match cannot be present without being present at some particular time; but it can be represented as present without being represented as present at any particular time. Colin's representation is a case in point. What I mean by this is not that Colin represents the beginning of the match as the very thing I have claimed it cannot be. I mean rather that Colin produces a representation whose content is that the beginning of the match is present at a particular time, but without himself making explicit reference to that time.

You may want to say that past, present, and future are free-floating in *this* sense. And you may (still) want to say that they constitute time. However, if you do say both of these things, then you must accept the consequence: that time itself is not a feature of reality, but only a feature of a certain way of representing reality.

If you do accept this consequence, then you will not be alone. Countless philosophers have held that time is unreal. They have said that it is merely a feature of how we view things. Indeed McTaggart arrived at this conclusion in pretty much the way just indicated, that is by arguing, first, that past, present, and future (understood as free-floating) cannot be features of reality and, second, that they constitute time.[6] Many who are reluctant to embrace McTaggart's conclusion accept the first part of this argument but not the second. They say that it is not time that is unreal, it is tense. Many others, however, accept the second part of the argument but not the first. Theirs is precisely the kind of position I oppose.[7]

—*"Even if what you say about time is correct, I still think there is a problem for you concerning sensory points of view. Nobody who is congenitally blind can fully understand Alison's representation. If a cockroach could speak, and said something about the taste of scrambled eggs, none of us could fully understand its representation.[8] Surely these facts are inexplicable if all representations answer to the same world. For if someone is part of the world to which a representation answers, in other words if he or she has access, in whatever attenuated sense, to all that is relevant to the truth of the representation, then surely there can at most be contingent obstacles in the way of his or her fully grasping that representation, not a constitutive impossibility."*—

In a way you are raising the question of how radical perspective is possible. The failures of understanding here stem from a radical

---

[6] J. M. E. McTaggart, *The Nature of Existence*, vol. ii, Bk. V, ch. 33.

[7] For articles representing each of these positions see Richard M. Gale (ed.), *The Philosophy of Time*, § II; and Robin Le Poidevin and Murray MacBeath (eds.), *The Philosophy of Time*, Pt. 1. Each of these includes a reprint of McTaggart's chapter and is accompanied by an extensive annotated bibliography. The claim that it is not time, but tense, that is unreal is associated particularly with D. H. Mellor, whose 'The Unreality of Tense' is in the latter.

[8] Cf. Wittgenstein, *Philosophical Investigations*, p. 223.

perspective that prevents representations of the same type being produced from other than the same point of view. But once again we must be careful not to conflate issues about type with issues about content. The type of a representation is a matter of the representation's psychological role. It is linked to a range of conceptual abilities. There is no mystery in the fact that somebody who is not suitably endowed lacks these abilities, and is constitutionally incapable of either grasping or producing a representation of the given type, despite having access to all that would be relevant to the truth of such a representation. This is not much different from the fact that somebody who is dumb is constitutionally incapable of yodelling. Congenitally blind people have access, in your attenuated sense, to Alison's apple, and to everything that is relevant to its being green. But because they cannot *see* it, they are incapable of engaging with it in the same way as she does.

—*"Your analogy with the dumb person omits the crucial cognitive element. What congenitally blind people lack is* knowledge, *knowledge of what the apple looks like. None of us knows what scrambled eggs taste like to a cockroach, or what it is like to be a bat. Absolute representations, even if they were possible, could never communicate these things, no matter how comprehensive the representations were. Even if there were absolute representations saying everything that could be said, at that level, about what was involved in the apple's being green, and even if a congenitally blind person could fully understand these representations, and even if he or she could know that they were all true, still there would be something about the apple concerning which he or she remained irremediably ignorant. This is reminiscent of Mr Meanour, in the case you described in the last chapter. No matter how much knowledge he has about his situation from other than his own point of view, he does not, as a result of that, know that he is wanted by the police. Let him find out never so many things about Mr Meanour. Still, until he realizes that* he *is Mr Meanour, he lacks the knowledge in question. The congenitally blind person's not knowing what the apple looks like; Mr Meanour's not knowing that he is wanted by the police; our not knowing what scrambled eggs taste like to a cockroach: surely these are examples of ignorance of perspectival facts?"*—

You have now given voice to what is probably the most compelling reason for the temptation. It is very natural to think that, in cases of this kind, where the states of knowledge are perspectival representations, there must be facts as finely individuated as they are; and hence that, at least in the case of these perspectival repre-

sentations, and by extension in the case of others, there must be
perspectival facts that are specially equipped to make them true.

There is a quick way to parry these thoughts and thereby to
answer your objection. This is to deny that the states of knowledge
in question *are* representations. More fully, the quick answer to
your objection can be set forth as follows.

The Quick Answer to the "Knowledge" Objection: Reconsider the
analogy with the dumb person. This does *not* omit the cognitive
element. Being able to yodel is a kind of knowledge. That is,
someone who is incapable of yodelling is *eo ipso* someone who
does not know something. But the "something" is not a fact. It is
how to pull off certain feats. In other words the knowledge is a
capacity rather than a kind of representation. What we need to
appreciate is that precisely the same is true of the knowledge to
which you have drawn attention. For instance, knowing what a
green apple looks like is knowing such things as how to select
the right paint on a palette in order to paint a green apple, or
how to pick out the only green apple in a given range of apples
just by looking. This too is knowledge of how to do certain
things. It is not knowledge of a fact. (A congenitally blind person
can know all the facts there are.) *A fortiori* it is not knowledge of
a perspectival fact.

This line of thought has recently become very familiar and very
popular.[9] I am sympathetic to the spirit of it, unsympathetic to the
letter. In Chapter Eight I shall return to these issues and try to
explain why I disagree with much of the quick answer. But the basic
idea—that one can know all the facts and yet still *not* know something—is, I think, the right counter to your objection. It means that
we can acknowledge the ignorance that you highlighted without
having to acknowledge facts of a special kind corresponding to it.

Where I fundamentally part company with the quick answer is
over the assumption that this idea—that one can know all the facts
and yet still not know something—can be sustained only if we deny
that the states of knowledge involved are representations. There is
no need to deny this. Nor indeed is it feasible to do so. Reconsider
Mr Meanour. Whatever capacities and dispositions to action may

---

[9] See e.g. David Lewis, 'Mad Pain and Martian Pain', Postscript; and D. H. Mellor,
'Nothing Like Experience'.

be involved in his eventually coming to realize that he is wanted by the police, the state that he gets into, a state of knowing *that* he is wanted by the police, is surely a (true) representation. Or consider again the congenitally blind. It is not just knowledge of what things look like that they cannot have. On the assumption that Alison's representation involves inherent perspective as well as radical perspective, they cannot have knowledge with that content. They can know all sorts of things in the neighbourhood, including things that they might reasonably express by using the same sentence: 'This apple is green.' But they cannot, strictly speaking, know what Alison knows when she knows that the apple is green. Yet she too, surely, is in a state of knowledge that is a (true) representation.

—*"How can you say that the knowledge in question is representational and at the same time claim that somebody who knows all the facts may nevertheless lack it?"*—

Because there are different ways of representing the facts. Here is an analogy. Suppose that the world were temporally symmetrical. In particular, suppose that there were some initial big bang, then millions of years of activity culminating in a big crunch, then an identical re-run, then nothing—just two cycles in all. Somebody could know all the facts, yet still not know, and have no way of knowing, whether she was living in the first cycle or the second.[10] Her ignorance would be a lack of representational knowledge.

—*"But are you not begging the question when you describe her as knowing all the facts? After all, there would be two different ways the world could be compatibly with all she knew."*—

Epistemically, there would; but not on any other way of slicing the possibilities. That is the point. States of knowledge sometimes slice the possibilities thinner than anything else. (Here is a useful comparison. It is epistemically possible that standard arithmetical principles and definitions require every even number other than 2 to be the sum of two primes. And it is epistemically possible that they do not: the matter remains unresolved. But only one of these is logically possible.) On any non-epistemic way of slicing the possibilities, there would be only one way the world could be compatibly with all this person knew. *Unless* we say this—unless we resist the assumption that there are different facts corresponding to each person's several states of representational knowledge—then we are

[10] Cf. David Lewis, 'Attitudes *De Dicto* and *De Se*'.

forced to recognize perspectival facts. And that, given what I have been arguing, is a *reductio ad absurdum* of the assumption.

This, incidentally, gives the lie to a popular argument against a certain kind of physicalism. The physicalism in question is the doctrine that all the facts are physical facts, facts about how physical things are physically. (This is exceedingly rough. Stated like that, the doctrine is as much in need of elucidation as of justification. But the point I am making here does not require anything more precise. I shall have more to say about physicalism in the next chapter.) The argument against such physicalism rests on the premiss that somebody could know all the physical facts yet still be ignorant, not knowing, for example, what a green apple looks like.[11] We can now see that this premiss, though no doubt true, is perfectly compatible with all the facts' being physical facts, as the physicalism in question has it.

A final point in this section: I have been trying to combat the temptation to posit perspectival facts and perspectival features of reality. Often the temptation takes the specific form of a temptation to posit subjective facts and subjective features of reality (meaning, beauty, grace, and suchlike). I do not think that, in this specific form, it raises any new questions of principle.

5

I hope now to have discharged the four tasks I set myself. There is a deep irony. To succumb to the temptation that I have been trying to combat is to endeavour to take perspective as seriously as possible, by promoting it from being a characteristic of representations to being a characteristic of reality, or rather of the facts that constitute reality. But this is precisely not to take perspective seriously. To suppose that there are, set against true perspectival representations of a certain kind, facts of a corresponding kind is not to accept the representations for what they are. It is to posit something special for them to answer to, when what is required is due acknowledgement of the way in which they are themselves special. A perspectival rep-

---

[11] See e.g. Howard Robinson, 'The Anti-Materialist Strategy and the "Knowledge Argument"'.

resentation of reality is just that: a *perspectival* representation of *reality*, the very reality that can be represented from other points of view and perhaps also from no point of view, the only reality there is. When cockroaches taste scrambled eggs they do not encounter something that is only part of "their" world, something gustatory to which the rest of us are denied access. They simply encounter scrambled eggs, in their own idiosyncratic way.

How does the discussion in this chapter bear on the question of whether absolute representations are possible? It is relevant to what would be involved in returning a negative answer to this question. If absolute representations are not possible, then the discussion in this chapter shows that we can nevertheless continue to operate with our idea of reality as that to which all representations answer. We need not suppose that we are only ever able to talk or think about our own private worlds, uniquely accessible from our own points of view, or that we are debarred from trying to form a conception of the common world in which we and others (other people, aliens, cockroaches, bats) find ourselves, or that we have no right to an idea of "the world" at all. That would be an alarming thought. It would leave us feeling weightless, cut off from one another, each trapped in a kind of autonomous dream-world. But it is not a thought that would be forced upon us by the impossibility of absolute representations. Nor, conversely, is there any quick argument from the untenability of this thought to their possibility.

—*"But there* is *a quick argument—is there not?—from your principal conclusion in this chapter. Or at least, there is on the anti-sceptical assumption that it is possible to form a conception of what the facts are like in themselves. For you deny that the facts are perspectival. So no such conception can itself be perspectival. It must be absolute. In other words it must be composed of absolute representations."—*

What do you mean by "a conception of what the facts are like in themselves"? If you in effect just mean an absolute conception, then this argument is question-begging. If not, then why need such a conception be composed of representations that are anything other than *true*? Remember, I no more want to think of the facts as absolute than I want to think of them as perspectival.

—*"But surely, if the facts themselves are not perspectival, then any perspectival conception of them imposes something on them that is not already there. It gives them a particular gloss. It is a conception of them as impinging in some way or other on a particular point of view, not as they are in themselves.*"[12]—

I simply cannot see any non-question-begging interpretation of these claims that gives us any entitlement to them.

This chapter, I hope, has clarified our main question. But work is still required to answer it.

FURTHER READING

The position I defend in this chapter is very much like that of D. H. Mellor: see e.g. 'Analytic Philosophy and the Self'; 'Nothing Like Experience'; and 'The Unreality of Tense'. Cf. also Laurence Nemirow, 'Review of Thomas Nagel's *Mortal Questions*'; Laurence Nemirow, 'Physicalism and the Cognitive Role of Acquaintance'; and John Perry, *The Problem of the Essential Indexical and Other Essays*.

Evidence that not only straw men succumb to the temptation identified in this chapter includes much of what has been written in response to McTaggart's argument, as cited above in n. 7. See e.g. C. D. Broad, 'Ostensible Temporality'; and Arthur N. Prior, 'Changes in Events and Changes in Things'. See also the work that Richard M. Gale identifies as employing the "A-theory of Time" in *The Philosophy of Time*, pp. 504–5; and the work that Robin Le Poidevin and Murray MacBeath identify as opposing the "tenseless theory of time" in *The Philosophy of Time*, pp. 223–4.

Others who succumb to the temptation include those who accept the "knowledge" objection to physicalism: see e.g. the pieces cited by Howard Robinson in n. 1 of 'The Anti-Materialist Strategy and the "Knowledge Argument"', including Frank Jackson, 'What Mary Didn't Know'. (Counter-objections to the "knowledge" objection include: David Lewis, 'What Experience Teaches'; Mellor, 'Nothing Like Experience'; and Nemirow, 'Physicalism and the Cognitive Role of Acquaintance'.)

I leave it to others to judge how far Thomas Nagel succumbs: see especially 'What is it Like to be a Bat?'; and *The View From Nowhere*.

---

[12] Cf. Richard Rorty, 'The World Well Lost', pp. 14–15.

CHAPTER FOUR

Why . . . this special deference to physical theory? This is a good question, and part of its merit is that it admits of a good answer. The answer is not that everything worth saying can be translated into the technical vocabulary of physics; not even that all good science can be translated into that vocabulary. The answer is rather this: nothing happens in the world, not the flutter of an eyelid, not the flicker of a thought, without some redistribution of microphysical states.

(W. V. Quine)

§ 1: The question whether absolute representations are possible is distinguished from various other questions with which it might be confused.

§ 2: Two arguments for the possibility of absolute representations are sketched. The first, which is a variant on the main argument of this chapter, is put on hold. The second is dismissed.

§ 3: The main argument of this chapter, the Basic Argument, is given. This is an embellishment of an argument due to Williams.

§ 4: The main premiss of the Basic Argument, the Basic Assumption, is identified. Some final brief comments are made about the role of science, and specifically of physics, within what has just been argued.

1

ARE absolute representations possible? That is the question. But it is as well to begin by rehearsing some of the things that the question is not, because confusion over this is both damaging and easy.

The question is not whether true representations are possible. Of course, being absolute is compatible with being false, but that is not the point I have in mind: I am prepared to grant that there is no significant gap between the possibility of absolute representations and the possibility of absolute truths. The point I have in mind is rather that being perspectival is compatible with being true—in an entirely straightforward sense of the term 'true'. This is a point that I have already laboured, but the point is worth making explicitly one more time because it is easy to think that perspectival truth (especially when it takes the form of subjective truth) gets its title of 'truth' by courtesy only. A very stark way of making my point is this. The question is not whether *representations* are possible. Perspectival representations are representations.

The question is not whether absolute representations actually exist. More specifically, the question is not whether the representations that constitute this or that actual scientific theory are absolute. Even if no physicist, say, has ever produced an absolute representation, this does not settle the question.

The question is not whether absolute representations are within easy reach. 'Possible' is intended minimally. It is intended to embrace *any finite extension of our powers*. An affirmative answer to the question does not preclude its being a practical impossibility to produce absolute representations. (Compare: it is possible to tell whether any given number is prime, even if the number has more than a trillion digits.) *A fortiori* an affirmative answer to the question does not preclude its being a matter of great effort to produce absolute representations, effort, conceivably, that no-one would think worth expending.

The question is not whether absolute representations lie at the end of some route that we are now travelling along. Again, an affirmative answer to the question does not preclude its being a matter of some radical volte-face to produce absolute representations.

The question is not whether the production of absolute representations is a desideratum of this or that kind of enquiry. I argued in Chapter Two that it is a desideratum of scientific enquiry. But I also indicated why the success of that argument does not require an affirmative answer to the question: absoluteness, even if it is unattainable, can serve as a regulative ideal. Nor, conversely, does the failure of the argument require a negative answer to the question. The sheer availability of absolute representations could not prevent scientists from having a perfectly justified lack of interest in producing them.

The question is not whether it is possible to frame sentences that can be classified as true or false independently of context. The question is not that, because not all representations are linguistic. But more importantly, even if attention is restricted to representations that are linguistic, to think that this is what the question amounts to is to make an unwarranted assumption about sameness of type. I shall say more about this in Chapter Five.

The question is not whether indisputable representations are possible. Indisputability is something quite separate. Even if absolute representations are possible, it may be that only highly abstruse scientific formulae can fit the bill. In that case true absolute representations will far more readily admit of dispute than most true perspectival representations. There is little room for dispute, for instance, when one person reminds another what day it is. In fact, true absolute representations will far more readily admit of dispute than a good many true *subjective* representations, those, for example, from points of involvement constituted by deeply shared humanitarian sensibilities. Suppose that the unusual appearance of pot-bellied famine victims on television makes a young child laugh. And suppose that the child is admonished by its parents, and told that starvation is not funny. There can be less dispute about that than there can be about the latest pronouncements in some recondite branch of quantum mechanics, however the latter are couched.

For much the same reason, the question is not whether certain (indubitable) representations are possible. Certainty differs from indisputability in that the certainty of a representation is a matter of the epistemic role it plays in the psychology of whoever produces it, whereas the indisputability of a representation is a matter of its epistemic standing in public discourse. But certainty, like indisputability, is quite separate from absoluteness. Descartes's search for certainty famously culminated in the perspective of the *cogito*: 'I think, therefore I am.'[1] Absoluteness does have connotations of firmness and stability. But these are of a non-epistemic kind.

[1] René Descartes, *Discourse on the Method*, Pt. IV.

The question is not whether there is some one privileged stock of concepts such that any representation involving only these concepts is guaranteed to be absolute. The question is not even whether there *can* be such a stock of concepts. If absolute representations are possible at all, then it may be that absolute representations of different kinds are possible, involving concepts drawn from different, "incommensurable" stocks: there need not be any single way of conceptualizing things that is necessary in order to represent them absolutely. I shall amplify on this in Chapter Five.

The question is not whether the world can be completely described using absolute representations. Perhaps the world cannot be completely described using *any* kind of representation. *A fortiori* the question is not whether there can be absolute representations knowledge of whose truth suffices for knowing everything. As I insisted in Chapter Three, even if the world *can* be completely described using absolute representations, assimilation of such a description leaves room for ignorance.

The question is not whether whatever can be said can be said using an absolute representation. The existence of inherently perspectival representations ensures that the answer to the latter question is no. But that in no way threatens the possibility of absolute representations.—*"What about the question of whether whatever can be said can be indirectly endorsed using an absolute representation?"*—As it stands, the question is not that either, although my treatment of it in this chapter will certainly indicate its dependence on that question.

The question is not whether it is possible to recognize something as an absolute representation. Even if absolute representations are possible, it may be that there is never any telling that something is an absolute representation because there is never any ruling out the possibility that a given representation contains some hidden element of radical perspective. To argue that absolute representations are possible is not to argue that representations are possible that are in any sense clearly labelled 'absolute'.

The question is not whether it is possible to produce a representation that betrays none of one's points of view. Even if the answer to this latter question is no, it may still be possible to produce a representation that is not *from* any point of view. Again, I shall amplify on this in Chapter Five.

The question is not whether there can be representations that are their own best explanation. More precisely, the question is not whether there can be representations such that the existence of each of them is best explained by some conjunction of them. In Chapter Two I defined a representation's "best explanation" as a true interpretative explanation of it which conforms better than any other to a paradigm involving maximum reflection and minimum perspective. But 'better than any other' is the operative phrase. This leaves open the possibility that the best explanation of a representation (if indeed there is such a thing) can never be absolute, simply because absolute representations are not possible. There are compelling reasons, in fact, for thinking that the best explanation of a representation can never be absolute even if absolute representations are possible. These have to do with the fact that the explanation must be interpretative. Arguably, there is no giving an interpretative explanation of anything without adopting some interpretative point of view. Come to that, there may be no giving an explanation of a representation, whether interpretative or not, without adopting some interpretative point of view. For the concept of a representation is itself ineradicably hermeneutical. This may mean that it cannot be exercised except from such a point of view, in which case any explanation that incorporates it must be (inherently) perspectival.[2] I talked about an ideal in Chapter Two which did involve absolute representations that were their own best explanation. But I did not commit myself to that ideal's being realizable if absolute representations are possible, only to its not being realizable if they are not. I think, in fact, that the ideal is an unrealizable, regulative one—whether or not absolute representations are possible. At any rate the possibility of absolute representations is quite separate from the possibility of representations that explain themselves in the way envisaged.

The question is not whether there can be representations that are made true simply by how the world is. My principal aim in Chapter Three was to argue that *any* true representation is made true simply by how the world is.

The question is not whether there can be representations that form a conception of how things are in themselves—unless those last eleven words are just a circumlocution for 'absolute represen-

---

[2] Cf. Bernard Williams, *Descartes*, pp. 301–3; Bernard Williams, *Ethics and the Limits of Philosophy*, p. 104; and Hilary Putnam, *Renewing Philosophy*, pp. 100–3.

tations'. This was basically the point I made at the end of Chapter Three.

The question is not whether there can be representations that are from all points of view at once. It is easy to think of the absolute as somehow encompassing the perspectival. But if this thought amounts to anything, it certainly does not amount to the absurd idea that being from no point of view is the same as, or even equivalent to, being from every point of view. Nor, for that matter, is being from no point of view the same as or equivalent to being from one very special point of view. The question is not whether there can be representations that are from "the point of view of the Universe".[3]

The question is not whether there can be representations whose subject matter is the world conceived as a whole. Swayed by a certain picture in which one moves nearer to an absolute view of something by backing off from it and seeing it in a broader context, we are inclined to say that one reaches an absolute view of something when one has backed off from it far enough to see it in the context of the world as a whole (*sub specie aeternitatis*). But this involves visual metaphors whose import, on reflection, is unclear, to say the least. And in so far as the idea of conceiving the world as a whole makes any sense at all—it does not make sense without some further gloss—then it remains to be shown why absolute representations have a better title to the claim of having the world conceived as a whole for their subject matter than perspectival representations.

These, then, are some of the things that the question is not. Of course, it is intimately related to many of them. I shall willy-nilly end up addressing many of these questions in what follows. In particular, I shall come back to the issue, which I touched upon in Chapter Two, of how the possibility of absolute representations bears on science, and specifically on physics.

2

In the first three chapters of this book I tried to articulate and to clarify my question. In this chapter I shall endeavour to answer it,

---

[3] This is another reference to the phrase used by Henry Sidgwick, *Methods of Ethics*, pp. 382 and 420.

arguing that absolute representations are possible. The argument will be an embellishment of a well-known argument of Williams.[4]

My interlocutor has already gestured towards two arguments for the possibility of absolute representations, one of which I said was a variant on the argument that I am about to present, the other of which I dismissed. First, at the end of Chapter Two, came the suggestion that if our sense of reality as something substantial is to be sustained, then absolute representations must be possible. Otherwise, the thought was, we would have no way of seeing how there could be anything underpinning the truism that representations answer to reality. It would look like just another way of saying that representations are representations. The term 'reality' would look as if were playing a purely syncategorematic role. In order to be sure that it was not playing that role we should need some conception of what the term stood for. But we should need more than that. To have a conception of what the term stood for would be to represent what the term stood for, namely reality, as being a certain way. And in order to stave off the objection that we were thereby producing "just more representations", and so still not seeing any deeper than the triviality that representations are representations, we should need a conception, or some guarantee of a conception, that was privileged in some way. In particular it would have to consist of representations whose indirect integration with other representations did not require "just more techniques of indirect integration". It would have to consist of absolute representations.

Of the countless questions raised by this rapid train of thought, perhaps the most basic is this: why *should* our sense of reality as something substantial be sustained? One of the main functions of Chapter Three was to rebuff one reason for thinking that it should not, namely that there are different worlds constituted by different perspectival facts. But there is more to be said in response to this question. I shall address it again in later chapters. Addressing some of the other questions is a task that remains for this chapter.

Meanwhile there is the second argument to which my interlocutor gestured. This was at the end of Chapter Three. This argument had an anti-sceptical premiss to the effect that it must be possible to

[4] Williams, *Descartes*, pp. 64–5, 239, 245–9, and 301–3, and *Ethics and the Limits of Philosophy*, pp. 138–40.

form a conception of reality as it is in itself. That premiss was then combined with the thought, for which I could see no non-question-begging justification, that only an absolute conception of reality is a conception of reality as it is in itself.

—*"But in dismissing this second argument do you not impugn the first? For now you seem to be conceding that perspectival representations can serve just as well, when it comes to providing a conception of what the term 'reality' stands for, as absolute representations."*—

So they can. But this is no threat to the first argument. In holding fast to our sense of reality as something substantial, we can perfectly well respond to the challenge to say what reality is like—what it is like "in itself" if you will—by producing perspectival representations. It is just that we do not *thereby* rid ourselves of certain sceptical worries. If we say that grass is green, for example, then we certainly say what reality is like (at least in part). But we do not rid ourselves of the worry that 'reality' is just a grammatical contrivance. To do that—to *sustain* our sense of reality as something substantial—we need to be able to call on absolute representations.

—*"What you now seem to be saying is that absolute representations, if they were possible, could serve as a philosophical palliative: they could serve to prevent our being afflicted by certain sceptical worries. That is scarcely an argument for their possibility."*—

I agree that there is a lacuna in what I have said so far. The argument for the possibility of absolute representations should indicate a genuine necessity where at this stage there appears to be a mere desirability. It will do this by proceeding, not from the premiss that we need to be able to *sustain* our sense of reality as something substantial, but from the premiss merely that reality *is* something substantial.

I shall now present the argument. As a mark of the central role that it will play in this book I shall refer to it as the Basic Argument.

3

The Basic Argument.

Representations are representations of what is there *anyway*. They are representations of reality. Each true representation is made true by reality. Each of any pair of true representations is made true by reality. Suppose that ρ_1 and ρ_2 are such a pair. In other words suppose that ρ_1 and ρ_2 are two true representations. Now it means nothing to say that each of them is made true by reality unless it is possible, in principle, to produce a representation that reveals how. Any reason for doubting that it is possible to do this is a reason for doubting that ρ_1 and ρ_2 really are two true representations. This is not a sceptical point. It is a point about what it is for something to *be* a pair of true representations. Any two true representations collectively have content, that things are a certain way, where things are indeed that way. This comes to nothing if it is not so much as possible to indicate what that way is.

To produce a representation that reveals how reality makes each of ρ_1 and ρ_2 true is, among other things, indirectly to integrate them. (For instance, suppose that ρ_1 is an assertion of the sentence 'It is humid.' And suppose that ρ_2 is an assertion of the sentence 'It is snowing,' made six months later in the same place. To produce a representation that reveals how reality makes each of these true is, among other things, to specify the weather conditions that obtain in the place concerned at the two times concerned.) In effect, then, I have just motivated the Fundamental Principle—again. But I have motivated something more. Given any pair of true representations, not only must it be possible indirectly to integrate them by producing another true representation. It must be possible to reveal them *as* having the content which is captured in the indirect integration. It must be possible to reveal them *as* representations made true by reality. (To reveal how reality makes the two assertions considered above true, it is necessary to say how the truth of an assertion of the sentence 'It is humid,' in a particular place at a particular time—and likewise in the case of the sentence 'It is snowing'—depends on the weather conditions that obtain in that place at that time.) This goes beyond the Fundamental Principle because indirect integration of two representations need not, itself, make reference either to them or to their content.

Now suppose that ρ_1 and ρ_2 are from incompatible points of view. (They may also be from at least one common point of view. That is, there may also be at least one element of perspective that they share. But the supposition is that there are elements of perspective that they—necessarily—do not share. This is true in the case of the two assertions considered above. No single representation can be, or could have been, produced from both of those temporal points of view.) On this supposition, ρ_1 and ρ_2 cannot be integrated by simple addition. In any account revealing how they are made true by reality, at least one of them—ρ_1 for the sake of argument—must be indirectly endorsed without adoption of the relevant point of view (the point of view that is incompatible with ρ_2's). This means that if the account is to reveal ρ_1 *as* a representation made true by reality, it must involve explicit reference to that point of view, showing how the point of view contributes to ρ_1's having the content it has. (Thus, on the supposition once again that ρ_1 and ρ_2 are the two assertions considered above, the account must involve reference to how the truth of ρ_1 depends on the time at which it is produced.) Now, call a maximal class of points of view, any two of which are incompatible with each other, a *range* of points of view. ('Maximal' here indicates that there is no point of view outside the class that is incompatible with each of those in it. The class of all points in time is a range—assuming that it is not possible to produce a representation from a point of view that is outside time altogether. If this *is* possible, then the class is not a range, because it is not maximal.) Say that a given range of points of view has been *superseded* when a representation has been produced that is not from any point of view in the range. Then only by superseding the range of ρ_1's point of view is it possible to show how that point of view contributes to ρ_1's having the content it has. For to show how ρ_1's point of view contributes to its having the content it has is also, *mutatis mutandis*, to show the same thing for any other possible representation from any point of view in the range. So the account must include a part that, metaphorically speaking, involves stepping up a level, a part that is not itself from any point of view in the range. (In practice this means that its treatment of ρ_1 and ρ_2 will be entirely symmetrical. The part of the account which is used to provide for the indirect integration of ρ_1 and ρ_2 will not be from either of the relevant points of view. In the case of the two assertions that we have been considering, it will be a specification of the weather conditions in the place concerned at the two times concerned, where these in turn will be specified by means of clock readings, dates, and the like.) The upshot of the discussion so far, then, is this. Given any pair of true representations ρ_1 and ρ_2 from incompatible points of view, it must be possible to produce a true representation ρ_3 which, even if it is perspectival, is not from either of those points of view, nor from any other point of view in the same range. In other words, it must be possible to supersede that range. Or in other words again: it must be possible to eliminate that element of perspective.

Suppose now that ρ_3 is perspectival. (If it is not, absolute representations are possible.) Then by definition, it must be possible to produce a representation ρ_4 with which ρ_3 cannot be integrated by simple addition. We can suppose without loss of generality that ρ_4 is true: if it were not, we could consider its negation. So the entire argument of the last three paragraphs can now be extended to ρ_3 and ρ_4. This means that it must be possible to supersede *that* range too. And so on indefinitely.

This is not yet an argument for the possibility of absolute representations however. Even granted the assumption that it is always possible to supersede a range without introducing a new element of perspective—call this the "no new perspective" assumption—there is still the problem that these ranges may extend indefinitely. It may be, for all that has been argued so far, that for each possible representation, there is another that contains fewer elements of perspective, though there is none that contains none. At this point it is tempting to try to extend the argument horizontally rather than vertically. It is tempting, in other words, to proceed as follows.

If the process just considered does not terminate in an absolute representation, then ρ_1 must be infinitely rich in perspective. That is, ρ_1 must be from infinitely many points of view—as it may be, a certain temporal point of view, a certain spatial point of view, a certain sensory point of view, and so on. Now for each of these points of view, there is a possible true representation from some incompatible point of view. And just as it must be possible to produce a single representation that reveals how ρ_1 and ρ_2 are made true by reality, so too it must be possible to produce a single representation that reveals how ρ_1 and all of these infinitely many other representations are made true by reality. Furthermore, just as this requires, in the case of ρ_1 and ρ_2, the possibility of a representation that has at least one less element of perspective than ρ_1 (the element that prevents ρ_1's integration by simple addition with ρ_2), so too it requires, in the case of ρ_1 and the infinitely many representations, the possibility of a representation that has *none* of the elements of perspective in ρ_1, and no others besides. In other words, it requires the possibility of a representation that is absolute.

That is the tempting way to try to extend the argument. It still rests on the "no new perspective" assumption, which at the very least requires justification. But more significantly, it rests on an assumption that must certainly be rejected. This is the assumption that there is no essential difference, for these purposes, between pitting ρ_1 against ρ_2 and pitting it against an infinitude of true representations. Everything that has so far been said about pairs of representations, including the Fundamental Principle, can readily be adapted to cover arbitrary finite sets. (See the discussion of indirect integration at the end of Chapter One.) But it cannot be readily adapted to cover arbitrary infinite sets. Apart from anything else, some infinite sets admit of no finite specification. It is absurd to think that, in such a case, there is any possibility of revealing, in a single representation, and with the relevant specificity, how all the members of the set are made true by reality. And lest it be protested that the infinite set in question *does* admit of a finite specification—on the grounds that it was finitely specified above—note that there is no such thing as "the" infinite set in question. We have been given no recipe for getting from ρ_1 to one particular infinite set of representations correlated with its infinitely many points of view. Such a recipe may exist. Indeed such a recipe may be recoverable from the process considered earlier, of advancing from ρ_1 to ρ_3 and so forth. But we are no more entitled to assume that this is the case than we are to assume that absolute representations are possible. All we are in a position to conclude so far is that, if ρ_1 is infinitely rich in perspective, then there is *an* infinite set of possible true representations such that each of ρ_1's elements of perspective can be eliminated by pitting it against some member of the set. This falls short of concluding that all of ρ_1's elements of perspective can be eliminated simultaneously, by simultaneously pitting it against all the members of the set.

Things would be different if there were any reason to think that a single account of how ρ_1 is made true by reality could serve for pitting it against *any* other possible truth. It would not then matter if ρ_1 could not be pitted against all the members of this set simultaneously. But in fact there *is* reason to think this. It is a further requirement of our sense of reality as something substantial. If reality is something substantial to which ρ_1 answers, once and for all, then it ought to be possible to give a single account, equipped to mesh with a similar account for any other possible truth, that reveals how. This is a return to ideas that guided the rapid train of thought considered above, the first of the arguments to which my interlocutor gestured. It is not a demand for a philosophical palliative. Indeed we can leave open the possibility that no such account is capable of serving as a philosophical palliative because no such account is recognizable as such. The point is rather that if such an account is not even possible—if a succession of different accounts is required for pitting ρ_1 against different possible truths—then that nullifies the thought that ρ_1 is made true by what is there *anyway*. There are then "just different techniques of indirect integration".

The conclusion that absolute representations are possible is still not secured however. It remains to deal with the "no new perspective" assumption, either by justifying it or by dispensing with it. It is simpler, in fact, to dispense with it. The best way to do this is to revamp the horizontal extension of the argument in a way that does not depend on the assumption. The starting point, again, is provided by ideas that guided the earlier rapid train of thought.

If reality is something substantial that representations answer to, the same reality in every case, then not only must it be possible to provide an account of the kind just described for any possible true representation, but the part of this account that is used for the indirect endorsement of the representation must be combinable with every other such part into a single conception of reality—call it C. This claim calls for elucidation of both 'combinable' and 'conception'. By 'combinable' I mean 'integrable by simple addition'. Anything less would once more be vulnerable to the objection that there were "just different techniques of indirect integration" applicable to "just more representations". The requirement of combinability here is the requirement that the representations constituting C should all be from the same points of view, if any. By 'conception' I mean 'set of true representations'. This allows for the possibility that a given conception, because it is infinite, cannot count as a single representation. I have already talked casually about conceptions of reality in this and previous chapters. I have also applied the term 'absolute' to them. Someone might protest that this is not licensed by my policy of applying 'absolute' only to individual representations. Very well. Think of the application of 'absolute' to a conception as an abbreviation. To say of a conception that it is absolute is to say that it contains only absolute representations.

Now consider any possible true representation ρ from any point of view π. One of the members of C must be derived from the account of how ρ is made true by reality. This account, since it serves for pitting ρ against any other possible true representation, including any possible true representation from a point of view incompatible with π, cannot itself be from π. So, given that all the members of C are from the same points of view, none of them can be from π. But π was chosen arbitrarily. So none of the members of C can be from any point of view. Absolute representations are possible.

4

This book could stop there. A question was raised. I now take myself to have answered it. Or at least, I take myself to have answered it on one basic assumption. The assumption is that representations are representations of what is there *anyway*. This is an assumption which, as we have seen, involves a cluster of interrelated ideas about the unity, substantiality and autonomy of reality, ideas which, among other things, inform the Fundamental Principle. I shall refer to it as the Basic Assumption.

There are certainly philosophers who do not share the Basic Assumption. I shall come back to it, and to their opposition, later in the book. But with the caveat that my answer to the question is to that extent hypothetical, this book could, as I say, stop there.

As I also indicated at the outset, however, addressing this question is not my only concern. Furthermore, it would be unsatisfactory to finish without responding to the many very important arguments that have been advanced for answering the question negatively. In the next chapter I shall broach some of these arguments. This will enable me at the same time to turn to my other concerns. More fully, my plan is this. In the next chapter I shall try to show that considerations in favour of answering the question negatively eventually become considerations in favour of something very radical: were it a necessary truth that all representations are perspectival, then this would have to be because of a single inescapable element of perspective of some deep and extraordinary kind. In Chapter Six I shall turn to this radical position and try to expose incoherence in it. Chapters Five and Six together will constitute further support for my own affirmative answer to the question. But they will also create a need for diagnosis. The radical position has an appeal that must be accounted for. In Chapter Seven I shall start on the diagnosis. That will lead me to the heart of the book, a study of ineffability.

Before I end this chapter, however, I need to say something about the role I see for science within what I have just been arguing. My discussion of science in Chapter Two, and much of what I have said elsewhere about indirect endorsement, probably suggest that my picture of an absolute representation is a picture of something built out of scientific concepts. It is—roughly speaking. But the first thing that needs to be emphasized in making this less rough is how indeterminate the picture is: as indeterminate as it can be compatibly with being describable in those terms. It is not a picture of something built out of the concepts that shape this or that extant scientific theory, nor yet concepts that can be obtained by any known methodological strategy from the concepts that shape this or that extant scientific theory. Here it is worth recalling some of the questions that I do not take myself to have answered. I do not take myself to have answered the question whether absolute representations actually exist; nor the question whether they are easy to produce; nor the question whether, in any of our current enterprises, we are *en route* to producing them; nor the question whether we can ever know that we have produced them. I am free to admit that the answer to each of these questions, suitably clarified, is no.

All I mean to be doing, in affirming the connection between absolute representations and science, or more specifically between absolute representations and physics, is signalling how I understand the term 'physics'. There is no point of great substance here. It is simply that, on this understanding, it is the business of physicists, as it is the business of no other enquirers, to find some minimal set of concepts that can be used for the indirect endorsement of any true representation: evidence that the concepts physicists currently employ are inadequate for these purposes is evidence that they have further work to do. (This is more or less Quine's position.)[5] It is important here to remember two things: the indirectness of indi-

---

[5] See e.g. W. V. Quine, 'Facts of the Matter'. See also the passage excerpted at the head of this chapter, from 'Goodman's *Ways of Wordmaking*', p. 98.

rect endorsement; and the fact that there need not be any question *in practice* of our being able indirectly to endorse any given true representation by producing a representation couched in purely physical terms. Thus in deciding whether the truth of some claim about desolation and consolation in the second movement of Beethoven's *Eroica* forces physicists to devise new concepts, we can afford to think in very schematic terms about the supervenience of aesthetic judgements on truths about the trajectories of fundamental particles (say). No doubt this will involve us in hard philosophical work, but it will not involve us in the manifestly hopeless task of actually trying to tell a long scientific story that weakly entails the aesthetician's claim.

That is how I understand the term 'physics', then. In saying this I do not mean to register indifference about whether it is how anybody else understands the term 'physics': there would certainly be cause for concern if, for instance, it were not at all how *physicists* understand the term. Nor do I mean to discount the possibility of forces, at work within that very understanding, that might lead me to deny this connection between absolute representations and physics: one understanding can evolve naturally into another. When I say that this is how I understand the term 'physics', the point I really mean to be making is that the physicalism to which I am thereby committed—I am certainly committed to *some* kind of physicalism, because it is in accord with my understanding of 'physics' to say that all facts are physical facts—does not amount to much. Crane and Mellor have argued that there is no kind of physicalism that is not either false, or unintelligible, or vacuous.[6] So be it: I can accept that this particular physicalism is vacuous. I would be happy to present the conclusion of this chapter by saying that absolute representations, couched in purely physical terms, are possible. But I would not thereby be saying much more than that absolute representations are possible. And even then, I would want to allow for a natural evolution of concepts that led me to stick with saying *just* that.

[6] Tim Crane and D. H. Mellor, 'There is No Question of Physicalism'.

FURTHER READING

Williams's argument is discussed in: Jane Heal, *Fact and Meaning*, § 7.2; Christopher Hookway, 'Fallibilism and Objectivity: Science and Ethics'; Nicholas Jardine, 'The Possibility of Absolutism'; Nicholas Jardine, 'Science, Ethics, and Objectivity'; and Hilary Putnam, *Renewing Philosophy*, ch. 5.

For variations on the Basic Argument see Simon Blackburn, 'Enchanting Views'; and Galen Strawson, *The Secret Connexion*, Appendix B.

Associated issues are taken up by Richard Rorty in 'The World Well Lost'; and pursued by Jonathan Lear in 'Leaving the World Alone'. See also Jonathan Dancy, *Moral Reasons*, ch. 9, § 2; and Gideon Rosen, 'Objectivity and Modern Idealism: What is the Question?'

On the relevance of physicalism to the ideas canvassed in this chapter, see David Charles and Kathleen Lennon (eds.), *Reduction, Explanation, and Realism*; James Hopkins, 'Wittgenstein and Physicalism'; Howard Robinson (ed.), *Objections to Physicalism*; and Bernard Williams, *Descartes*, pp. 296–7.

CHAPTER FIVE

If . . . my experience formed a closed system, if the thing and the world could be defined once and for all, if the spatio-temporal horizons could, even theoretically, be made explicit and the world conceived from no point of view, then nothing would exist; I should hover above the world, so that all times and places, far from becoming simultaneously real, would become unreal, because I should live in none of them and be involved nowhere. If I am at all times and everywhere, then I am at no time and nowhere.

(Maurice Merleau-Ponty)

§ 1: *This chapter consists of a survey of arguments for the impossibility of absolute representations. One such argument, the Opposition Argument, is sketched. Its main premiss, the Outlook Assumption, is identified and rejected. Many arguments for the impossibility of absolute representations are variations on the Opposition Argument. The Opposition Argument accordingly serves as a reference point throughout the chapter. In particular, it structures the next three sections.*

§ 2: *First, arguments are considered in which the evaluative element in any outlook is taken to support the Outlook Assumption. Putnam is adopted as a representative proponent of arguments of this kind.*

§ 3: *Next, arguments are considered in which incompatibilities between outlooks are taken to support the Outlook Assumption. These fall into two sub-categories. Goodman is adopted as a representative proponent of arguments in the first sub-category.*

§ 4: *Arguments in the second sub-category are considered in connection with the work of Kuhn, Whorf, and Saussure.*

§ 5: *Threats to the possibility of absolute representations arising from reflections on language are considered.*

§ 6: *Threats to the possibility of absolute representations arising from reflections on science are considered.*

§ 7: *Nietzsche's perspectivism is considered. This is an example of an attack on the Basic Argument that rejects the Basic Assumption.*

§ 8: *Attacks on the Basic Argument that share the Basic Assumption, such as Putnam's, can be resisted. Those that reject the Basic Assumption typically lead to an impasse. However, a species of idealism is sketched that affords the prospect of a reconciliation.*

1

AT THE end of Chapter One I sketched an argument for the impossibility of absolute representations. That argument, somewhat filled out, runs as follows. (I shall refer to it as the Opposition Argument.)

The Opposition Argument: Any conceptual apparatus used to represent the world must involve its own distinctive systems of classification, its own principles of assimilation and discrimination. Assimilation and discrimination are always in respect of something. Things that are alike in one respect are always different in many others; and things that are different in one respect are always alike in many others. Thus, for instance, we use the concept *green* to liken an apple to Uranus and to distinguish it from a banana, even though the two pieces of fruit are like each other in innumerable ways in which neither is like the planet. Concepts are tools for drawing attention to certain features of the world and relegating others as irrelevant. Through the exercise of concepts the world is structured into foreground and background. But the structuring must have a point. And only a being capable of seeing that point is able to exercise the concepts. It is a familiar enough fact that concepts can reflect the needs, interests, and concerns of those who exercise them. This is why it is unsurprising that those who speak tone languages, such as Cantonese, make finer discriminations with respect to intonation than those who speak English, or that human beings generally have so many concepts pertaining to food. But there is more to it than that. Any representation is shaped by concepts that simply cannot be used by beings whose nature is not such as to see the world in one way rather than another, in other words from a particular point of view. So any representation is perspectival—indeed both radically and inherently perspectival, and perhaps also, depending on how far the link between a concept and its associated point of view is a matter of interests, concerns, or values, subjective. Absolute representations are impossible.

The Opposition Argument is just one of a plethora of arguments against the possibility of absolute representations. I have accorded it special prominence simply because many of the others are variations on it. It will serve as a reference point throughout this chapter. An important preliminary is to say where it goes wrong.

One simple objection to the Opposition Argument is that it takes for granted that all representations are conceptual, in other words that the production of a representation always involves the exercise of concepts. This is not a very damaging objection, though. The idea of a non-conceptual representation offers little solace to the defender of absolute representations. Typically, when people talk of non-conceptual representations, they have in mind one or other of two extremes. The first is the kind of representation that a primitive organism could produce just by interacting with its environment and processing data. (Thus, perhaps, the cockroach tasting scrambled eggs.) Such a representation would be radically perspectival. Its type would be determined by the constitution of the organism, and would not be capable of instantiation except from the point of view of that organism. The other extreme is the kind of representation that an infinite or divine being might produce. Here what is envisaged is a completely unmediated unconditioned assimilation of the very content of the representation, the sort of thing that Kant referred to (using these terms in his own semi-technical way) as an exercise of intuitive understanding.[1] There is good reason, however, at least in the context of this discussion, to withhold from anything of this second kind the title of 'representation'. This is because what has tacitly been at issue all along is whether *we* can produce absolute representations. (Admittedly there is the question of who "we" are. I shall come back to this in the next chapter.)

---

[1] Immanuel Kant, *Critique of Pure Reason*, B145.

The fundamental objection to the Opposition Argument, I think, is that it makes a certain assumption about points of view themselves. In order to state this assumption I need first to define an *outlook*. By an outlook I mean a way of seeing the world: to have a particular outlook is to treat some things as relevant to others, to be disposed to make various connections between things, to be struck by certain similarities and differences, to find some things natural foci of attention. The assumption in question is this: to represent the world in accord with an outlook is to represent it from a point of view. Call this the Outlook Assumption.

It certainly follows from the Outlook Assumption that absolute representations are impossible. For to represent the world is always to represent it in accord with some outlook—as the Opposition Argument shows. But we can resist the Outlook Assumption. Provided that the outlook associated with any given representation does not preclude the representation's integration by simple addition with any other representation, then, whatever principles of relevance and conceptual stage-management are presupposed in that outlook, whatever *Gestalt* switches are required in order to acquire that outlook, whatever interests and concerns are shared by those who have that outlook, the representation may be absolute.

—*"But surely, to have an outlook is always to have it to the exclusion of certain others. How can a representation produced in accord with one outlook be integrated by simple addition with a representation produced in accord with another, incompatible outlook?"*—

If it were true that to have an outlook is always to have it to the exclusion of certain others, then the Outlook Assumption would hold. But I say that some outlooks are non-exclusive. In particular, the outlook involved in producing any absolute representation is non-exclusive.

— *"That sounds ad hoc. In what sense of 'non-exclusive'? Surely there is no non-question-begging sense in which the outlook involved in producing some highly complex physical law is compatible with the outlook of (say) a beetle. Or at least, there is no non-question-begging sense in which these outlooks are compatible but in which the latter is not also compatible with the outlook of a cow—even though, presumably, a beetle and a cow represent things from incompatible points of view."*—

I agree. In fact I see similar question begging in the definition of an absolute representation. An absolute representation is a representation that can be integrated by simple addition with any other possible representation. So there needs to be a sense of 'can' in which the thoughts of a beetle can be integrated by simple addition with the physical law (assuming it is absolute) but not with the thoughts of a cow. And I am prepared to admit that, ultimately, there is no way of elucidating these senses except by resort to something circular, for instance by qualifying the 'can' with: 'as far as being from any point of view is concerned'. But circularities in my position do not impugn its coherence. There is still plenty to be said about how the various notions are interrelated. Take non-exclusiveness. The idea is this. The criteria for having any given outlook include manifesting certain capacities and dispositions and producing representations of certain types. This means that some outlooks, in some respects, rule out others. Thus the criteria for having the outlook of a beetle and the criteria for having the outlook of a cow include responding in incompatible ways to the sudden arrival on the scene of a bull. In that respect the outlook of a beetle rules out the outlook of a cow. In like respect the outlook of a beetle rules out the outlook of a physicist. ('Physicist' here is just a convenient shorthand for any being that produces absolute representations: see the discussion at the end of the last chapter.) The criteria for having the latter include responding to certain situations with a degree of sophistication that no beetle-minded creature could ever attain. But that is not my concern. There is a respect in which the outlook of a beetle does not rule out the outlook of a physicist. The criteria for having the outlook of a beetle and the criteria for having the outlook of a physicist do not include producing representations from incompatible points of view. In this respect the outlook of a physicist is not ruled out by *any* others. This is the sense in which the outlook of a physicist is non-exclusive.

True, had this discussion taken place in Chapter One, it would have forced us back to the drawing board. It seems clear now that the definition of an absolute representation with which we have been working, like some of those rejected earlier in that chapter, makes essential use (albeit less directly than those rejected then) of the very ideas that it was intended to explicate. But no matter. We can afford to be pragmatic about this. The definition is not wrong; and it was adequate for its purpose, which was to help formulate the Basic Argument. Moreover, now that that argument is in place, there is not the same need for a definition. *The Basic Argument itself gives us a grip on what it is whose possibility it is an argument for.* It is an argument for the possibility of representations that can figure in a conception of reality capable of being used to indicate how any two representations, if true, are true: a conception of reality fit to sustain our sense of reality as something substantial that is there *anyway*.

This entitles us to a certain cavalierness in our approach to arguments against the possibility of absolute representations. There is now a specific case to be answered. The possibility of absolute representations is now much more concrete in our thinking. In envisaging absolute representations, we are envisaging representations with a distinctive role to play in relation to representations of other kinds. We can dismiss any argument against the possibility of absolute representations which, finding in the very idea of a representation criteria for being perspectival, does not directly foreclose the possibility that these criteria should be met by representations playing just the role envisaged.[2] In particular, we can dismiss any argument that simply helps itself to the Outlook Assumption, as the Opposition Argument does. Variations on the Opposition Argument may pose more of a challenge, but for the time being we can distinguish between representing the world in accord with an outlook and representing it from a point of view, by reckoning some outlooks non-exclusive.

Given the close link between non-exclusive outlooks and absolute representations, it makes sense to register that link in some suitable terminology. I shall therefore coin the adjective 'Absolute', with a capital 'A', to play the role that 'non-exclusive' has been playing; and I shall coin 'Perspectival' as its complement. (I cannot use 'absolute' and 'perspectival' themselves, because I have expressly committed myself to applying these only to representations.) From now on, then, any outlook will be said to be either Absolute or Perspectival.

The connection between the Absolute/Perspectival distinction and the absolute/perspectival distinction is simply this. The representations produced in accord with an Absolute outlook may be absolute, whereas the representations produced in accord with a Perspectival outlook cannot be. Thus what makes an outlook

[2] An example would be an argument purporting to show that any representation must contain a perspectival reference to whoever produced the representation, based, say, on David Lewis, 'Attitudes *De Dicto* and *De Se*'.

Perspectival on this conception is that it conforms to the Outlook Assumption: to represent the world in accord with it is, necessarily, to do so from a point of view. Equivalently, what makes an outlook Perspectival is the distinctive way in which the outlook rules out certain others. Consider the outlook of someone who is sighted. Clearly there are respects in which this outlook rules out the outlook of someone who is congenitally blind. Having one of these outlooks involves responding to appropriate light stimulation in a way that is incompatible with having the other. But as far as that goes, the outlook of the sighted person is no different from an Absolute outlook. An Absolute outlook likewise rules out the outlook of any being that lacks the intellectual capacity to produce absolute representations. What makes the outlook of the sighted person Perspectival is not that there are people who are blind. It is rather that there are creatures, or there could be creatures, with a sensory apparatus that is itself precluded by normal human vision, for instance because it is monochromatic, or (as in the example in Chapter One) because it makes a particular substance look red to them though it looks green to all normal-sighted humans. And what 'precluded' signifies in that last sentence is that certain true representations produced by exercising the alternative sensory apparatus cannot be integrated, even indirectly, with certain true representations produced by exercising normal human vision unless, in at least one case, a step is taken, however small, in the direction of a physical paraphrase.

Keeping in focus the somewhat attenuated modalities at work in this account helps us to respect a distinction that I drew towards the beginning of the last chapter. This is the distinction between a representation's *betraying* a point of view and its being *from* that point of view. A representation betrays a point of view when no such representation could have been produced by a being that did not have that point of view. This definition can be taken in a more or less restrictive sense depending on how the 'could' is understood. In one of its least restrictive senses, a representation that distinguishes between various tonemes betrays the point of view of a Cantonese speaker (or a speaker of some other tone language), a point of view defined, in part, by the interests and concerns that make it worthwhile to classify phonemes in that way. In a more restrictive sense, a representation with a certain degree of sophistication betrays the point of view of beings with a particular evolutionary history. At

the limit it is conceivable that absolute representations can be produced only by beings whose very survival is linked, epiphenome-
nally, to their delighting in certain mathematical relations. In an
even more restrictive sense, any representation with a temporal
location betrays the temporal point of view of whoever produced
it, at the time of its production. In none of these cases need the representation be *from* the specified point of view. If I assert that $e = mc^2$,
for example, the sheer fact that my representation occurs in
time does not mean that it is from the temporal point of view I have
when I produce it. This distinction is an important weapon in com-
bating many arguments against the possibility of absolute representations. But it is not always an easy distinction to keep a grip on.
Often the feature of a representation that makes it betray a particular point of view is its type. This is true of the Cantonese speaker's representation. There is then a sense in which the representation cannot be integrated by simple addition with a representation
not from that point of view. This in turn may suggest, incorrectly,
that the original representation is from that point of view. The confusion here is a confusion of modalities. What determines whether
the representation is from that point of view is whether integration
by simple addition is possible in the attenuated sense relevant to
perspective. It may well be. Indeed it may be possible in less attenuated senses too. One does not have to relax one's standards much
to say that those who do not share the Cantonese speaker's point of
view nevertheless *can* distinguish the different tonemes.

2

There have been countless arguments against the possibility of
absolute representations. My aim in this chapter is to survey some
of the most important. (This will mean being highly selective. For
a glimpse of some of the material that I am ignoring see the further
reading at the end of this chapter.)

The best known and most eloquent critic of absolute representations was Nietzsche. I shall turn to his work later in the chapter,
though many of the ideas that I shall parade before then are of
more or less Nietzschean inspiration. I shall begin by discussing
attempts to supplement the Opposition Argument by establishing

the Outlook Assumption (which can now be expressed in the form: 'Any outlook must be Perspectival'). These attempts are roughly of two kinds. On the one hand there are those that emphasize the evaluative element in any outlook. On the other hand there are those that emphasize how deep the incompatibilities between outlooks lie.

Among contemporary analytic philosophers, Putnam stands out as a proponent of arguments of the first of these kinds. Putnam has argued forcefully that fact and value are inextricably linked. His argument, in a nutshell, is this. The concept of a fact, or the concept of what is true, is constitutively tied to the concept of rationality. Something is true if and only if it would be rational, in some suitable idealization, to believe it. But rationality is value-relative. There is no sense in talking about what it would be rational to believe except with respect to some particular set of commitments, projects, aspirations, and ideals. One basic reason for this is that there is no sense in talking about what it would be rational to believe except relative to what questions it would be rational to address. And what questions it would be rational to address would depend on what, in a given context, counted as relevant, where this in turn would depend on a certain conceptualization dictated by what mattered. But nothing would matter, in any context, save with respect to some such set of values.[3]

Putnam draws much the same conclusion from considerations about the social nature of language. He argues that any conceptualization is necessarily bound up with some linguistic tradition; and that a tradition always carries with it its own value-imbued criteria of rationality. He writes:

Using any word . . . involves one in a history, a tradition of observation, generalization, practice and theory.—It also involves one in the activity of *interpreting* that tradition, and of adapting it to new contexts, extending and criticizing it. One can interpret traditions variously, but one cannot apply a word at all if one places oneself entirely outside of the tradition to which it belongs. And standing inside a tradition certainly affects what one counts as "rational . . .".[4]

Once again, then, we seem to have reason to conclude that to

---

[3] Hilary Putnam, *Reason, Truth and History*, esp. chs. 6 and 9. It should be noted that Putnam has subsequently modified his views: see e.g. 'Pragmatism', p. 299.

[4] Putnam, *Reason, Truth and History*, p. 203, his emphasis.

represent the world is always to represent it in accord with some outlook. (The focus on linguistic, or conceptual, representations is, as before, harmless.) This was what the Opposition Argument showed. But Putnam's critique goes further. It includes special emphasis on the way in which having an outlook is a matter of *evaluation*—of respecting certain things, cherishing certain things, regarding certain things as important. On the face of it this is a crucial supplement. It seems enough to establish the Outlook Assumption. Once it is conceded that an outlook involves evaluation in this way, then the manœuvring of the previous section, whereby some outlooks were said to be Absolute, really does look drastically Procrustean. The point is: radically different and incompatible things can be valued.

Some might deny this. Or rather, they might say, concerning a minimal stock of goods, such as truth and rationality themselves perhaps, that these cannot but be valued. This would give them a way of acknowledging that every outlook involves evaluation while still reckoning some outlooks, those whereby only these goods are valued, privileged and, more specifically, Absolute. Others might insist that only certain goods can be *rationally* valued, or, what on some natural assumptions would not be an independent position, that the valuing of certain goods is part of the idealization in which truth is identified with what it would be rational to believe. Such people might then say that, for all Putnam has shown, *every* outlook is Absolute. While I am sympathetic to such views, I cannot myself appropriate them as a way of resisting Putnam's argument. This is because I accept the Engagement Principle articulated in Chapter Two, the principle that all the representations that directly engage us are perspectival. Part of accepting this principle is thinking that all evaluation has an irreducibly perspectival character. (I shall return to these issues in Chapter Eleven.)

It is worth noting in this connection how subtle Putnam's own ideas about evaluation are. He certainly does not think that there is nothing more to what is valuable than what is valued. He is adamant that people's values can themselves be criticized and assessed, and not just in the sense that they can come up against other people's values. Even so, he ultimately espouses a pluralism that makes the evaluative nature of outlooks seem enough to clinch the Outlook Assumption.

How then do I combat Putnam's argument?

By denying that it does after all show (even) as much as the Opposition Argument shows. What the Opposition Argument shows is that it is impossible to produce a representation except in accord with some outlook. What Putnam's argument shows is that it is impossible to exercise the *concept* of a representation except in accord with some outlook—or more strictly, that this is true of certain concepts constitutively linked to the concept of a representation, principally that of truth. This is a vital difference. It is the difference between concluding that all representations must be perspectival and concluding that all representations about representations must be perspectival.

—*"Surely, for your purposes, this response to Putnam's argument misses the point. The point is not whether Putnam's argument shows as much as the Opposition Argument shows. The point is whether Putnam's argument shows something that the Opposition Argument does not show: namely, the Outlook Assumption, which by your own admission is all that is required to secure the impossibility of absolute representations. It still looks as though Putnam has said enough to establish that."*—

But once we have seen how Putnam's argument falls short of the Opposition Argument we can see that he has not in fact said enough to establish the Outlook Assumption. He has not shown that any outlook must be Perspectival, only that this is so for any outlook involved in reflecting on the truth of a representation.

—*"Can the gap here not be bridged? To produce a representation is to produce it as true. The producer of a representation always aims or purports to aim, however tacitly, at the truth, and thus exercises, again however tacitly, the concept of truth. If exercising that concept is impossible except in accord with a given outlook, then so is producing the representation."*—

I disagree. Let us grant that to produce a representation is to produce it as true, in the sense indicated. (Actually, this is already dubious.) And let us grant that there is something perspectival about the concept of truth, as I think Putnam's argument shows we ought. All that follows is that the producer of any representation has a point of view operative in the production of the representation. This is certainly not something I want to deny. At most it gives us reason to think that any representation must betray a point of view, not that it must be from a point of view. The possibility remains that some representations—no matter how crucial evaluation may be to any critical assessment of their purpose, point, or status; no matter what indispensable contribution evaluation may make to any reason for producing them; no matter how involved evaluation may be in the history of whatever conceptual apparatus is used in them—nevertheless play the privileged role that absolute representations, and they alone, are equipped to play.

There is a basic tactic here: to distinguish between all that informs the production of a representation on the one hand and the role that the representation can play in such processes as indirect integration on the other. (The distinction between a representation's betraying a point of view and its being from a point of view is one application of this broader distinction.) Evaluation is often crucial to the former. But whether the representation is absolute or not depends on the latter. One attractive feature of this tactic is that it leaves considerable room for concession whenever anyone insists on the parochial, conditioned, nay, perspectival character of any act of producing a representation. They are right to insist on this, if it is properly understood. Apart from anything else, any act of producing a representation is indeed an *act*, and agency itself is impossible without some (evaluative) point of view giving sense to the question of what to do. But one possible thing to do is to represent the world from no point of view.

3

Let us now turn to arguments of the second kind, attempts to establish the Outlook Assumption by emphasizing how deep the incompatibilities between outlooks lie. These can themselves be divided into two sub-categories. In the first of these sub-categories are arguments purporting to show that, for any possible outlook, there is another that controls exercise of the very same concepts, but incompatibly. In the second sub-category are arguments purporting to show that, for any possible outlook, there is another that controls exercise of incompatible concepts. In both cases the conclusion is that the incompatibility in question is deep enough to prevent the outlook from counting as Absolute.

Goodman has produced arguments belonging to the first of these sub-categories. With the help of some highly suggestive examples he argues that any possible outlook consists, in part, of presupposed theories and arbitrary choices: without these the application of concepts would be impossible. Furthermore, on Goodman's view, for any possible outlook, there is another in which incompatible theories are presupposed and incompatible choices made. It seems to follow that, for any possible outlook, there is another in accord with which concepts are applied in incompatible ways. One of the simplest of Goodman's examples (an example used in a different connection in Chapter Two) concerns the combination of theory and choice that governs application of the concept of motion. One person can say, truly, that the earth rotates while the sun is motionless; another, equally truly, that the earth is motionless while the sun revolves around it.[5] Their representations are from different, incompatible points of view.

Mere accumulation of examples settles nothing, however. We already knew that instances of perspective were many and varied. Goodman needs to show that what occurs in these examples is ineluctable. He does have some general arguments. But the fact is that the examples themselves are meant to do important work. And when he turns his attention to mathematical contexts his examples appear inadequate to the task. He says that, in a discussion of a square segment, one person can say truly that every point is made up of a vertical and horizontal line; another, equally truly, that no point is made up of a line or anything else.[6] It is admittedly not obvious what to say about this example. But that is partly because the ways of resisting its alleged import are too many, not too few. Here are three. We could deny that the type of one of these representations is the negation of the type of the other. 'Is made up of' is not clearly univocal in its two occurrences. Second, we could insist that any perspective here is easily eliminated by explicit relativization to a background system. Goodman expressly admonishes against doing this, but there is much to be said in response to his admonishment. Third, in line with a suggestion considered in Chapter One, we could deny that it is even appropriate to talk in terms of truth and falsity in a mathematical context of this kind.

Putnam likewise has reservations about this example. But when he gives his own example, intended to do the same work, it is hardly more convincing. In a world consisting of three atoms, Putnam

---

[5] Nelson Goodman, *Ways of Worldmaking*, p. 113.
[6] Ibid., pp. 114–16.

says, "you can either say that there are three objects (the atoms), or that there are seven objects (the atoms and the various aggregates of two or more atoms)."[7] No doubt. But why think that it is impossible, having noted this variation in what we count as an "object", to eliminate any perspective that it reveals, for instance by saying that what there are in this world are *three atoms*, which is precisely what Putnam himself says at the outset? (We should not think that Putnam is vindicated by the mere fact that there is as much of a decision involved in talking of atoms rather than objects as there is in talking of three objects rather than seven. Of course there is. But whatever else it is, the impossibility of absolute representations is not a *platitude* about the nature of representation. We ought to find it very suspicious that Putnam summarizes his discussion of this example by saying, 'You can't describe the world without describing it.')[8]

Goodman is surely right that any outlook must involve presupposed theories and arbitrary choices. What is not so clear—and this accounts for the strain in a number of his examples—is that other outlooks are therefore possible whereby the same concepts are used incompatibly. When different arbitrary choices are made, this often means that different concepts result. Had a "week" been defined as consisting of ten days rather than seven, this would not have been our concept of a week, or not exactly. And when different theories are presupposed—theories themselves being representations—this often means that any incompatibility that results is the straightforward incompatibility of one representation with a contradictory representation, so that what follows is not that anyone is liable to say, or to have said, anything perspectival, but that someone, somewhere, is liable to say or to have said something false. There is not enough in Goodman's discussion, despite the range and force of his examples, to justify the generalization that absolute representations are impossible.

Goodman, it should be noted, is following his own radical agenda. In a way it is a misleading dilution of what he is doing to say that he is arguing that absolute representations are impossible. But of this more anon.

---

[7] Hilary Putnam, *Renewing Philosophy*, p. 120.
[8] Ibid., p. 123.

4

Arguments in the second sub-category are on the whole deeper. One thing that follows from the Opposition Argument is that, for any possible outlook, there is another that controls exercise of quite different concepts. Arguments in the second sub-category take this idea one radical step further. They extend 'quite different' to 'incommensurable'. Part of what is meant by calling two concepts, or two sets of concepts, incommensurable is that no single outlook can control the exercise of both. So the two outlooks in question cannot be combined or amalgamated into one. Hence there is a sense in which the concepts, and more pertinently the outlooks, are incompatible. More pertinently still, the outlooks are incompatible in the sense necessary for them to be Perspectival.

There are examples of such incommensurability in the history of science, according to Kuhn. Kuhn holds that scientific practice has to be understood in terms of the idea of a "paradigm". Paradigms are particular revolutionary achievements that create new modes of scientific activity. In Kuhn's words, "some accepted examples of actual scientific practice . . . provide models from which spring particular coherent traditions of scientific research."[9] Copernicus's hypothesis that the earth and other planets circle the sun; Newton's three laws of mechanics; Einstein's conjecture that the speed of light is constant from one frame of reference to another, but simultaneity relative: these are major examples of paradigms. Paradigms dictate what is relevant to what, what counts as evidence for what, what is a suitable analogy for what, and so forth. In a word—in my word—they dictate outlooks. But as the examples show, or can be used to show, they also dictate what concepts to use. Each paradigm has its own associated set of concepts. And because accepting a particular paradigm is accepting a particular scientific procedure, to the exclusion of others, it seems to follow that some of the outlooks cannot be combined, and hence that the concepts in question are incommensurable.

Work in anthropology also seems to deliver examples of such incommensurability. Whorf's famous case-study of the Hopi Indians in Arizona is a compelling illustration that some of the most fundamental categories that we Anglophones use in repre-

---

[9] Thomas Kuhn, *The Structure of Scientific Revolutions*, p. 10.

senting the world, categories that we might well have taken to be universal, are a mere reflection of one particular culturally and linguistically determined outlook, with no direct counterpart under the control of other outlooks. In particular, Whorf argues, Hopis have nothing that directly corresponds to our concepts of space and time. He proceeds to describe some quite different categories in terms of which Hopis organize their experience and to which we have nothing that directly corresponds.[10] Outlooks in such cases amount to something very grand: *Weltanschauungen*, forms of life even. At any rate they look to be uncombinable and the concepts under their control incommensurable.

Such examples are gripping. But even if we grant what is said about them, they are really only examples of radical perspective, and it is of little moment at this stage in the enquiry to learn that some representations are radically perspectival. It is of some moment to learn that some representations in science are radically perspectival, though even this may seem less significant in view of my disclaimer in the last chapter that the question whether absolute representations are possible is not a question about actual scientific theories. It remains to be seen what reasons there are for thinking that these examples are examples of something ineluctable (to echo the point I made in connection with Goodman).

One important source for such reasons is Saussure's work in linguistics. Saussure held that languages were to be understood as structures, or systems of structures, whose elements have no existence beyond those structures, rather as there is nothing more to the King in chess than the moves it can make in any given chess position, or nothing more to the positive integer 2 than its being the second element in the infinite progression 1, 2, 3, ... Saussure applied this idea in the first instance to the phonetic elements of a language. A phoneme can only be identified by where it stands in relation to other phonemes in a system of contrasts. Phonemes are not "sounds", in any neutral language-independent sense of that term. (Think again how in some Oriental languages there are distinctions between tonemes to which nothing corresponds in English, and conversely, how there is a distinction in English between the liquid consonants *l* and *r* to which nothing corres-

[10] Benjamin Lee Whorf, 'An American Indian Model of the Universe'.

ponds in those Oriental languages.) It follows that there is no identifying one phoneme in one system with another in another, just as
there is no saying how the Ace of Spades moves in chess. Likewise,
Saussure argued, in the case of the semantics of a language. The
meaning of a word, or the concept exercised in the use of a word,
has no life outside the language to which the word belongs.[11]

Two premisses now seem to be enough, in fact more than
enough, to advance from Saussure's argument to an argument for
the ineluctability of radical perspective in linguistic representations.
Each premiss is pretty much incontrovertible. The first is that having a language involves having an outlook; or more specifically, that
having a language involves having its own distinctive outlook.
Given this premiss, and given Saussure's argument, it follows that
the outlooks of monolingual speakers of different languages cannot be combined. At most they can be held in tandem. Any bilinguist must simply alternate between representing things in accord
with one outlook and representing them in accord with the other,
a sure sign, it seems, of the incommensurability of the concepts
involved. The second premiss is that there are at least two languages.

Neither premiss is incontrovertible to the extent that nobody
would dream of trying to controvert it. Even in the case of the second premiss there is an issue about how 'language' is to be understood. If it is to be understood as meaning 'empirically identified
language such as English, German, or Hopi', then the second premiss is a brute fact. But somebody might think that the relevant
part of Saussure's argument is plausible only if 'language' is understood in a metaphysically more ambitious way, as meaning something like 'conceptual scheme', and they might then dispute the
second premiss.[12] I do not want to quarrel with either premiss,
however. The real issue, it seems to me, here as elsewhere, is what
sort of incompatibility has been demonstrated.

A minor point first: we should not be suspicious about whether
Kuhn and Whorf have even given us examples of incommensurability just because they manage to describe to us in our own terms
the concepts that are said to be incommensurable with ours. There
is nothing incoherent in the idea that techniques should be available

---

[11] Ferdinand de Saussure, *A Course in General Linguistics*.
[12] Cf. Donald Davidson, 'On the Very Idea of a Conceptual Scheme'.

to exploit one set of concepts in introducing another, even if the concepts are incommensurable; nor in the idea that the two corresponding outlooks, though they cannot be combined, can be held in tandem. There would be an inconsistency here only if Kuhn and Whorf presented *equivalents* of the alien concepts.

The problem lies not with the examples but with the argument. Specifically, it lies with the assumption that the uncombinability of outlooks associated with different languages is the uncombinability relevant to Perspective. This assumption can also be expressed as follows. The bilinguist who first represents things in accord with one outlook and then represents them in accord with the other can never thereby count as having produced a single representation (can never thereby count as having integrated the two representations by simple addition). I see no reason to accept this assumption. Again it is a question of the role the representations play. The uncombinability of the outlooks may simply mean that the concepts under the separate control of each must always lead their own separate and independent lives. This has no bearing on whether either of these representations can figure in a conception of reality capable of being used to indicate how they and other representations are true, if they are. It is still possible that one of these representations is absolute.

Is it possible that both are? This again depends on how 'language' is to be understood. If it is understood in such a way that a language is defined by a discipline, as in 'the language of art history', then there is only one language—the language of physics—in which it is possible to couch absolute representations. Hence it is not possible that both the representations are absolute. They belong to different languages. But I see no reason why 'language' should not be understood in such a way that it *is* possible that both the representations are absolute. I do not think that we need balk at the idea that there should be absolute representations of two distinct kinds, produced in accord with two separate outlooks. The sort of thing that I am envisaging is the sort of thing that Quine is envisaging when he suggests that a pair of scientific theories might be "empirically equivalent", in the sense that "whatever observation would be counted for or against the one theory counts equally for or against the other", yet such that each involves "theoretical terms not reducible to" the other's.[13] It is no part of the belief in the possibil-

[13] See W. V. Quine, *Pursuit of Truth*, §§ 41–2. The quoted material occurs on pp. 96–7.

ity of absolute representations that anyone representing the world absolutely is constrained to see the world in one particular way, structured as it were into one particular combination of foreground and background.

Arguments in the second sub-category, all of which are variations on this theme, can, I think, be resisted. Still, the discussion in this section does suggest that it would be salutary to look in more depth at two things whose relation to the possibility of absolute representations has come to appear intimate, and which, for reasons that I have alluded to, may yet pose problems for my position: namely, language and science.

5

Saussure's reflections on language have led others, notably Derrida, to an even more radical position. The meaning of a word, as used in a specific context, has no life even outside that context (or that "text"). The very idea of meaning, as something fixed and determinate that transcends particular acts of communication, comes to seem an illusion.[14]

Conclusions that are in some ways strikingly similar have been reached in the analytic tradition by Quine. Quine is impressed by the way in which language and theory contribute inextricably to the production of any linguistic representation. Both are part of the outlook in accord with which the representation is produced. But this makes it hopeless, Quine thinks, to try to factor out any "meaning" controlling the production of the representation, as though this were something that might equally control the production of some other representation, in some other language, against some other background of presupposed theory. Quine does admit that we can construct bilingual dictionaries that allow us to translate some representations by means of others. But he also thinks that such dictionaries are subject to a radical indeterminacy. That is, he thinks that two such dictionaries may both satisfy all possible criteria of adequacy yet diverge in their verdicts about whether one rep-

---

[14] e.g. Jacques Derrida, *Margins of Philosophy*.

resentation is a correct rendering of another. In such a case, he insists, "there is no fact of the matter" concerning which is right.[15]

One thing that follows from both Derrida's and Quine's anti-Platonism about meaning (as we might justly call it), at least in the absence of disclaimers or qualifications, is the context-dependence of any declarative sentence. By this I mean that, granted their views, the mere fact that the same declarative sentence has been used in two different contexts is never a guarantee that the same thing has been said, in any acceptable non-question-begging sense of 'same thing'. How *can* it be, if there is no meaning attaching to words apart from how they are used in different contexts? This creates internal tension for Quine, who is adamant that some declarative sentences are "eternal"—true or false independently of context. What he has in mind are sentences free of such devices as tense and the use of the first person, devices which introduce *systematic* context-dependence. (Obviously a sentence like 'It is nearly midnight,' or 'I am thirsty,' cannot be classified as true or false independently of context.) Eternal sentences, for Quine, include most of the "theoretical sentences in mathematics and other sciences", but are not confined to them. Examples are '2 + 2 = 4' and '$e = mc^2$'.[16] But consider: what can it mean to say that a declarative sentence is "eternal"? It cannot just mean that any utterances of it have the same truth value. A sentence could satisfy this condition as a result of some irrelevant contingency, for instance by being uttered just a few times or indeed by never being uttered at all. It must mean that any utterances of it are *guaranteed* to have the same truth value. But guaranteed by what? The only possible candidate is the sentence's "meaning", the very thing that Quine repudiates.

This route from anti-Platonism about meaning to the conclusion that every declarative sentence is context-dependent can also be traced in a rather different way. If the meaning of a word is nothing apart from its continued usage, then any word has, at any stage in its history, different possibilities of further meaning-preserving use woven into it. Its history is not irrelevant to this. These possibilities are possibilities of developing something. The use of the word comes to be seen as a *process*, always capable of being continued in different ways, for different purposes, to different effects. There is

[15] W. V. Quine, *Word and Object*, ch. 2.
[16] Ibid., § 40.

no legislating in advance for the possibilities of creative language-use that such processes afford. For example, there is no legislating in advance for the success of metaphors, which may be contrived to describe situations completely unlike anything that anyone has ever encountered before and which may then give way to new, previously unimagined literal uses. Consider, for instance, the smooth adaptation of the word 'hear' to cover what we do to somebody's voice over the telephone. Processes being what they are, however, it follows that any declarative sentence is at the very least dependent on temporal context. No use of a word can be understood except as occurring at a particular stage in its development. Think about the sentence, 'Earshot of somebody is the distance within which his or her voice can be heard.' This was once more or less definitional. Now utterances of it would be false. Yet it scarcely seems to have undergone any change of meaning. (It is interesting to see here how Saussure's synchronic approach to meaning has yielded to something radically diachronic.)

Suppose now we accept the anti-Platonism about meaning, as I think we must. The conclusion seems inescapable that absolute representations are impossible. (Once again it is harmless to restrict attention to linguistic representations.) For to admit that, given any utterance of a declarative sentence, another utterance of that same sentence can be made without saying the same thing is surely to admit that, given any linguistic representation, another representation of that same type can be produced that does not have the same content. And this is decisive against the representation's being absolute.

Before I counter this, it is worth noting that Derrida's views, and to a lesser extent Quine's, also pose another (if less urgent) problem. They reveal the power of interpretation. A representation is nothing but interpreting makes it so. Moreover, a representation may be different things according to different interpretations. This means, as Putnam's work has already helped to show and as was acknowledged to an extent in the last chapter, that there is perspective in our very concept of a representation, and associated concepts. Associated concepts include the concept of truth, the concept of type, the concept of content, and the concept of absoluteness itself. What, from one interpretative point of view, are two representations with the same content are, from another point of view, two representations with different content. From a third point of view they are not representations at all. *A fortiori* nothing is an absolute representation except from some point of view. Absoluteness does not itself enjoy the stability of absoluteness. But is this not self-stultifying? Is not the whole idea of an absolute representation beginning to buckle under its own weight?

Well *is* it? I have never claimed absoluteness on behalf of any of my own representations nor denied that any of the basic concepts that I have been using have something deeply perspectival about them. I am as happy to admit perspective in the concept of absoluteness as I was earlier to admit it in the concept of truth. Yes, in talking about absolute representations I am myself producing representations from a point of view. (Just which point of view is immaterial to the validity of my claims. There is an analogue to this in Descartes's use of the first-person singular at the heart of his philosophy. Descartes produced representations from his own point of view, but in such a way that, if his arguments were successful, other people would be assisted in producing representations of the same types from their points of view with equal validity.) Whether my position is correct depends not on whether any representation I have produced is absolute. It depends on whether absolute representations are possible.

What then of the threat posed by the context-sensitivity of all declarative sentences? Well, noting the perspectival element in interpretation in fact helps us to see how to evade that threat. We can see that whether two representations are of the same type or not itself depends on interpretation. It is certainly not dictated by whether the same declarative sentence has been used. To think it is is to underestimate just how context-dependent declarative sentences are. There is no inconsistency in the idea that an absolute representation should be produced by using a sentence which can also be used, in another context, metaphorically perhaps, to produce a representation with some quite different content—and thus of some quite different type. All that matters, as ever, is the role that the original representation plays, or might play.

If there is any self-stultification here, it lies rather with those who deny that absolute representations are possible though they are prepared to concede the possibility of representations that are absolute from "our" point of view.[17] At any rate I do not think there

---

[17] I am thinking, perhaps unfairly, of Richard Rorty. See e.g. *Philosophy and the Mirror of Nature* , pp. 344–5.

is anything in anti-Platonism about meaning to force me to retract anything I have said; nor in any other doctrine about meaning that respects, as it must, the fluidity of the relationship between using the same words and saying the same thing.

6

Concerning science there is the distinction between actual scientific practice—past, present, or indeed future—and an idealization of scientific practice. The connection I have affirmed between absolute representations and science is loose enough for me to be relatively unperturbed by demonstrations of radical perspective in the former. This is why I do not mind conceding many of the conclusions that Kuhn draws, convincingly, from his historical studies. True, this leaves the task of accounting for the relation between actual scientific practice and the idealization, a huge task which I cannot now so much as embark upon. But I see the belief in the possibility of absolute representations as directing the discharge of that task, not as frustrating it.

Kuhn is not alone in drawing attention to the way in which perspective pervades science. Many others have emphasized how values and interests shape scientific research. The point is often made that vast sociological, economic, and political assumptions are built into decisions about what is worthy of investigation in the first place. Scientific research costs a lot of money. It is also publicly funded. Decisions about how to spend public money on that scale require justification and accountability. And although these do not always take the form they should, there is no question of the research proceeding without being significantly informed, at some level, by self-conscious assessment of its purpose—and by a self-conscious need to impress. This is all the more true given the inseparability of scientific research and technology. Technology, clearly, introduces a further dimension of practice-cum-evaluation that must affect decisions about how to use public resources. None of this is enough to show that scientists do not routinely produce absolute representations. But it does help to show how much is demanded by the idealization in which they do. Any perspective in the rationale that they give for their endeavours, which may be crucial to their delivering any results at all, must somehow be kept out of the outlook in accord with which they state those results. I am quite ready to believe that scientists have not got there yet.

Something else that is often said is that science is the new religion. All manner of things are meant by this; all manner of things are presupposed by it. As a sociological generalization about the attitudes of the laity, what they count worthy of respect and what they regard as authority—indeed as a similar sociological generalization about the attitudes of practitioners—it is just about compatible with the view that scientists routinely produce absolute representations. But as an observation about power bases and control, with corresponding implications about what scientists are up to (however unselfconsciously) when they present their results, it once again puts that view in great jeopardy. Here is Feyerabend, with characteristically forceful hyperbole:

[Science] is one of the many forms of thought that have been developed by man, and not necessarily the best. It is conspicuous, noisy, and impudent, but it is inherently superior only for those who have decided in favour of a certain ideology . . . And as the accepting and rejecting of ideologies should be left to the individual it follows that the separation of state and *church* must be supplemented by the separation of state and *science*, that most recent, most aggressive, and most dogmatic religious institution.[18]

Certain feminists have recently added a further twist to all of this. They would agree with the quotation from Feyerabend. But they would also emphasize 'man' in the first sentence. A good deal of scientific practice, they argue, is governed and shaped by the values of a particular group of people who have most of the relevant power and whose point of view is fundamentally male, though not only male. Harding writes:

What we took to be humanly inclusive problematics, concepts, theories, objective methodologies, and transcendental truths are in fact far less than that. Instead, these products of thought bear the mark of their collective and individual creators, and the creators in turn have been distinctively marked as to gender, class, race, and culture . . . Western culture's

---

[18] Paul Feyerabend, *Against Method*, p. 295, his emphasis.

favoured beliefs mirror in . . . sometimes distorting ways not the world as
it is . . . but the social projects of their historically identifiable creators.[19]

There is much in this critical assault on scientific practice that I
agree with. There is even more that I could agree with as far as my
views about the possibility of absolute representations are concerned. Furthermore I would add that if, contrary to the assault,
scientists do routinely produce absolute representations, or even if
they *sometimes* do, it would be a desperate task to demonstrate that
this was so. What considerations could be adduced? Technological
success (the fact that we can build bridges and fly to the moon)
could at most count as evidence for the *truth* of scientific representations, not for their absoluteness, even if the deep perspective in
the very idea of technological success should not give pause. Any
convergence among scientists, arriving independently at representations of the same type when addressing the same problem, would
be of greater relevance. But 'independently'; 'same type'; 'same
problem': all of these would create a risk of question begging. And
which scientists? Not those whose research is flawed. Some would
have to be discounted. Could we be sure that we were not dis-
counting those whose representations are from a different point of
view from the others'? And even if we could be sure of that, could
we be sure that the scientists who remain have not all produced representations from some common point of view? It would be significant, lastly, if we could establish that scientific representations can
be used to indicate how true representations of other kinds are
true. But could we establish this with respect to all *possible* truths, as
we should need to in order to prove absoluteness?

In maintaining that it would be a desperate task to demonstrate
that scientists produce absolute representations I am effectively
maintaining that it would be a desperate task to do this not only in
our current circumstances, but in any possible circumstances. We
might never be able to tell that something was an absolute representation. This does not concern me. As I said in the last chapter, the
question of whether it is possible to produce absolute representations is not the same as the question of whether it is possible to tell
that we have done so.

How does any of this affect my claim that absolute representa-

[19] Sandra Harding, *The Science Question in Feminism*, pp. 15–16.

tions are possible in science, and specifically in physics? Hardly at all. That claim was never intended to go much further than the claim that absolute representations are possible. There is little to be said against the former that is not straightforwardly something to be said against the latter. Admittedly some of the arguments against the possibility of absolute representations that we have looked at have variations couched specifically in terms of science. For example, Popper long endorsed a variation of Putnam's argument, insisting that scientific investigation was impossible without some (evaluative) point of view determining what counted as worthy of attention, what ought to be selected for observation, and what classifications were to be used. He once quoted Katz with approval: 'A hungry animal divides the environment into edible and inedible things . . . Generally speaking, objects change . . . according to the needs of the animal.' He went on, 'We may add that objects can be classified, and can become similar or dissimilar, *only* in this way—by being related to needs and interests.'[20] But whatever can be said to resist general arguments against the possibility of absolute representations can be adapted to resist more specific arguments of this kind. In this case we can invoke the tactic that I proclaimed earlier, of distinguishing between what informs the production of a representation and what role that representation might play.

7

There is scarcely anything in any of these arguments against the possibility of absolute representations that cannot be found somewhere, in some form, in Nietzsche. With brilliant rhetoric Nietzsche presented an unparalleled case for the necessary perspectivalness of any representation. Here is a selection of quotations:

Everything of which we become conscious is arranged, simplified, schematized, interpreted through and through . . .

The apparent world . . . [is] a world viewed according to values; ordered,

[20] Karl Popper, *Conjectures and Refutations*, pp. 46–7, his emphasis. The passage quoted is from David Katz, *Animals and Man*.

selected according to values, i.e., in this case according to the viewpoint of utility in regard to the preservation and enhancement of the power of a certain species of animal.

Let us, from now on, be on our guard against the hallowed philosophers' myth of a "pure, will-less, painless, timeless knower"; let us beware of the tentacles of such contradictory notions as . . . "absolute knowledge" . . . [which] presuppose an eye such as no living being can imagine, an eye required to have no direction, to abrogate its active and interpretative powers—precisely those powers that alone make of seeing, seeing *something*. All seeing is essentially perspectival, and so is all knowing. The more emotions we allow to speak in a given matter, the more different eyes we can put on in order to view a given spectacle . . . the greater our "objectivity". But to eliminate the will, to suspend the emotions altogether, provided it could be done—surely this would be to castrate the intellect, would it not?

Physicists believe in a "true world" in their own fashion . . . But they are in error. The atom they posit is inferred according to the logic of the perspectivism of consciousness—and is therefore itself a subjective fiction. This world picture that they sketch differs in no essential way from the subjective world picture: it is only construed with more extended senses, but with *our* senses nevertheless.[21]

Nietzsche's perspectivism includes, as well as much that we have sampled, much that we have not yet sampled. It draws on his doctrine of the will to power. For Nietzsche, the need-driven, value-directed perspective that pervades all representation is itself a manifestation of the will to power. In any act of representation, some agent, some centre of force, imposes an interpretation—an interpretation that, in part, it would like to compel other centres of force to accept. This interpretation is not just a passive response to something that is antecedently given, in which meaning is to be found. It is rather a creation of meaning. It is an act of the will to power. The world is a dramatic text whose interpretation is part of acting out a

[21] Respectively: Friedrich Nietzsche, *The Will to Power*, § 477; ibid., § 567; *On the Genealogy of Morals*, Essay III, § 12; and *The Will to Power*, § 636, all emphasis his. (In the third quotation I have taken the liberty of replacing the translators' 'perspective' by 'perspectival'.) Cf. *The Will to Power*, §§ 293 and 481; Nietzsche, *Beyond Good and Evil*, §§14 and 16; and Nietzsche, *The Gay Science*, § 373. (Caveat: *The Will to Power* is compiled from Nietzsche's notebooks. It is not a book that he wrote for publication. Attributions to him based on this book should be correspondingly circumspect.)

particular life, creatively adopting a particular style, telling a particular story: the story that will become the narrator's autobiography. The interpreted world and the interpreting agent are constituted together. Any representation is from a point of view that is partly the *creature* of that representation. Points of view themselves are interpreted into existence. Not that one interpretation is therefore as good as any other. 'As good as' is in turn evaluative, and hence interpretative. The relative assessment of interpretations must be made in accord with an interpretation and is not constrained to treat all interpretations alike. Such perspectivism does however check a certain hubris, the hubris that will not even acknowledge other interpretations, still less the possibility that some change of interpretation or change of style may be to the good.

—*"If your portrayal of Nietzsche is correct, then surely he is guilty of self-stultification. For surely to attempt this kind of overview of perspective—an overview that is deconstructionist in this way—is to attempt to transcend perspective."*—

Not at all. It is true that there are passages in which Nietzsche suggests that all there "really" is is the will to power, active in different interpreting subjects. It can look as if he is purporting to represent the world from no point of view.[22] But as we have seen, it is part of his vision that interpreting subjects themselves exist only from suitable interpretative points of view. He is at perfect liberty to cast everything that he himself says, in presenting his vision, as perspectival. And so he does. Here is an important quotation:

"Everything is subjective," you say; but even this is interpretation. The "subject" is not something given, it is something added and invented and projected behind what there is . . . [Is] it necessary to posit an interpreter behind the interpretation? Even this is invention, hypothesis.[23]

Elsewhere he makes clear that we humans, considering how things might look from non-human points of view, can at most check our own hubris with the thought that they might look *some* way. We can never transcend our human points of view to attain to anything more determinate than this.

---

[22] See e.g. Nietzsche, *The Will to Power*, §§ 569 and 1067.
[23] Ibid., § 481.

The human intellect cannot avoid seeing itself in its perspectives, and *only* in these. We cannot look round our own corner: it is a hopeless curiosity that wants to know what other kinds of intellects and perspectives there *might* be . . . I should think that today we are at least far from the ridiculous immodesty that would be involved in decreeing from our corner that perspectives are permitted only from this corner.[24]

The charge of self-stultification is in fact often levelled against the claim that any representation must be perspectival, not just in connection with Nietzsche.[25] It is one charge that I have scrupulously avoided. I have acknowledged that there is perspective in the concept of a representation, and indeed in that of perspective. I would not at all mind granting to anyone claiming that all representations must be perspectival the perspectivalness of his or her own representation. (What I would mind granting is its truth.) There *is* self-stultification hereabouts. For instance it is self-stultifying to identify some point of view by superseding its range, and then to claim that all our representations must be from that point of view. The very process of identifying the point of view belies the claim. It is also self-stultifying to say that, since all representations must be perspectival, then something or other—for instance, some principle about the transcendent nature of things in themselves— holds absolutely.[26] But the mere statement that all representations must be perspectival does not, it seems to me, in any way cancel itself out.

What it does cancel out, if the Basic Argument is correct, is a cluster of interrelated ideas about the unity, substantiality, and autonomy of reality, the ideas encapsulated in the Basic Assumption. I said in the last chapter that I had argued for a hypothetical: *if* the Basic Assumption holds, then absolute representations are possible. This leaves me at the mercy of attacks on my position that do not share the Basic Assumption, attacks that are, as I shall say, *nihilistic*. And in fact Nietzsche, in so far as his work admits of any label, is the arch-exponent of nihilism.

In depicting the will to power as the progenitor of points of view and their associated realities Nietzsche is precisely challenging that robust sense of something independent to which representations

---

[24] Nietzsche, *The Gay Science*, § 374, his emphasis.
[25] e.g. W. V. Quine, 'On Empirically Equivalent Systems of the World', pp. 327–8.
[26] Cf. Bernard Williams's castigation of "vulgar relativism" in *Morality*, pp. 34–5.

must answer. (This is why I cannot resist his onslaught in the same way as I resisted the Opposition Argument. I cannot just say: Nietzsche shows only that any representation must be in accord with an outlook, not that it must be from a point of view. That would be to disregard the direct assault on the Basic Argument itself.) Nor is it simply a question of Nietzsche's denying the Basic Assumption. He is challenging the very categories that give the assumption sense, the categories that give sense to my entire discussion: the idea of a representation, the idea of truth, the idea of that to which representations must answer. If sometimes he himself makes use of these ideas, then, dialectical playfulness apart, his doing so can be construed in the spirit of a *reductio ad absurdum*. He writes:

There is no "other", no "true", no essential being—for this would be the expression of a world without action and reaction.

The world with which we are concerned is false . . .; it is "in flux", as something in a state of becoming, as a falsehood always changing but never getting near the truth: for—there is no "truth".[27]

Here is something radical that I still need to confront.

8

The first thing to be said is that I have no defence of the Basic Assumption. It is precisely that: an assumption, a complex multi-faceted assumption that is vulnerable on different fronts.

Several of the writers whose views we have canvassed in this chapter are nihilists. Goodman and Derrida, for instance, both deny the unity of reality.[28] There are two ways of doing this. (These two ways may ultimately be equivalent.) The first is to acknowledge a multiplicity of realities. The second is to repudiate the very idea of reality, in the sense intended. These are Goodman's and Derrida's respective positions, more or less.

Goodman holds that true representations are sometimes incompatible. Their truth has to be construed as truth in different worlds.

---

[27] Respectively, Nietzsche, *The Will to Power*, §§ 567 and 616, emphasis removed. Cf. Nietzsche, *The Gay Science*, § 481; and Nietzsche, 'On Truth and Lies in a Nonmoral Sense'.

[28] I am indebted to Putnam in what follows. See Putnam, *Renewing Philosophy*, esp. ch. 6.

This is in direct violation of the Fundamental Principle. Goodman admits that his claim that there are different worlds is itself rivalled by the equally true but incompatible claim that there is a single world with different aspects.[29] But he then turns his multi-world conception on itself to resolve the contradiction: in one world there are different worlds, in another there is just the one. It is this nihilism that ultimately drives his rejection of the possibility of absolute representations. If there is a multiplicity of worlds, then any representation must at least be from one of *these* points of view. Nothing I said in response to Goodman above gainsays that.

Derrida, with his anti-Platonist conception of meaning, recoils *à la* Nietzsche from the very categories that have informed my entire discussion. There are not, in Derrida's view, separate "representations" set over against "reality", "true" or "false" according to whether or not they represent it as it is. Rather there is an infinite net of context-dependent meaning, each part of which is intelligible only in relation to the whole and in relation only to the whole, no part of which is finally resoluble into representer and represented. Like Nietzsche, Derrida does not simply deny the Basic Assumption. He declines even to think in those terms. He declines to accept the framework of my enquiry.

The same is true of many feminists. I have been operating with a set of dichotomies—the true and the false, the objective and the subjective, the absolute and the perspectival, the one and the many—which they regard as part of an androcentric ideology.[30] In its most extreme form this ideology elevates the first element in each dichotomy and then links these together with masculinity. This ideology has certainly been of historical significance. One could scarcely deny its influence on, say, the veneration of scientific practice as a kind of detached, authoritative, rational domination of nature. But I want no part of it. As I have repeatedly emphasized, I do not recognize the coincidence of these dichotomies. Still less do I recognize their coincidence with the dichotomy between the masculine and the feminine, or with that between the worthy and the unworthy, or (worst of all) with both. And I have no other reason for aligning them in this way. It is an urgent question for me, then, whether the dichotomies can survive the ideology. I see no reason why not. But some feminists will say that this is just because my outlook is male; that only from a male point of view is it possible to ignore the resonances that these dichotomies have. At a superficial level this need not concern me. I have said that I am happy to grant perspective in the concepts I have been using. Why should I not be happy to grant, in particular, male perspective in those concepts, so long as what I say when wielding them is true? At a deeper level, however, such nonchalance is misplaced. This is for two reasons. First, it is quite alien to my own sense of what I am doing to suppose that I am writing from a male point of view. If I could be persuaded that that were the case, it would, to say the least, be unsettling. Secondly, if it is true that only from a male point of view is it possible to ignore the ideological resonances of the dichotomies, then the most natural explanation for this is that the ideology and the dichotomies are not after all separable, which means that I cannot even take refuge in the truth of what I am saying: for I think the ideology is false. In any case, if there are sound feminist reasons for no longer even using these concepts, then to use them in an effort to rebut such reasons—to say, 'It does not matter if my own claims are perspectival so long as they are true'—is merely to provide further evidence of the extent of the problem.

Against none of these forms of nihilism do I have any decisive objection. I cannot establish the truth of the Basic Assumption. All I can do is to play it out in enough different ways to give it the ring of truth. Where does this leave the possibility of absolute representations? I have argued that that possibility is entailed by the Basic Assumption. Some nihilists might accept this argument. Indeed they might be nihilists precisely because they accept it, arguing by *modus tollens* that the Basic Assumption is false because absolute representations are not possible. Other nihilists might share my belief that absolute representations are possible. There is no obvious impediment to this in their mere rejection of the Basic Assumption. Most nihilists, however, will reject my conclusion as well as the Basic Assumption. Some will be forced to do this, those, for instance, who do not even countenance the use of the concept of a representation. My greatest quarrel, in a way, is with anyone such as Putnam who rejects the conclusion but shares the Basic Assumption. With nihilists I reach something more like an impasse.

Not that this is the end of the matter. I shall have a good deal

more to say about the Basic Assumption in later chapters. But there
is also an extremely important form of nihilism that I still need to
address.

Part of the Basic Assumption is that how reality is is independent of how it is represented as being. This idea is challenged by *idealists*. Idealism can certainly be used to resist my conclusion.[31] In
fact idealism can be used to resist the Fundamental Principle. For
on a suitably extreme idealist view, what true representations can
be produced is not dictated by what reality is like; rather, what reality is like is dictated by what true representations can be produced.
I want to close this chapter by considering one very radical and very
significant species of idealism that can be pitted against my conclusion.

I begin with two definitions. Let us say that something is *immanent* if it is the sort of thing that we can identify, where this is to be
understood in the minimal sense that it is in the domain of a quantifier that can appear in one of our representations. (We do not have
to have the means to single it out from other things.) And let us say
that something is *transcendent* if it is not immanent. Again there is
the question of who "we" are. But it seems not to matter. For whoever "we" are, everything, it seems, is immanent. This is because
the quantifier 'everything', understood unrestrictedly, itself appears
in our representations.

According to the idealist view I have in mind, however, there is
an element of perspective even in the idea of unrestricted quantification. What is understood as everything from one point of view
may not be from another. What is immanent from one point of
view may be transcendent from another. It follows that there is an
element of perspective even in the concept of reality. For reality
comprises all there is: the constituents of reality are all and only the
things in the domain of the quantifier 'everything', understood
unrestrictedly. Our references to reality are therefore, on this conception, references to what qualifies as reality *from our point of view*.
It would not *be* reality unless there were representations, from our
point of view, conferring such a privilege on it. This is what makes
the view idealist.

---

[31] Two twentieth-century examples of this, in different traditions, are M. Merleau-Ponty,
Phenomenology of Perception, Pt. II, ch. 3; and Michael Dummett, 'Reply to McGuinness',
where he uses a kind of idealism to deny that non-divine beings can produce absolute representations of physical reality.

But what *is* "our point of view"? Still leaving indeterminate who "we" are, we can at least say this. Our point of view must be a point of view from which we cannot help producing our representations. Anything less, anything that we could abandon without ceasing to be able to represent reality, would lack the authority and the power to delimit what we understand reality to be.

The following, then, is a consequence of this idealist conception:

(P1) There is a point of view such that any representation of ours must be from that point of view.

(P1) is of course stronger than

(P2) Any representation of ours must be from some point of view or other,

which is the simple negation, or which appears to be the simple negation, of my conclusion. (I shall come back to this point in a lit-tle while.) (P2) is compatible with our being able to abandon any given point of view when producing a representation. It takes something more than idealism, I think, to block the move from there to the conclusion that we can simultaneously abandon them all. But I shall not argue for that now. What concerns us here is (P1).

(P1), to repeat, is stronger than (P2), and (P2) appears to be the negation of my conclusion. So prima facie, at least, (P1) is incom-patible with my conclusion. However, complications in the imma-nent/transcendent distinction mean that the matter is not quite as straightforward as it seems. To see exactly how (P1) does bear on my conclusion, and more generally how this idealist conception does, we need to take into account the application of the imma-nent/transcendent distinction to various key notions in this very discussion.

The distinction is applied, first, to points of view themselves. This is related to an observation I made earlier: that it would be self-stultifying to supplement (P1) with the claim that we can *identify* the point of view in question, in a way that involves superseding its range. If we cannot identify the point of view in that way, then there must be a reason why not. The reason, on this idealist con-ception, is that we cannot identify it all. It is transcendent.

The distinction is applied, secondly, to modalities. Immanent modalities constitute possibility with respect to what is immanent, transcendent modalities with respect to what is transcendent. It is immanent modalities that represent real possibility. Transcendent modalities are purely formal. The 'must' in (P1) is an immanent 'must'. What (P1) says is that there is a point of view such that we, here, in reality, cannot help producing representations from that point of view.

The distinction is applied, thirdly, to the absolute/perspectival distinction itself. This is a simple corollary of its application to points of view and to modalities. A representation is immanently absolute if it can be integrated by simple addition with any representation that is immanently possible. But such a representation may yet be from a transcendent point of view. Granted that the point of view concerned in (P1) is transcendent, then what (P1) precludes is our producing representations that are transcendently absolute.

We can now see why the relationship between (P1) and my conclusion is not as straightforward as it seems. (P1) only contradicts my conclusion if my conclusion requires the *immanent* possibility of representations that are *transcendently* absolute.

Still, if the immanent/transcendent distinction can be applied here at all, then my conclusion does indeed require this—and (P1) does contradict my conclusion. For the question addressed by the Basic Argument is whether we, here, in reality can produce representations that are not from *any* kind of point of view. My conclusion is that we can. (P1) entails that we cannot.

Such, then, is the radical idealist view in question. It is heady, beguiling—and incoherent. At least it looks incoherent. It looks vulnerable to the suggestion made at the outset: that the very idea of that which is transcendent is self-contradictory, and the immanent/transcendent distinction, therefore, without force. Anything that exists, precisely because it is something that exists, is immanent. Nor is this conclusion mitigated by the fact that its references to what exists are references to what exists *from our point of view*. We can have no grasp on the possibility that what exists from our point of view is anything less than what exists, so long as our point of view is indeed ours. What *we* understand to be all there is, we understand to be *all* there is. What *we* understand to be reality, we understand to be *reality*. A transcendent point of view is therefore not a point of view. And a representation that can be integrated by simple addition with any representation that is immanently possible—which is to say, really possible—is a representation that can be integrated by simple addition with any possible representation. It is absolute.

These, at any rate, seem to be compelling objections to the view. But we do well to pause before dismissing it. It is of great historical importance; its motivation goes very deep, as I shall try to show in the next chapter; and most significantly of all in the context of this enquiry, it seems to point a way round the impasse between the nihilist and me, doing justice both to the Basic Argument and to the arguments, or to many of the arguments, that we have looked at in this chapter that stand opposed to it. Roughly, the idea is this. The Basic Assumption holds, and the Basic Argument is correct, at the immanent level. But at the transcendent level, the Basic Assumption is false, idealism supplants it, and many of the reasons canvassed in this chapter for the impossibility of absolute representations are sound, or have sound counterparts.

A little more fully. At the immanent level, it is true that representations are representations of what is there anyway and hence, as the Basic Argument shows, that absolute representations are possible. But these representations are still from our transcendent point of view. That point of view is determined by our own most inclusive outlook, that which ultimately counts as the outlook of a physicist. At the transcendent level the Outlook Assumption holds. Any outlook is Perspectival inasmuch as there is the formal possibility of outlooks that it excludes. Moreover, the reasons for this are more or less the reasons considered in this chapter. Any outlook involves evaluation, presupposition, and non-Platonistically construed meaning, all of which admit of alternatives. When I resisted this conclusion I conceded a good deal in the reasons for it, but I urged that there could still be representations with a distinctive role to play that qualified them as absolute. Now, however, that role appears merely immanent. My resistance is quite ineffectual against transcendent perspective. Finally, the *coup de grâce*: to the extent that the Basic Assumption holds, which is to say at the immanent level, it can be *justified*. For what gives reality its substantiality, its unity, and its autonomy, at that level, is precisely its being held together at the transcendent level—at a transcendent point of view.

Patently, this is a view that demands further discussion. I said in the last chapter that I would try to show that considerations in favour of the necessary perspectivalness of any representation were considerations in favour of something very radical. What I had in mind was this view. The point is this. If the view is *not* incoherent, then it provides a way of respecting those considerations without surrendering the Basic Argument—provided that care is taken over levels. I shall devote the next chapter to discussion of the view. We need to see whether we can after all make sense of transcendent perspective. We need to see whether we can make sense of an exclusiveness in our own most inclusive outlook that is not vitiated by the fact that the outlook excludes nothing else that we can identify as an outlook, an exclusiveness that is altogether more profound, altogether more mysterious, than whatever keeps apart the coleopterous and the bovine.

FURTHER READING

Books that in one way or another present problems for the possibility of absolute representations include: Richard J. Bernstein, *Beyond Objectivism and Relativism*; Gilles Deleuze, *The Logic of Sense*; H.-G. Gadamer, *Truth and Method*; E. H. Gombrich, *Art and Illusion*, especially Pt. III; R. L. Gregory, *The Intelligent Eye*; Martin Heidegger, *Being and Time*; Edmund Husserl, *Ideas*; Jean-François Lyotard, *The Postmodern Condition*; Michael Polyani, *Personal Knowledge*; Richard Rorty, *Philosophy and the Mirror of Nature*; Mark Sacks, *The World We Found*; and Hans Vaihinger, *The Philosophy of 'As If'*, especially pp. 64–77, 157–78, and 313–18.

Putnam's views are discussed in: Simon Blackburn, 'Enchanting Views'; Richard Rorty, 'Putnam and the Relativist Menace'; and Ernest Sosa, 'Putnam's Pragmatic Realism'.

Nelson Goodman defends his views in *Of Minds and Other Matters*, ch. 2.

Thomas Kuhn further develops his views in 'Second Thoughts on Paradigms'.

Derrida's views are discussed by Iris Murdoch in *Metaphysics as a Guide to Morals*, ch. 7; and by Hilary Putnam in *Renewing Philosophy*, ch. 6. See also Christopher Norris, *Derrida*.

On Quine, see Christopher Hookway, *Quine*.

On Nietzsche, see: Alexander Nehamas, *Nietzsche: Life as Literature*; and Michael Tanner, *Nietzsche*.

On the threat posed to absolute representations by feminism, see: Sandra Harding, *Whose Science? Whose Knowledge?*, which, in conjunction with her *The Science Question in Feminism*, contains references to a wealth of further relevant material; Luce Irigaray, *This Sex Which is Not One*; and Luce Irigaray, 'An Ethics of Sexual Difference'.

CHAPTER SIX

It argues an utter want of consistency to say, on the one hand, that
the understanding only knows phenomena, and, on the other hand,
assert the absolute character of this knowledge, by such statements
as "Cognition can go no further"; "Here is the *natural* and absolute
limit of human knowledge." But "natural" is the wrong word here.
The things of nature are limited and are natural things only to such
extent as they are not aware of their universal limit, or to such
extent as their mode or quality is a limit from our point of view, and
not from their own. No one knows, or even feels, that anything is a
limit or defect, until he is at the same time above and beyond it . . .
A very little consideration might show that to call a thing finite or
limited proves by implication the very presence of the infinite and
unlimited, and that our knowledge of a limit can only be when the
unlimited is *on this side* in consciousness.

(G. W. F. Hegel)

*§ 1: Idealism, empirical idealism, and transcendental idealism are each defined.
Reasons are given both for the appeal of transcendental idealism and for its incoherence.*

§ 2: Kant's transcendental idealism is sketched.

*§ 3: A kind of transcendental idealism suggested by the later work of Wittgenstein
is sketched.*

*§ 4: Between them, these indicate the possibility of a response of the kind consid-
ered at the end of Chapter Five to the Basic Argument. They do nothing, however,
to rebut the reasons given for the incoherence of this response. Some comments are
made about the use of the pronoun 'we' in this discussion, and a variation on
transcendental idealism is briefly considered.*

1

SO FAR I have talked about idealism without explicitly defining it. By *idealism* I mean the view that some aspect of the form of that to which our representations answer depends on some aspect of the representations. We can distinguish between empirical idealism and transcendental idealism. *Empirical idealism* includes the rider that this dependence is immanent. *Transcendental idealism* includes the rider that it is transcendent.

For the time being we need not worry about whether this usage coincides with anybody else's, nor about who, if anybody, has been either an empirical idealist or a transcendental idealist in these terms.[1] The positions themselves are our immediate concern. The view outlined at the end of the last chapter is a species of transcendental idealism.

—*"What do you mean by the "form" of that to which our representations answer?"*—

I mean whatever is a matter of its being not only how it is but *however* it is. This includes: its essential constituents, if any; whatever qualifies it as reality; and its very existence. Were it not for each of these, that to which our representations answer would not *be* that to which our representations answer. They determine how it must be. Idealism in its various guises is intimately related to necessity.

The distinction between what is necessary and what is contingent has long preoccupied philosophers. Most have regarded it as a basic philosophical tool. But many have been sceptical of it. Even those who have accepted it have often been keen to recognize contingency in what seems necessary. There is an irony here. Usually people are happy when they can recognize necessity in what seems contingent. This helps to satisfy their desire for explanation. If, for instance, it could be shown that the most fundamental physical laws were a kind of play of mathematics, admitting of no coherent alternative, then this would satisfy *par excellence* the basic urge we have to account for how things are by indicating some respect in which they could not have been otherwise. But philosophers tend

---

[1] But cf. Bernard Williams, 'Wittgenstein and Idealism', p. 148. For discussion of what 'dependence' means in this context, cf. Mark Sacks, *The World We Found*, § 1.2.2. For discussion of Kant, from whom the terminology derives, see further below.

to find necessity an unsatisfactory resting-place. They tend to find it mysterious that we can have commerce with all the ways things might have been. So there has been a trend among philosophers to seek a grounding for the ways things might have been in how they actually are.

Finding such a grounding is not simply a question of finding contingency in what once seemed necessary. We all of us do that all the time. It is an important part of growing up. Rather it is a question of finding contingency in what *is* necessary; in other words, of locating a contingent ground for what *seems* necessary, in such a way as to continue to be able to acknowledge the necessity. Whether this can be done is obviously dubious, though philosophers have variously supposed themselves capable of doing it. At any rate there is a link with transcendental idealism. Precisely what transcendental idealism affords is the prospect of locating a contingent base, within our representations, for necessary features of that to which the representations answer, without in any way compromising the necessity. The necessity is not compromised because the base is located somewhere beyond what we can represent, which means that we can continue to regard the features in question as necessary. For as far as anything we can represent is concerned (as far as anything we can think or imagine or say is concerned) they are.

This link between transcendental idealism and necessity is a crucial one. We shall return to it later in this chapter and in subsequent chapters. It is one of transcendental idealism's greatest enticements. So too is that through which we first encountered the doctrine, the fact that it affords the prospect of reconciliation in the face of apparently irreconcilable arguments for and against the possibility of absolute representations. In fact these enticements are variations on a single theme. They are not the only ones. There is a class of problems in philosophy to which transcendental idealism provides a general solution. The problem in each case is how to acknowledge an apparent philosophical truth which we seem to have no way of acknowledging without saying something false.[2] For example, there seems to be a philosophical insight in the thought that, had sentient creatures never existed, neither would the physical universe. As Dummett puts it: 'What would be the

[2] Cf. Williams, 'Wittgenstein and Idealism', p. 163.

difference between God's creating [a universe that was throughout its existence devoid of sentient creatures] and his creating nothing at all, but merely conceiving of such a universe . . .?'[3] Yet on the other hand, it seems the merest contingency that conditions in the physical universe were such as to generate sentient life. It seems straightforwardly false to say that, had those conditions never been met, the physical universe as a whole would never have existed. Transcendental idealism provides a way round this problem. Taking the physical universe to be that to which our representations answer, the transcendental idealist can argue as follows.

> *The Dependence of the Physical Universe on Our Representations*: The physical universe does depend on the existence of our representations ("we" here being all sentient creatures). But this dependence is not itself a feature of the physical universe. It is transcendent. And because the physical universe is that to which our representations answer, it follows that we cannot produce a representation to the effect that the physical universe depends on the existence of our representations without saying something false. That the physical universe depends on the existence of our representations is a transcendent truth but an immanent falsehood.

Once transcendental idealism is seen at work in this way one senses further potential. Thus consider the platitude that how things can be truly represented as being is how they really are; or alternatively, that the content of any true representation is the fact that things are a certain way. The 'is' here is the 'is' of identity. The content of my thought that grass is green, for example, and the *fact* that grass is green—the fact that that stuff out there is that colour— are one and the same. They do not merely correspond. (The content of my thought *is* that grass is green. The fact *is* that grass is green.) Platitude or no platitude, this seems to require explanation. Why should reality be constituted by just the sort of thing that we grasp in our thoughts? Transcendental idealism provides an explanation. It lets us say that the form of reality is determined at the transcendent level by the form of thought. But there is nothing we can truthfully say about this relationship at the immanent level that is not the merest truism. If we attempt to say more, we are

[3] Michael Dummett, 'Reply to McGuinness', pp. 351–2.

liable to produce absurdities about, for example, the mental make-up of physical reality.[4]

There is even quasi-technical work that transcendental idealism might do for us. Consider the quantifier 'everything'. What is the domain of this quantifier, when it is understood unrestrictedly? The obvious answer is: the set of all things. This is in line with the answer we would give concerning an unrestricted understanding of other quantifiers. The domain of 'everyone' is the set of all people, that of 'always' the set of all times. But what conception of a set do we have here? On one very natural conception, a set is something whose existence is parasitic on that of its members: they exist "first". So no set can belong to itself. But since sets themselves are things, this means that there cannot be a set of all things.[5] True, this conception of a set is not the only one available. Many will not recognize this as a real dilemma. But, for those who do, some form of transcendental idealism presents itself as a solution: the domain of 'everything', as used unrestrictedly in our representations, contains everything immanent, but is itself transcendent.

Despite all these enticements, however, transcendental idealism still looks incoherent. Specifically, it looks self-stultifying. Here are some apparently decisive objections to it.

First, there is no way of stating the view without producing a representation of the very kind it says we cannot produce. Take the claim that the physical universe depends on the existence of our representations. It is no good treating this claim as transcendently true but immanently false. The transcendent interpretation does not exist. If it did, it would not be transcendent. If we really cannot produce a representation to the effect that the physical universe depends on the existence of our representations without saying something false, then the physical universe does not depend on the existence of our representations. At a more general level, we cannot represent limits to what we can represent. For if we cannot represent anything beyond those limits, then we cannot represent our not being able to represent anything beyond those limits. Again, the very idea of that which is transcendent is incoherent. To be

[4] Cf. Ludwig Wittgenstein, *Philosophical Investigations*, §§ 93–7; and John McDowell, *Mind and World*, pp. 27–8—where each, however, tries to resist the allure of transcendental idealism, the former in reaction to his own earlier work (see further Chapter Seven below).

[5] Cf. Michael Dummett, *Frege: Philosophy of Language*, pp. 529 ff.

transcendent is to fail to be one of the things that constitute all there is. It is to fail to be.

I said these objections appeared decisive. I think they are. Transcendental idealism *is* incoherent. But that is by no means the end of the matter. There is a good deal more to be said about where it stands in relation to our enquiry. There is also an important counter-objection that needs to be addressed. The transcendental idealist may say, 'There is nothing wrong with transcendental idealism *per se*. What these objections are objections to is the attempt to state it. Transcendental idealism is a truth that cannot be stated.' This too I think is incoherent. But trying to formulate a proper reaction to it will take us very deep.

Let us turn first to the two philosophers who are of greatest significance to this discussion, though their relations to transcendental idealism are very different: Kant and Wittgenstein.

2

Kant was a transcendental idealist. This is a little like saying that Marx was a Marxist, but only a little. It was Kant who coined the expression 'transcendental idealism' and who first advocated any such position. It was Kant too who drew the contrast with 'empirical idealism', likewise his coinage. But remember: I have been operating with my own definitions of these expressions. These definitions are not the same as Kant's. Kant had in mind a pair of doctrines specifically about space and time.[6] I have been following the current trend of using the two expressions in an extended sense that is supposed to arise naturally out of Kant's. It is this sense that I tried to capture in my definitions. It remains to be shown that Kant was a transcendental idealist in my terms.

Kant takes as his starting point the existence of what he calls synthetic a priori knowledge. There are two contrasts here. A priori knowledge is opposed to a posteriori knowledge. A priori knowledge concerns the form of that to which our representations answer. It is knowledge not merely of how things are but of how they must be. It does not require observation. A simple example is

---

[6] e.g. Immanuel Kant, *Critique of Pure Reason*, A490–1/B518–19.

my knowledge that there are no male aunts. However, this is analytic. That brings us to the second contrast. Analytic knowledge is that to which synthetic knowledge is opposed. Analytic knowledge depends solely on the interrelations of concepts. It cannot be denied without contradiction. Synthetic knowledge, by contrast, depends on something beyond its constituent concepts. As far as they are concerned it admits of alternatives. A simple example of synthetic knowledge is my knowledge that there is a vicious wind blowing outside. However, this is a posteriori. What is distinctive in Kant's system is the suggestion that there is knowledge that is *both* synthetic *and* a priori: the two contrasts are not aligned. His examples include: arithmetical knowledge, such as our knowledge that $7 + 5 = 12$; geometrical knowledge, such as our knowledge that between any two points there is one and only one straight line; and some of our knowledge concerning the essential workings of the physical world, such as our knowledge that matter is never created or destroyed, and our knowledge that nothing happens without a cause.[7]

Most of this has subsequently been contested. Some philosophers query Kant's distinctions. Others accept the distinctions but query Kant's application of them, claiming, for instance, that arithmetical knowledge is analytic. Certainly Kant's belief in synthetic a priori knowledge cannot be accepted in all its detail. Advances in science have shown that some of his purported examples of synthetic a priori knowledge, so far from being that, are not even examples of knowledge: indeed the things that are said to be known are not even *true*. (Between two points there can be more than one straight line.) Moreover, the fact that these advances have been made partly through experimentation means that not only are those particular examples discredited, but the a priority of other examples is called into question. Geometry nowadays seems a decidedly empirical discipline.

Suppose, however, that Kant is right, and that there *is* synthetic a priori knowledge. What follows?

There is a puzzle. It seems impossible that we should have knowledge of what is independent of us except through observational contact with it, or through the analysis of concepts. Yet the knowledge in question is based neither on observation (it is a priori) nor

[7] Ibid., A1–16/B1–30; and Kant, *Prolegomena to Any Future Metaphysics*, §§ 1–5.

on conceptual analysis (it is synthetic). Kant's solution to this problem is to deny that it is knowledge of what is independent of us. On Kant's view, our knowing anything about the world is possible only because we have appropriate epistemic faculties. Through these we ourselves make a contribution to the form of what we know. It is as if we have native spectacles through which we view the world. Synthetic a priori knowledge is knowledge of how things must look through these spectacles. It is knowledge, as we might say, *pertaining to* these spectacles. It is knowledge pertaining to our own epistemic faculties.

Because this knowledge includes knowledge of the structure of space and time, Kant concludes that even these are contributed by us. They are not features of "things in themselves". But they are features of that to which our representations answer, at least if "our representations" are taken to be those that make any real sense to us. Kant's view is a species of idealism. What makes it a species of transcendental idealism is the fact that, whatever the process whereby we contribute the spatiality and the temporality of the spatio-temporal world, it is not a physical process. It is not itself the sort of thing that we can identify in any of our representations. It is transcendent,[8] a condition of the possibility of the spatio-temporal world rather than an identifiable part of it. To identify it we should need to have knowledge of things in themselves, and this, Kant insists, is impossible. We cannot take our spectacles off.

This is a variation on the position highlighted in the previous section. The claim that the physical universe depends for its existence on sentient creatures is one that Kant takes to be transcendently true and immanently false. Taking it to be immanently false distances him from the empirical idealist. Again, however, we must query whether the transcendent interpretation is available for Kant. Certainly it is not available in the way he suggests, encapsulating something that can be known through philosophical argument: we are not supposed to know anything about things in themselves. The boldest affirmations Kant makes of transcendental idealism—the ones most likely to be interpreted as affirmations of empirical idealism, despite his efforts to distinguish these—are in the first edition

---

[8] Kant himself draws a distinction between the 'transcendent' and the 'transcendental' which would be crucial to a full discussion of these matters but which, for the sake of simplicity, I shall pass over: see e.g. *Critique of Pure Reason*, A296/B352-3.

of his *Critique of Pure Reason*. By the second edition he has dropped them.[9] In the intervening *Prolegomena to Any Future Metaphysics* he shows himself to be very sensitive about the danger of being interpreted as the wrong kind of idealist, a fate which he claims has already befallen him, and he even suggests that his own position should be known henceforth not as 'transcendental idealism' but as 'critical idealism'.[10] It is as if he is engaged in an on-going struggle to suppress the immanent interpretation of his idealist claims and, in at least some crucial cases, eventually gives up.

However that may be, Kant's transcendental idealism is of the sort that entails the perspectivalness of all our representations, where "our representations" are again taken to be those that make any real sense to us. Simplifying somewhat, we can say that Kant's use of the phrase 'things in themselves' has something of the syncategorematic about it, and that when he denies the possibility of our having knowledge of things in themselves, or indeed of our representing things in themselves, what he is denying is the possibility of our achieving absolute knowledge or producing absolute representations. Our representations are from the point of view of possible human experience. They involve concepts that concern the way things appear to beings with certain epistemic faculties, most obviously faculties that involve the imposition of a spatio-temporal structure on what is known. Representations of the same type could not be produced from other points of view. (This means that the representations are not only perspectival, but radically perspectival.) But the transcendent possibility of beings occupying other points of view is not ruled out.[11]

—*"You say that, on Kant's view, our representations are from the point of view of possible human experience. Why 'human'? Other animals experience things in space and time as well."*—

Yes: sooner or later we are going to have to confront the question of how the pronoun 'we' functions in these various discussions. But Kant is certainly interested in representations that exhibit a sophistication unavailable to penguins or mice (say), whose own

---

[9] See e.g. the discussion of the Fourth Paralogism, 'Of Ideality', *Critique of Pure Reason*, A366 ff.

[10] Kant, *Prolegomena to Any Future Metaphysics*, § 13, Remark III.

[11] See e.g. Kant, *Critique of Pure Reason*, A26/B42 ff., A45–6/B62–3, and A146–7/B185–7; and cf. Kant, *Groundwork of the Metaphysics of Morals*, pp. 105 ff. in the pagination of the original 2nd edition.

representations are even further away from being absolute than ours are. Kant's concern is with rational animals, animals whose representations involve the use of concepts signalling where they (the representations) stand in logical relation to one another. These representations he calls *judgements*. A judgement, through its constituent concepts, points beyond itself to all the other possible judgements in which the same and related concepts occur. But it also points beyond itself to reality. The conceptual components of any judgement are configured in such a way as to say, '*This is how things are.*'[12] And this most fundamental of ideas, the idea of things being a certain way, which so primordially characterizes the form of reality, is itself brought within the ambit of Kant's idealism.

Kant holds that there is an essential link between judgement and self-consciousness. In judging, 'This is how things are,' one brings together various raw materials of knowledge and unites them in a certain way. In doing this, one also, at the same time, enables oneself to acknowledge those raw materials of knowledge as one's own. One enables oneself to judge, '*I judge*: this is how things are.' Without this potential for self-consciousness there would be no judgement. But it is impossible to unite the raw materials of knowledge in this way, so as to bring them within the purview of one consciousness, except through the exercise of certain basic concepts, concepts that can serve as a kind of noetic glue. (A prime example is the concept of causation.) Hence, just as we impose a spatio-temporal structure on what we know in experiencing it, so too, Kant argues, we impose a certain conceptual structure on what we know in judging of it. It is this that allows for, and indeed constitutes, the very possibility that things should *be* one way or another. 'A judgement,' Kant writes, 'is nothing but the manner in which given modes of knowledge are brought to the objective unity of apperception. This is what is intended by the copula "is".'[13]

This train of thought can lead to justification of the Fundamental Principle, at least in application to "our representations". For such a representation to be true is for things to be a certain way. For things to be a certain way is for one to be able to

[12] The Wittgensteinian allusion here is deliberate: see Ludwig Wittgenstein, *Tractatus Logico-Philosophicus*, 4.5. See further Chapter Seven below.

[13] Kant, *Critique of Pure Reason*, B141. More generally for the ideas in this paragraph see ibid., 'Transcendental Deduction of the Pure Concepts of Understanding', B129–69, a replacement for A95–130.

judge, at least in principle, that things are that way. So if two representations are true, then one can judge that things are as each says. But given the unifying function of judgement, if one can judge that things are as each says, then one can judge that things are as both say. So, since all these judgements are true, things are as both say and there can be a true representation to that effect.

This illustrates an idea mentioned summarily at the end of the last chapter, the idea that the unity of reality is determined by its being held together at the transcendent level. This holding together is part of the transcendent process whereby we contribute a conceptual structure to reality, allowing for things to be some way or other. It is something that we effect ourselves. Indeed it is something that each of us effects severally. For the unity in question, though shared, is essentially the unity of each individual consciousness. This explains why Kant sometimes toys with what might be called transcendental solipsism. He writes, 'All objects with which we can occupy ourselves . . . are one and all in me, that is, are determinations of my identical self.'[14] Here the idealism reaches its point of greatest intensity. (Revealingly, this is another of the passages he excises from the first edition of the *Critique of Pure Reason*.)

In sum, then: Kant provides us with both the basic structure and the main components of the view outlined at the end of the last chapter. He explicitly draws the contrast between "real", immanent possibility and purely formal, transcendent possibility; and he implicitly draws the contrast between immanent points of view and transcendent points of view.[15] He thus allows for the possibility of our producing absolute representations at the immanent level and the impossibility of our doing so at the transcendent level. His allowing for these things is not itself explicit.[16] Nor do his own reasons for thinking that all our representations must be from a transcendent point of view bear much resemblance to anything canvassed in the last chapter. But his historical relevance to our discussion is clear. Transcendental idealism is Kantianism. He cannot but serve as a touchstone for us, and we shall constantly return to him.

Not that there is anything in Kant to mitigate the suspicion of incoherence. That suspicion finds clear enough targets. For

[14] Ibid., A129.
[15] e.g. respectively: ibid., Bxxvi, note; and ibid., A26/B42 ff.
[16] But cf. ibid., 'The Architectonic of Pure Reason', A832–51/B860–79.

instance, in so far as it makes sense to say that "all objects with which we can occupy ourselves are in me", it seems plainly false. And if we really cannot know anything, or intelligibly say anything, except from the point of view of possible human experience, then, in particular, we cannot know, or intelligibly say: we cannot know anything or intelligibly say anything except from the point of view of possible human experience. The doctrine still appears to foreclose its own acknowledgement.

3

Wittgenstein was not a transcendental idealist. His relevance to our discussion is more oblique than Kant's. At least, it is in that respect. The arguments considered in the last chapter for the necessary perspectivalness of all our representations, arguments showing that our representations are intelligible only within a general framework of evaluations, presuppositions, and non-Platonistically construed meaning, have clearer echoes in Wittgenstein than in Kant. Those echoes will guide us at various points in what follows.

My assertion that Wittgenstein was not a transcendental idealist needs two immediate qualifications. It is customary to divide Wittgenstein's work into two phases. Despite profound continuities between the two phases, some of which will be of concern to us later, this is entirely apt. The first qualification is that I am talking exclusively in this section about Wittgenstein's later work. His earlier work will be a main focus of the next chapter. The second qualification is that, when I say that Wittgenstein was not a transcendental idealist, I do not mean that he confronted these issues and rejected transcendental idealism, still less that he embraced some other "ism" in its stead. Wittgenstein's conception of philosophy would not have allowed for that. For Wittgenstein philosophy was a kind of therapy. Its purpose was to cure us whenever, through the misuse of our own language, we became troubled by unanswerable pseudo-questions posing as deep problems. Reconsider a suggestion that appeared in Chapter One, the suggestion that self-ascriptions of pain are not representations but something more like interjections. Suppose this is correct. And imagine someone grappling with the following perplexity: 'Why can nobody else know with the certainty I do that I have been hurt?' This would be a case in point. It would be like grappling with the gibberish, 'Why can nobody else know with the certainty I do that *ouch!?*' Philosophy could be used to show that there was no real question here, relieving the person of the urge to find an answer. On this conception, then, it is not the point of philosophy to advance "isms". If, in the course of doing philosophy, one affirms anything, then it will be by way of showing the use of certain words. What one affirms will as likely as not be a platitude, or an item of common empirical knowledge, not something to be debated. So transcendental idealism is either of no concern to philosophy or, more probably, a bit of nonsense to be flushed out of the system by means of some suitable philosophical medicine.[17]

However, Wittgenstein's relevance to our discussion does not, as these remarks suggest, lie in his supplying the methods for finally disposing of transcendental idealism—as though Kant and he were the main proponent and opponent in what has come to be the crucial debate. On the contrary, for reasons that I hope will eventually make this claim sound less paradoxical, his relevance lies in the further inducement his work gives to embrace transcendental idealism, in the version outlined at the end of the last chapter. Transcendental idealism, for all that its outright endorsement would be so utterly un-Wittgensteinian, has an important place in Wittgenstein's work; or better, it has an important place in Wittgensteinian exegesis.

For Wittgenstein, philosophy involves self-conscious attention to the use of language. This means commanding a clear view of how words are used, reflecting on what does and does not make sense, feeling one's way around inside one's outlook, or one's various outlooks. It also means recognizing certain things as necessary. These are things that cannot intelligibly be denied. Wittgenstein's view of such necessities is a little like Kant's view of analytic truths. They are not used to make substantial claims about the world. They register the interrelations of concepts. For Wittgenstein, saying, 'Aunts are female,' is enunciating a rule rather than making an assertion. (Saying, 'Aunts are not female,' would be enunciating a different rule, using homonyms.) Saying, 'Aunts *have* to be female,' is

---

[17] e.g. Wittgenstein, *Philosophical Investigations*, §§ 122–33.

alluding to this fact. We will not count somebody as an aunt unless we also count that person as female.

Notice again how contingency is located in necessity. Wittgenstein is keen to dispel the view that, in exploring meaning in the way described, we are exploring some unchanging super-physical landscape, as though the concept of an aunt and the concept of femaleness were things we just stumbled across, the one an inseparable part of the other. It is on our own contingent practices that we are focusing. Moreover, part of Wittgenstein's genius is his special gift for drawing attention to how deep the contingencies lie. It is of course contingent that we use particular words (particular sounds and particular inscriptions) in the way that we do. (We might have used the word 'aunt' to denote uncles.) But when we reflect self-consciously on our actual classifications, we are inclined to see these as subject to certain constraints. Imagine people who in some circumstances use a word to denote green things, and who in other circumstance use that same word to denote blue things. We are inclined to say that they cannot have one concept in mind: they do not count as carrying on in the same way. Wittgenstein, applying some of his own philosophical methods to this very inclination of ours, urges us to think again about what is involved in "carrying on in the same way". It is not that he has in mind some favoured view of this that he wants to argue for. Rather, by means of a careful interlacing of hints, suggestions, and descriptions of different imaginable cases, he gets us to explore in greater depth the view we already have. We come to see what a huge amount we take for granted whenever we count someone, or refuse to count someone, as carrying on in the same way. Had various facts of nature, including facts of human nature, been different from how they are, then all sorts of behaviour might have constituted carrying on in the same way. (Thus imagine the blue / green case supplemented as follows. Suppose there are periodic atmospheric conditions that temporarily turn green things blue, and blue things green.) The contingencies of language use include all such facts. In particular, and centrally, they include our shared sensibilities, our shared senses of the natural and the salient: our shared outlooks. Without these, communication would break down. As Cavell marvellously and famously puts it:

That on the whole we . . . [make, and understand, the same projections of words into further contexts] is a matter of our sharing routes of interest and feeling, modes of response, senses of humour and of significance and of fulfilment, of what is outrageous, of what is similar to what else, what a rebuke, what forgiveness, of when an utterance is an assertion, when an appeal, when an explanation—all the whirl of organism Wittgenstein calls "forms of life".[18]

Wittgenstein describes "forms of life" as "the given". They are what has to be accepted.[19] Part of what he means is that it is in our biological nature to have certain outlooks. This comes out in the fact that, ultimately, we just do act in certain ways, ways that help to sustain communication among us. But the phrase 'form of life' indicates more. We have also been inculcated into certain social practices. As a result, we value certain things, we take certain things for granted, we defer to certain authorities, we accept certain canons of rationality, and we adopt certain modes of interpretation. All these things help to mould our natural outlooks into the full sophisticated outlooks in accord with which we produce our linguistic representations.[20] They are also the things whose contributions to forming these outlooks were marshalled in the last chapter in support of the Outlook Assumption, on which the Opposition Argument rested: the assumption, namely, that having such an outlook is having it to the exclusion of others; that representing the world in accord with such an outlook is representing it from a point of view. Not that Wittgenstein can yet be called upon as an ally by those who deny the possibility of absolute representations. Recall the tactic that I used there, of distinguishing between what informs the production of a representation and what role the representation might play. Wittgenstein in fact has a keen sense of the different roles representations might play, and a keen sense of the importance of distinguishing them. Even the virulent anti-scientism that marks so much of his writing could be conducive to my conclusion that science, and science alone, enables us to find the concepts to produce absolute representations. The connecting thought here would be: 'Science is all right, *in its place.*'[21]

---

[18] Stanley Cavell, 'The Availability of Wittgenstein's Philosophy', p. 52.

[19] Wittgenstein, *Philosophical Investigations*, p. 226.

[20] Cf. John McDowell on "second nature" in *Mind and World*, pp. 84 ff.

[21] On this last point, cf. Wittgenstein, *Philosophical Investigations*, §§ 410 and 571. For various points in the discussion so far, see e.g. ibid., §§ 217, 241, 372, and 569–70, and Pt. II, § xii;

Let us stay with Wittgenstein's anti-scientism for a while. One of its principal targets is the urge to make philosophy itself scientific. Wittgenstein is adamant that the exploration of language that characterizes philosophy cannot be a scientific exploration. There are many things he means by this. For instance, he means that philosophy must be shorn of any pretensions to theory and systematicity. He means that philosophy must be descriptive rather than explanatory.[22] But something else he means, or at least something that is very closely related to this and that he certainly thinks, is that philosophy cannot be *detached*. We might have thought that the kind of description of our own linguistic practices required in philosophy would be something whose content could in principle be grasped by one who did not already understand the language. Nothing less, we might have thought, could have any purchase on one who *mis*understood the language. But for Wittgenstein, such detachment is neither necessary nor possible. Williams puts well the kind of thing that Wittgenstein envisages instead:

[On a Wittgensteinian conception] we can . . . make [our language] clearer to ourselves, by reflecting on it, as it were self-consciously exercising it; not indeed by considering alternatives . . . but by moving around reflectively inside our view of things and sensing when one begins to be near the edge by the increasing incomprehensibility of things regarded from whatever way-out point of view one has moved into. What one becomes conscious of, in so reflecting, is something like: *how we go on*. And *how we go on* is a matter of how we think, and speak, and intentionally and socially conduct ourselves.[23]

How then are we supposed to engage with those who misunderstand the language (very probably ourselves in another guise)? Well, through what we say in the course of these reflections, we give them the same kind of exposure to the language as we give infants. We do not so much tell them what the language is like as show them what is like. By exposing them to the language we

Wittgenstein, *Remarks on the Foundations of Mathematics*, Pt. I, § 4; and Wittgenstein, *On Certainty*, § 204. (Note: references to Wittgenstein's later work should carry a similar caveat to that in Chapter Five, n. 21, in connection with Nietzsche. Only Part I of *Philosophical Investigations* was written for publication, and some of that he would no doubt have changed if he had lived to see his book published.)

[22] See e.g. Wittgenstein, *Philosophical Investigations*, § 109.
[23] Williams, 'Wittgenstein and Idealism', p. 153, his emphasis, tenses adapted.

prompt them (encourage them, invite them) to reach a proper understanding of the language not from without, that is to say not by interpreting it in terms of some other language that they antecedently understand, but from within. However, this is not just a matter of our using the language while they watch. We do also describe the language: we make conceptual connections explicit, we distinguish between different forms of speech, we expose pieces of nonsense, and suchlike. The significant thing is that even when we do all this, we do it in terms that are unintelligible except to those who already understand. We have no choice. Our descriptions cannot be endorsed except from the point of view of such understanding. In my terminology they are inherently perspectival. The exploration of language that Wittgenstein is envisaging is thus a reflective, reflexive, self-conscious process: it is a moving to and fro in which we maintain a certain conceptual point of view, partly by producing representations that cannot be produced except from that point of view, with the constant aim of keeping the point of view itself in focus.

But what *is* this point of view? I have characterized it as the point of view implicit in an understanding of our language; but what exactly is that? This question is connected to two others. The first relates back to the discussion in Chapter Five about the different ways in which the term 'language' can be understood. How is 'language' being understood here? The second is an instance of the recurrent problem about the first-person plural. Who, in this discussion, are "we"? These questions come together as follows. What, in this discussion, is "our language"?

Not English. It is not any empirically identified language of that kind. The example about aunts being female might have looked like an example concerning English. But if it were, there would be no reason to think that the relevant linguistic practices cannot be described except to those who already understand the language. There is no impediment to describing the use of the words 'aunt' and 'female' in, say, French. No, the example has nothing specifically to do with English. The relevant linguistic practices are such as our refusing to count somebody as an aunt unless we also count that person as female. And "we", here, include monolingual speakers of French, who participate in this practice through their use of the expressions 'tante' and 'le sexe féminin'.

"Our language", then, is something more like our range of conceptual resources. Certainly this makes it clearer why anyone should think it impossible to describe our language without using it. It also absolves Wittgenstein of a kind of empirical idealism, a rather crazy and uninteresting kind of empirical idealism at that. As I observed before, it is contingent that the English word 'aunt' is used in the way that it is. Had Wittgenstein meant to ground necessity in such contingencies as this—had he meant that the necessity of aunts being female was due to English speakers using 'aunt' and 'female' in a certain way—then he would in effect have been saying that the form of reality depends on a set of historical accidents involving the actual mechanics of linguistic representation.

One thing that belies such idealism is that it would still have been necessary that aunts were female, and *a fortiori* aunts would still have been female, even if the words 'aunt' and 'uncle' had had their meanings interchanged. True, it would not then have been correct to utter the sentence, 'Aunts are female,' but that is another matter. In fact, aunts would still have been female whatever we had got up to. That is part of what is meant by saying that aunts have to be female.

There are forces in Wittgenstein, however, that make it very difficult to keep a grip on this. Wittgenstein does not ground necessity in simple contingencies of word use. But he does ground it in contingencies. "Our language" might have been different. Does this not mean that we might have admitted the possibility of male aunts? And if so, does it not follow that there might have been male aunts? A variation on this quandary occurred at the end of Chapter One, in the discussion I had with my interlocutor about the sum: $2 + 2 = 4$. I suggested (without, I should add, endorsing the suggestion) that there might have been those who had a different arithmetic from ours and for whom this sum did not hold. My interlocutor resisted this suggestion on the grounds that I was envisaging a "merely linguistic" difference that was irrelevant to the sum itself. Now prima facie Wittgenstein sides with my interlocutor. On a Wittgensteinian view, not only does $2 + 2$ equal 4, but $2 + 2$ must equal 4. '$2 + 2 = 4$' is a rule. And yet—it is a rule only because of our contingent linguistic practices (and not just in the sense that we might have used different sounds or inscriptions to express it). Are there not Wittgensteinian reasons for saying that, had those practices been different, $2 + 2$ would not have equalled 4, a conclusion which, when it is not giving us a thoroughly unnerving sense of

vertigo, seems to be just false, another affirmation of a crazy empirical idealism?

Well, Wittgenstein need not in fact say any such thing. These
quandaries are real enough for him. But they are real in a way that
is compatible with his having a clear solution to them. (I shall have
more to say in due course about what I mean by this.) Wittgenstein
can respond as follows. It is not that, had our practices been different, 2 + 2 would not have equalled 4. Rather, had our practices been
different, we would not have had such a rule. We would not have
thought in those terms. It remains the case that 2 + 2 must equal 4.
Nothing is to count as a proper calculation if it stands in violation
of that. Again, "our language" might have been different, not in the
sense that we might have admitted the possibility of male aunts—
which is not something we could have done, for our concept of an
aunt and our concept of maleness would not have been those concepts if they had not excluded each other—but rather in the sense
that we might not have *had* those concepts. Similarly, the contingency of our linguistic practices is the simple contingency of their
existing at all. And as we have seen, it is a deep contingency. We are
lucky, for instance, that we do not come to blows over whether ele-
mentary sums have been performed correctly.[24] But in so far as this
means that there is a contingent grounding for what is necessary, it
neither threatens the necessity nor indicates any dependence of the
form of reality on any aspect of our representations.

As regards the question of who "we" are, there is no reason why
this question should not admit of a perfectly definite answer once
various matters have been resolved—though there is also no press-
ing need to resolve them, since nothing in what has just been said
hinges on their resolution. The matters in question include:
whether being one of "us" means sharing various outlooks, or
merely being able to share them; if the latter, in what sense of
'able'; and either way, which outlooks. However these matters are
resolved, "we" are not just English speakers. On some ways of
resolving them, "we" are a certain group of human beings. On
others, "we" are all human beings. On others again, "we" include
any beings, actual or potential, with whom humans can communicate, or any beings whom humans can recognize as producing linguistic representations.

---

[24] Cf. Wittgenstein, *Philosophical Investigations*, § 240.

Wittgenstein can be exonerated, then. The problem is that it is
extremely difficult to stop there. It is extremely difficult not to
envisage the 'we' expanding as it were to infinity. Once we have
considered the various possibilities above, we find it hard ultimately not to think of "ourselves" as all *possible* producers of linguistic
representations. One of two things can then happen. First, the contingency can disappear altogether. "Our language" comes to admit
of no alternative. Any evidence that something is a use of language
at all is *eo ipso* evidence that it is a use of "our language".[25] The references to "us" and to "our language" are then in effect redundant,
and philosophy must once again be seen as the exploration of some
unchanging super-physical landscape. The second thing that can
happen is that the contingency is retained. "Our language" does
admit of alternatives. But given the nature of its expansion they are
not "real" alternatives. 'We', and 'our language', are to be understood transcendently. Neither possibility is acceptable to
Wittgenstein.

Somehow, if his view is to be safeguarded, the urge to see the
'we' expanding in this way must be resisted. But again, there are
forces in Wittgenstein himself that make that urge almost irresistible. Indulging in the kind of self-conscious reflection that
Wittgenstein advocates, we cannot help asking, 'But what, ultimately, does somebody's being an aunt *consist in*? What does something's being green consist in?' We cannot help asking these questions because we cannot help wondering about the basic form of
that to which our representations answer, that whose character
gives our language its point and helps to make it possible. We know
that aunts have to be female, and we know that females have to
have a certain biological constitution. Such are our rules. But what
does it *take*, ultimately, for things to be configured in such a way
that somebody is an aunt? Or in such a way that something is
green? On a Wittgensteinian view, there is nothing we can summon
in response to such questions that is clearly demarcated from the
language itself. Someone who wants to know what something's
being green consists in cannot just focus attention on a green thing
and think, '*That* is what it consists in.' It is not clear what they are
referring to by 'that'. Anyone who wants to know what some-

---

[25] Cf. ibid., § 207; and Donald Davidson, 'On the Very Idea of a Conceptual Scheme'.

thing's being green consists in must observe us communicating with one another and exercising various discriminatory capacities that we possess. Not only that. Such a person must understand our acts of communication and see the point of our classifications. Such a person must become, or already be, one of us. What something's being green consists in is, at least in part, how we carry on. And the only way to prevent this from being a crazy empirical idealism is to let the 'we' expand to infinity; or in other words, assuming that the concept of being green cannot be regarded as part of some super-physical landscape, to let the idealism turn transcendental. Anything less entails the immanent truth of various immanent falsehoods, for instance: 'Had our language been different, grass could not have been green.' As regards the point of view that we are focusing on when we do philosophy, that now appears as a transcendent point of view, a point of view with no "real" alternatives. It is that residual point of view from which we produce representations even when we produce them in accord with our most inclusive outlook. Like Kant's position, this is transcendental idealism of the kind considered at the end of the last chapter. It entails the impossibility of absolute representations. It also has an analogue of the 'I judge' that Kant took to be appendable to any judgement: namely, a 'we judge', which, as in Kant, betokens some transcendent unifying principle holding our world together.

So—how can Wittgenstein resist such transcendental idealism, which looks no more acceptable than it did before?

By disallowing the questions that led to it. We must not ask, 'What does something's being green consist in?' Or at least, we must not ask it with a certain metaphysical intent. (It may be a perfectly good scientific question, with a perfectly good scientific answer concerning wavelengths and the rest.) Somehow we have to see these questions themselves as pseudo-questions, symptoms of an illness awaiting Wittgensteinian therapy.

The fact remains that it was assimilation of Wittgenstein's work that led us to pose the questions. It was assimilation of Wittgenstein's work that tempted us to affirm the transcendental idealism. Moreover—a point but for which this entire exegetical approach to Wittgenstein would be altogether harder to justify—there is evidence that Wittgenstein himself feels the force of the temptation. The question about how far our mathematics depends on us, for instance, is one that he himself grapples with, very uncomfortably. Consider this quotation:

"But mathematical truth is independent of whether human beings believe it or not!"—Certainly, the propositions "Human beings believe that twice two is four" and "Twice two is four" do not mean the same. The latter is a mathematical proposition; the other, if it makes sense at all, may perhaps mean: human beings have *arrived* at the mathematical proposition. The two propositions have entirely different *uses*.—But what would *this* mean: "Even though everybody believed that twice two was five it would still be four"?—For what would it be like for everybody to believe that?— Well, I could imagine, for instance, that people had a different calculus, or a technique which we should not call "calculating". But would it be *wrong*?

And consider this:

We have a colour system as we have a number system.—Do the systems reside in *our* nature or in the nature of things? How are we to put it?—*Not* in the nature of numbers or colours.—Then is there something arbitrary about this system? Yes and no. It is akin both to what is arbitrary and to what is non-arbitrary.[26]

And consider Williams's just reply:

The diffidence about how to put it comes . . . [from the problem:] how to put a supposed philosophical truth which, if it is uttered, must be taken to mean an empirical falsehood, or worse . . . [Wittgenstein's theory of meaning] points in the direction of a transcendental idealism . . . [We are] driven to state it in forms which are required to be understood, if at all, in the wrong way.[27]

4

To take stock, then: both Kant and Wittgenstein, in their different ways, indicate the possibility of a deep nihilistic response to the Basic Argument. This response leaves us with room to countenance the argument, at one level. Yet it still entails that there is a point of

---

[26] Respectively: Wittgenstein, *Philosophical Investigations*, pp. 226–7, his emphasis; and Wittgenstein, *Zettel*, §§ 357–8, his emphasis.

[27] Williams, 'Wittgenstein and Idealism', p. 163.

view such that any of our representations must be from that point of view. Kant gives us the structure of the response, and Wittgenstein, in spite of himself, gives us ideas about how to complete it. In neither Kant nor Wittgenstein, however, is there anything that rebuffs our initial sense that the response is incoherent. If it is, and if I am right that it is the most powerful available response to the Basic Argument, then this is further reason for accepting that argument.

Concerning the incoherence of the response, I have little to add to what I have already said. The attempt to use words such as 'we' with a transcendent interpretation, though enticing, is effectively doomed to failure by definition. It also typically falls foul of its very purpose: to circumscribe how words can be used, precisely so as to show that they cannot be used in *this* way. The "transcendent" denial that absolute representations are possible undercuts itself and collapses into an unregenerate affirmation that they are.

Of course, as I have already indicated, demonstrating the incoherence of transcendental idealism is itself a Wittgensteinian undertaking. The doctrine is one whose very statement is a mishandling of the language of just the kind that Wittgenstein is keen to expose. There is clearly an ambivalence in Wittgenstein's philosophy, if not in Wittgenstein himself. What is not so clear yet is the diagnosis. More needs to be said about this. That is one reason why I cannot let the matter rest there. Another, closely related, reason is that, despite the seemingly decisive objections to transcendental idealism, it retains an allure that is still at times almost irresistible. And a third reason, itself closely related to both these, is that there is still the transcendental idealist's envisaged counter-objection, namely that any faults here lie not with transcendental idealism itself, but with the attempt to state it. In the next chapter I shall start to say something in connection with each of these.

There is one final task for this chapter. This concerns the vexed question of who "we" are. I have remonstrated against the attempt to give 'we' a transcendent interpretation, and I have said a little about how Wittgenstein, who makes constant use of the pronoun, might respond to the question of whom *he* means by it. But there remains the question of whom I mean by it. For I too have made constant use of the pronoun, sometimes implicitly and crucially. The very issue that has structured this whole enquiry, the issue of whether absolute representations are possible, is, I acknowledged

earlier, the issue of whether *we* can produce absolute representations.

—*"You are in trouble, surely. For you cannot take the approach you
said Wittgenstein could take. Suppose you try. Suppose you say that, subject to the resolution of various inessential matters, 'we' can receive different determinate interpretations. Then it behoves you to give an example.
But there are no examples for which the Basic Argument works. Given any
suitable specification of who "we" are, the Basic Argument leaves open the
possibility that we cannot (even between us) produce absolute representations. It does nothing to show, for instance, that Anglophones can produce
them, nor that all living humans can produce them, nor yet that all
humans ever can produce them. Maybe they can. But the Basic Argument
does nothing to show that. For it does nothing to show anything as specific as that. All that remains for you to do, surely, is to let the 'we' expand
to infinity, embracing all possible producers of representations, the very
thing that you argued, on Wittgenstein's behalf, was unacceptable."*—

I detect two confusions here. In the first place, I think the Basic
Argument does show the things you say it does not. Remember
how the 'can' is to be understood. As I said near the beginning of
Chapter Four, it is to be understood in a minimal sense. It is meant
to encompass any finite extension of our powers. Practical possibility is not at issue. It is perfectly acceptable, then, for me to specify
that "we" are all humans; or all living humans; or all living
Anglophone humans; or even you and I. If the Basic Argument is
successful, then each of these groups can, in this minimal sense,
produce absolute representations. I in fact have greater latitude
than Wittgenstein has.

—*"But if the 'can' extends this far, then are you not in effect letting
the 'we' expand to infinity? It is surely much the same whether you take a
particular group and envisage all possible extensions of its powers or
envisage all possible groups."*—

Quite. And that brings me to the second confusion. There is
nothing wrong with letting the 'we' expand to infinity, *per se*. We
can certainly talk about all possible producers of (linguistic) representations. What we cannot do is to use 'we', so interpreted, to do
what Wittgenstein wants to do, namely to identify the contingent
grounding for necessity. This is because, on this interpretation, 'we'
itself takes in all possibilities. It does not pick out a group whose
existence and practices are a matter of contingent fact.

—*"But now it is not clear what work your own uses of 'we', explicit or*

implicit, are supposed to be doing. Why insist that the question whether
absolute representations are possible is the question whether we can pro-
duce them, if, as now seems to be the case, that sets no limits?"—

It does set limits. It rules out what an infinite being can do. That
is why I insisted on it in the first place, in Chapter Five. I am envisaging all possible *finite* extensions of powers. It is as if the 'we' and
the 'can' work together as an existential quantifier, whose variable
has an infinite range but no infinite values. (Neither, of course, does
it have any transcendent values.)

In the sense in which we can produce absolute representations,
we also, I believe, can know anything. That is, for any representation, there is a finite extension of our powers enabling us to know
whether or not it is true.[28] It may still be that we cannot know
everything. That is, it may still be that there is no single finite extension of our powers enabling us to know whether or not each representation is true. This is a simple scope distinction. It is one of
many that arise in this connection. Another relates to the claim that
we cannot fully understand our own intellect. This is sometimes
argued on the grounds that, in order fully to understand any intellect, we need an intellect of greater sophistication. This shows that
'our own intellect' is understood as falling within the scope of the
'cannot'. That is, it is not understood as picking out our actual intellect, the intellect of (say) turn-of-the-millennium *Homo sapiens*. It
remains an open question whether we can fully understand *that*.
But to return to my claim that we can know anything: I make this
claim as a preliminary to some final brief comments about an oft-
encountered variation on transcendental idealism. This variation is
like the original, but restricted to representations such that we can
know whether or not they are true. What the variation comes to,
roughly, is that some aspect of the form of what we can know
depends on some aspect of our knowledge, though we cannot have
knowledge of this dependence. Kant's view can be regarded as a
version of this doctrine; witness my caveat, when discussing his
view, that by "our representations" I meant those that we can make
any real sense of. (Kant would regard being able to make any real
sense of a representation as equivalent to being able to know
whether or not it is true.) For although Kant denies us knowledge

[28] I do not say that, for any true representation, there is a finite extension of our powers
enabling us to know that it is true. See Joseph Melia, 'Anti-Realism Untouched'.

of things in themselves, he does not deny that we can have *thoughts* about things in themselves.[29] One reason for considering this variation is that it looks as if it may be able to do much of the work of the original but without self-stultification. Can it? Well, not if we are supposed to be able not just to state it, but also, by dint of philosophical reasoning, to know of its truth, as Kant thinks we are. But more to the point, if I am right that there is nothing we cannot know, then the variation and the original are in any case the same.

FURTHER READING

On Kant, see: Henry E. Allison, *Kant's Transcendental Idealism*; P. F. Strawson, *The Bounds of Sense*, to which H. E. Matthews replies in 'Strawson on Transcendental Idealism'; Hilary Putnam, *Reason, Truth and History*, ch. 3; and Garrett Thomson, 'The Weak, the Strong and the Mild—Readings of Kant's Ontology'.

The *locus classicus* for rejection of Kant's analytic/synthetic distinction (and, less directly, of his a priori/a posteriori distinction) is W. V. Quine, 'Two Dogmas of Empiricism'.

The *locus classicus* for rejection of Kant's view that arithmetical knowledge is synthetic is Gottlob Frege, *The Foundations of Arithmetic*.

There is revealing evidence of Kant's own struggle with transcendental idealism in work that he was in the throes of producing at the end of his life, published as his *Opus Postumum*.

On Wittgenstein, see: Michael Dummett, 'Wittgenstein's Philosophy of Mathematics', which he embellishes in his 'Wittgenstein on Necessity: Some Reflections', and to which Cora Diamond replies in 'The Face of Necessity'; James Edwards, *Ethics Without Philosophy*; Peter Hacker, *Insight and Illusion*; David Pears, *Wittgenstein*, and, in greater depth, *The False Prison*; Hilary Putnam, 'On Wittgenstein's Philosophy of Mathematics'; and Crispin Wright, *Wittgenstein on the Foundations of Mathematics*.

The idea that there is a form of transcendental idealism in the later work of Wittgenstein is associated primarily with Bernard Williams: see 'Wittgenstein and Idealism'. The idea is pursued in various ways by Jonathan Lear: see 'Leaving the World Alone'; 'The Disappearing "We"'; and 'Transcendental Anthropology'. Mark Sacks explores the idea in 'Transcendental Features and Transcendental Constraints'. So do I in

---

[29] Kant, *Critique of Pure Reason*, Bxxvi, and note.

'Transcendental Idealism in Wittgenstein, and Theories of Meaning'. The idea is attacked by Derek Bolton, in 'Life-form and Idealism'; and by Norman Malcolm, in 'Wittgenstein and Idealism'. Less directly, it is attacked by John McDowell, in 'Following a Rule'.

The contradictions inherent in transcendental idealism surface in Graham Priest, *Beyond the Limits of Thought*. Priest himself concludes that some contradictions are true.

CHAPTER SEVEN

We do not know how to pray as we ought, but the Spirit himself
intercedes for us with sighs too deep for words.

(St Paul)

§ 1: *The suggestion that transcendental idealism is inexpressibly true is pro-
pounded and rejected. But the idea that there is a connection between transcendental idealism and inexpressibility, and that this serves to explain the continuing allure of transcendental idealism, is kept in play.*

§ 2: *Wittgenstein's earlier work is considered, to see whether it can help to substantiate this idea.*

§ 3: *A proposal is made, deriving from Wittgenstein's earlier work, namely that
we are shown that transcendental idealism is true, where this means that we have
ineffable knowledge and that transcendental idealism is what results when an
attempt is made to put that knowledge into words.*

§ 4: *This proposal will be defended in the next two chapters. A kind of prole-
gomenon to these two chapters is given.*

1

—"YOU talked more than once in the last chapter about a counter-objection that the transcendental idealist might bring to all that you have levelled against the doctrine: namely, that there is nothing wrong with transcendental idealism itself but only with the attempt to state it; that transcendental idealism is inexpressibly true. I think I have a way of giving
graphic vindication to this counter-objection.

—"Consider the following horrific possibility, familiar from a number
of recent philosophical discussions. A human brain is kept alive in a vat
and is so manipulated by scientists as to give the subject the illusion of liv-

ing a perfectly normal life with a perfectly normal body. This possibility raises deep questions. First, and most basically, in what sense is it a possibility? Is it a technological possibility? Or is it perhaps only a narrative possibility, the stuff of third-rate science fiction, not ultimately fully intelligible? Just what sorts of thoughts can the subject have? What sorts of representations can he produce?"—He?—*"I agree, the use of this pronoun here is problematical, even if the brain was originally that of a man. But let us imagine the story fleshed out in such a way as to warrant the attribution of a sex to the subject, in whatever tenuous sense. To continue: does it make a difference, and if so what difference, if the brain has been in this state from birth? What if there are several brains in the vat, connected in such a way that the subjects can "communicate" with one another? What if there are no brains not in the vat? What if the vat and its contents have been brought into existence as a result of some bizarre cosmic accident?*

—"I do not propose to enter into the huge controversy excited by these questions. I just want to consider one plausible reaction to the scenario (which I shall not try to defend) and then to relate that back to your discussion of transcendental idealism. According to the reaction I have in mind, the subject can have thoughts and can, more generally, produce representations, but these exhibit a kind of local idealism. What they answer to is not the whole of reality, but merely that part of the brain's environment with which it has a certain immediate commerce. In a drastic but convenient oversimplification, they answer to what is in the vat. (It may be important here to stipulate that the brain has been in this state since birth.) This is a kind of local idealism because that to which the subject's representations answer is limited by features of the representations themselves, most obviously by their location.

—"The subject is not, on this view, the victim of any deep error. Let us say that he simulates doing something when it is, for him, as if he really is doing that thing, or, very roughly, when his brain undergoes the kind of workings that the brain of a normally embodied person undergoes when he or she does that thing. Now suppose that the subject simulates seeing the sun, say. We may want to say that he has the illusion of seeing the sun. But 'illusion' is not really the right word. The subject does not have all sorts of false thoughts about the real sun. He has mostly true thoughts about configurations of things in the vat. It is just that he conceptualizes these in his own highly idiosyncratic way.

—"Any representation that the subject produces is, on this view, perspectival. Its content depends not only on its type but also on its location.

Another brain in another vat generating another representation of the same type would be reckoning with a different local "reality". It would be reckoning with what was going on in a different vat. Even when the subject has mathematical thoughts, their content is restricted by his limited access to reality. He cannot reproduce any of our mathematics, because our mathematics is vulnerable to the possibility that goings-on outside the vat should call it into question, if not by showing it to be false, then at least by showing it to be inapplicable. His mathematics is not vulnerable to that possibility. To be sure, any goings-on outside the vat can be mimicked inside it. If there are circumstances in which our mathematics would be called into question, then there are circumstances in which his would be. But the point is, there are circumstances in which our mathematics would be called into question but not his. Whereas we think that $7 + 5 = 12$, he thinks that $7 + 5 = 12$ "in the vat". True, it is for him as if he thinks that $7 + 5 = 12$. In the terminology introduced above, he simulates *thinking that $7 + 5 = 12$. But remember, this just means that his brain undergoes the kind of workings that your brain or my brain undergoes when either of us thinks that $7 + 5 = 12$.*

—"*Here is another thing he might simulate thinking, in that same sense: absolute representations are possible. He might simulate reading this book and being convinced by the Basic Argument. If he does, and if the Basic Argument is in fact successful, then his actual thinking in this regard is, I claim, quite correct.*"—

Explain. Prima facie what he actually thinks, on this way of construing him, is that absolute representations are possible "in the vat". But they are not, according to you. He cannot produce absolute representations.

—"*This is to overlook the fact that, granted his limited access to reality, his conception of absoluteness is itself limited. What he actually thinks is that representations that are absolute "in the vat" are possible "in the vat". And so they are. One can give this a deliberately paradoxical twist by saying that absoluteness is relative, or, somewhat less hyperbolically, that there are restricted versions of absoluteness. This is not the point that you made in Chapter Five about there being perspective in the concept of absoluteness. That was a point about the perspectival character of interpretation. This is a point that arises once interpretation has done its work—once interpretation has fixed what representations there are and what their contents are. This is the point that, relative to some limited range of possibilities, a perspectival representation can count as absolute.*

—"*Transcendence and immanence exhibit the same relativity. Relative* to some limited range of possibilities, what is immanent can count as transcendent. Thus, for instance, the scientists and the computer hooked up to the brain's nerve endings are transcendent "in the vat". But when the subject simulates thinking that nothing can be transcendent, again his actual thinking is quite correct. What he actually thinks is that nothing "in the vat" can be transcendent "in the vat".

—"Imagine, then, that the subject simulates thinking all the things that you have been maintaining: that the form of reality is independent of his representations; that absolute representations are possible; that nothing can be transcendent; that transcendental idealism is incoherent. Provided that you are right about all these things, then he is right too, in each particular. Yet, for all that, the form of reality "in the vat" does depend on his representations; absolute representations are not possible "in the vat"; some things are transcendent "in the vat"; and transcendental idealism, "in the vat", is quite coherent, in fact true. Transcendental idealism is true "in the vat" because, while the form of that to which his representations answer depends on some aspect of his representations, this dependence is transcendent "in the vat".

—"All of this is beyond his powers of representation. If he were to try to affirm any kind of transcendental idealism with respect to his own representations, he would say something false, or meaningless. Even so, he can surely at least have an inkling of what is going on. Imagine that one of the scientists gets him to simulate being told that he is really just a brain in a vat. That is, imagine that one of the scientists so manipulates him that it is, for him, as if someone tells him that he is really just a brain in a vat. To be sure, he knows that what he is told is false. Or rather, he knows that what he is told "in the vat" is false. He knows that he is not just a brain in a vat "in the vat". But surely he can have a non-representational insight into the possibility that really he is just a brain in a vat, that really transcendental idealism, with respect to his own representations, is true. And if he can, then can we not do likewise?

—"Usually, when the possibility of the brain in the vat is mooted, it is mooted in connection with a sceptical challenge. How do we know that we are not in that position? Whatever resources we marshal to show that we are not, the subject can simulate marshalling those same resources to show that he is not. As soon as we reflect on this, the sceptical doubts return. Similarly, when we affirm that representations are representations of what is there anyway, or that absolute representations are possible, or that nothing can be transcendent, and then reflect on the fact that this subject can simulate affirming those very same things (that is, it can be, for this *subject, as if he affirms those very same things), then our affirmations are somehow compromised. We seem bound to conclude that, just as he can have a non-representational insight into certain sceptical possibilities, so can we. In particular, we seem bound to conclude that we can have a non-representational insight into the possibility that transcendental idealism is true. But once we admit that we can have a non-representational insight into the possibility that transcendental idealism is true, it is a small step to the conclusion that we can have a non-representational insight into its actual truth. For transcendental idealism, at least in the version that you have been dealing with in the last two chapters, is itself a doctrine about possibilities. It is a doctrine involving the possibility of representations that cannot be integrated by simple addition with our absolute representations. And the possibility of the possibility of such representations is, in effect, their possibility. Kantian-cum-Wittgensteinian arguments can put flesh on the bones of this possibility, the flesh, say, of imaginary creatures whose conceptual resources are in principle inaccessible to us. But the insight itself has now been attained in a very direct way which bypasses those arguments. And the transcendental idealist's envisaged counter-objection has surely at last been vindicated."—*

I disagree. I do not think that the incoherence of transcendental idealism has in any way been mitigated by anything that you have just said, not even granted the legitimacy of this way of construing the brain in the vat. And the appeal to inexpressibility gains nothing on earlier appeals to transcendence. 'It is inexpressibly true that . . .' is subject to just the same strictures as 'It is transcendently true that . . .'. When the brain in the vat undergoes the kind of workings that our brains undergo when we deny that we are brains in a vat, or reject transcendental idealism, or affirm the possibility of absolute representations, his thinking is, for the reasons you gave, perfectly sound. But so is ours. We are not brains in a vat; transcendental idealism is incoherent; absolute representations are possible. He cannot express or think about possibilities that transcend his world. Neither can we. There are no possibilities that transcend our world.

—*"But that is much too cavalier. He cannot express or think about possibilities that transcend his world because his powers of representation are limited. But such possibilities exist. Some are realized. Surely it is an arrogation to deny that we might be subject to the same kind of limitations. Admittedly, it is self-stultifying for us to talk about, or even to think about, possibilities that transcend our world. But what about the claim, which*

*you have still not addressed, that we can have a non-representational
insight into their existence?"—*

If these possibilities do not exist, then we cannot have an insight
of any kind into their existence. And if it is self-stultifying for us to
say or to think that they do exist, then they do not.

—*"Very well, my formulation was unhappy. Indeed—who knows?—
there may be no satisfactory way of putting the suggestion. That may be a
further consequence of the non-representational character of the insight.
But you surely do not begrudge a Fregean pinch of salt."*[1]—

A Fregean pinch of salt is precisely what I begrudge. It is not that
I am unsympathetic to the idea of a non-representational insight.
On the contrary, one of my chief aims in this book is to defend the
idea. I want to try to make sense of transcendental idealism's great
allure (which I by no means deny), and I want to do so by arguing
that the transcendental idealist is trying to express inexpressible
knowledge. (Throughout this book I shall use 'inexpressible', 'non-
representational', and 'ineffable' interchangeably: likewise their
cognates.) But I will not be satisfied except in so far as I am satisfied
that I have tried to say nothing but what can be said, and that I have
avoided self-stultification, that ever-present threat in any discussion
of the inexpressible. If the project can be carried out at all, then it
can be carried out without pinches of salt.

The idea that transcendental idealism is a truth that cannot be
expressed is every bit as incoherent as transcendental idealism. It
compounds the absurdity of things being a certain way, even
though it is impossible in principle to indicate what that way is,
with a self-stultifying shot at providing just such an indication. It is
what transcendental idealists resort to when their awareness of the
incoherence of their position has still not overcome their commitment to it. The temptation to say that we have a non-representational insight into the truth of transcendental idealism is little more
than an extension, under the influence of self-conscious reflection,
of the temptation to affirm transcendental idealism in the first
place. To succumb to the former as a way of accounting for the
latter is hopeless. We must proceed much more cautiously.

If we are to make proper sense of the inexpressible, then we
must abandon forthwith any notion that things can inexpressibly be

---

[1] Frege famously relied on his reader not to begrudge a pinch of salt when he found that
there was no satisfactory way of putting a central thesis of his logical theory: see Gottlob
Frege, 'On Concept and Object', p. 52.

a certain way. For things to be a certain way is for it to be possible, in principle, to represent them as so being. The inexpressible, whatever else it is, is not that which carves up logical space awkwardly.

Sometimes logical space is carved up awkwardly. And sometimes, when it is, we are deeply moved as a result. Most of us have said something like, 'Words cannot express how I feel at the moment,' and have known a certain anguish in saying it. But still, ultimately, we have been talking about contingent limitations. It is a familiar enough fact that contingent limitations can make it a practical, social, or indeed physical impossibility for one to express things in a certain way, even sometimes to express them at all. One's vocabulary might be limited. The vocabulary of the language one speaks might be limited. One might lack the skills to use non-linguistic means of expression: gestures, looks, deeds, music. One might be paralysed. But as far as inexpressibility is concerned this is all beside the point. The inexpressible is what cannot be expressed even in principle, even in that minimal sense of 'can' distinguished towards the beginning of Chapter Four. If the inexpressible relates to logical space at all, then it relates not to particular ways of carving up logical space but to its *being* logical space, not to how things are but to their being any way at all.

Among the contingent limitations that make it impossible for one to express how logical space is carved up are limitations that make it impossible for one to reckon with all the relevant parts of logical space in the first place, limitations that prevent one from reckoning with all the possibilities. The brain in the vat is limited in this way. But again, as far as inexpressibility is concerned, that is beside the point. If we are to make proper sense of the inexpressible, and if we are to formulate a proper reaction to transcendental idealism, then we do well, I think, to pay the story no further heed.

—*"But surely what the story shows is that various concepts, like the concept of inexpressibility, are relative to different limited conceptions of what the possibilities are. Given the brain's limitations, he might simulate talking about complete inexpressibility and mean only inexpressibility "in the vat", that is inexpressibility relative to his limitations. Surely we are bound to pay heed to the story. We are bound to acknowledge the possibility that, when we talk about complete inexpressibility, we likewise only mean inexpressibility relative to our limitations."*—

What limitations? It is precisely one of the failings of transcendental idealism to suppose that there can be a satisfactory answer to this question. When we talk about complete inexpressibility we mean complete inexpressibility. In the rest of this chapter, and in the next two, I shall try to make sense of this.

2

I shall start with Wittgenstein, but this time with his earlier work. In the *Tractatus*, the one major work of Wittgenstein's to be published during his lifetime,[2] he embraced a kind of transcendental idealism, then famously acknowledged, at the end of the book, that what he had written was nonsense. The book's thoroughly Kantian project, combined with its remarkable final renunciation, make it a natural focus for this discussion.

'Thoroughly Kantian': there are features of the *Tractatus* that make this seem an odd choice of epithet. The book contains only one reference to Kant, and that rather dismissive. It also contains a good deal that sounds anti-Kantian.[3] But I hope to give some indication of how steeped the *Tractatus* is in Kant for all that. (I am not saying that Wittgenstein consciously drew on Kant. Schopenhauer was an important intermediary. Wittgenstein did consciously draw on Schopenhauer,[4] and he on Kant, though the main conduit was a set of ideas concerning ethics and the will that I shall barely touch on.)

Wittgenstein's aim in the *Tractatus* is to draw the limits of what can be represented. By considering the essence of representation he attempts to say what the world must be like in order to be represented at all. And by "the world" he means "all that is the case", all that *can* be represented. He is led to a powerful vision of alluring crystalline purity. The basic structure of this vision is as follows. (We need not concern ourselves for current purposes with the interpretation of the details.) The world is the totality of facts. Facts are determined by states of affairs. States of affairs are configurations of simple objects. Simple objects constitute the unanalysable, ungenerable, indestructible substance of the world. These would

[2] Ludwig Wittgenstein, *Tractatus Logico-Philosophicus*.
[3] e.g. ibid., 4.0412 and 5.634. The one reference to Kant is at 6.36111.
[4] See Erik Stenius, *Wittgenstein's 'Tractatus'*, ch. 11; Allan Janik and Stephen Toulmin, *Wittgenstein's Vienna, passim*; and Peter Hacker, *Insight and Illusion*, pp. 87–100.

have existed however the facts had been. If the facts had been different, it would have been because the objects had been configured differently, not because there had been different objects. Objects constitute the form of the world, the form of that to which our representations answer. Representations share this form. They are themselves facts. They are determined by configurations of simple signs, each of which stands for a simple object. When a representation is produced, the fact that those signs are configured in that way represents that the corresponding objects are configured in the same way. If they are, the representation is true. If they are not, it is false.[5]

So far there is nothing in this vision that is clearly idealistic. The form of that to which our representations answer is given by the form of our representations, but there is nothing that unequivocally suggests a dependence of the former on the latter, not even as one half of a symmetrical mutual dependence. However, even if there is nothing yet in the vision that is clearly idealistic, Wittgenstein brings it to completion, towards the end of the book, with a compressed combination of solipsism and mysticism in which the strain of Kantian idealism is unmistakable. (In fact the later idealism encourages a non-idealistic construal of much of the earlier material. We must remember that for Kant, transcendental idealism went hand in hand with empirical realism.)[6]

The idealism comes out as follows. Wittgenstein's vision has a very atomistic quality. Objects are independent of one another. States of affairs are independent of one another. But, as Wittgenstein himself observes, this independence, which is a matter of the possibilities that things enjoy, is itself a kind of dependence, a dependence on the world's logical form.[7] In a sense, his preoccupation is with the unity in which everything is held together, an abstract, logical unity which contributes nothing to what the world is like but constrains what it could be like. It is the unity that attends every possibility. It is also the unity of self-consciousness. I recognize it when I view the world self-consciously from my own particular point of view, and come to see everything as being how it is from that point of view. The world's unity *is* the possibility of

---

[5] Wittgenstein, *Tractatus, passim.*, esp. the 1s, the 2s, and the early 3s.

[6] "Empirical realism" is just the negation of empirical idealism.

[7] Wittgenstein, *Tractatus*, 2.0122.

its being represented from a single point of view. What cannot be represented from my point of view cannot be represented, and is not part of the world. So the world is *my world*. How things are is how they can be truly represented as being, and how they can be truly represented as being is how they can be truly represented as being *for me*. (Again there is a link with the Fundamental Principle. If a representation is true, then that is because of how things are for me. If another representation is true, then that too is because of how things are for me. So *for me* things are as both representations represent them as being.) What makes this a kind of idealism is, first, that the world's being my world is an aspect of its form, and, second, that it is determined by an aspect of representations, namely that any representation is a representation of how things are for me.[8]

But the idealism is manifestly transcendental rather than empirical. The world's being my world is not itself one of the facts that constitute the world. What would an immanent interpretation of the claim that the world is my world be? That I own everything? That I am God? At any rate the claim would be false.

Wittgenstein's idealism, and the remarks that support it, are not to be interpreted immanently, then. On the other hand, as he himself makes clear by the way in which he draws the limits of what can be represented, these claims do not admit of a transcendent interpretation either. What can be represented is only how the facts are that constitute the world. And that is why Wittgenstein admits, at the end of the book, that what he has written is nonsense: his reader must use what he has written as a ladder to climb up beyond it and must then, so to speak, throw away the ladder.[9]

Now the sheer fact that a book consists largely of nonsense is no ground for indictment. Books are written for all sorts of purposes. Some of these might well be served by nonsense. An obvious example is entertainment. Another is parody. Another is Wittgenstein's own purpose in writing the *Tractatus*. I have already said that his aim is to draw the limits of what can be represented, but I am talking now about his ulterior purpose, the point of drawing these limits. This relates back to our discussion of his later work. It marks a profound continuity between the *Tractatus* and that later work. In both, Wittgenstein sees philosophy as an activity whose task is to

---

[8] Principally ibid., the 5.6s.   [9] Ibid., 6.54.

stop us from being troubled by unanswerable pseudo-questions
that pose as deep problems, a task that is accomplished by our being
led to a clear understanding of what can and cannot be said.[10] His
purpose, in fact, is to *combat* nonsense of a certain kind. But it is not
a paradox to suppose that this purpose should be well served by
producing a lot of that kind of nonsense. One can easily imagine
how doing this would be one good way of getting others to see that
they had been doing likewise, though in their case with damaging
consequences. True, there are parts of the *Tractatus* that prevent
this from counting as a full vindication of it in its own terms, for
example the claim that "the [only] correct method in philosophy
would . . . be . . . to say nothing except what can be said",[11] and the
claim in the Preface that, if the book has any value, it consists, in
part, in the fact that he has produced true representations in it. (Or
are these claims themselves nonsense?) But still, we have here a
sense of how, even in its own terms, the *Tractatus* can count as a
successful tissue of gibberish.

In fact, however, this is too quick. The nonsense that we find in
the *Tractatus* cannot be regarded merely as a sequence of strategi-
cally chosen instances of the kind of thing that he is trying to put
us on our guard against. For one thing, some of it, at least, is supposed to subserve his aim of drawing the limits of what can be represented. (It is as though he has affected to draw these limits in the
very way in which, as he himself says several times in the *Tractatus*,
it cannot be done: by stepping beyond them.)[12] It is plain that
Wittgenstein has written this nonsense as a result of an impulse to
express what he takes to be genuine insights, insights, ironically,
that go with a clear understanding of what can and cannot be said.
It is plain also that we are supposed to attain that clear understanding by sharing the insights—by, as one would like to say, "understanding" the nonsense. What is going on here?

The fact is that Wittgenstein does believe in things that are
beyond representation. In his own terminology, there are things
that, though they cannot be said, *can* be *shown*.[13] The *Tractatus*, for
the most part, consists of doomed attempts to put just such things
into words.

This distinction between what can be said and what can be

[10] Ibid., 4.003 and 4.112–4.115.   [11] Ibid., 6.53.
[12] See e.g. ibid., the Preface, 2.173–2.174, 4.113–4.115, 4.12, and 5.61.
[13] See e.g. ibid., 4.022, 4.12 ff., 5.62, 6.12, and 6.522.

shown—the saying/showing distinction—is a linchpin of the whole book. Moreover, it is what can be shown that principally concerns Wittgenstein. It is this that he takes to be truly important. His interest in drawing the limits of what can be represented has more to do with what lies beyond them than with what lies within them. Whatever is of value, he believes, lies outside the world, and can only be shown. Value is a feature of the world as a whole, not of any fact within it. I engage with value when I am, in Wittgenstein's word, "happy", or, in another word that he also uses in this context, "good". I then view the world as a whole: I adopt a certain attitude towards it whereby its limits, so to speak, expand. Wittgenstein presents these ideas towards the very end of the book.[14] He is deliberately laconic about them. To gesture to them in the way he does is as much as he is prepared to allow himself in view of the inexpressibility. (But he famously wrote in a letter to Ficker, 'My work consists of two parts: the one presented here plus all that I have *not* written. And it is precisely this second part that is the important one.')[15]

The idealism can also be shown, but not said. Anything to do with the world's form can be shown, but not said. The world's form is a matter of how it must be, not of how it is, and what can be said is only how the world is, or in other words what the facts are that constitute the world. I am shown the idealism when I am shown that the world is my world and that I am not myself anything in the world but rather its transcendent limit, that which holds it together in unity. This is connected with the way in which, when I focus self-consciously and introspectively on myself, or on my point of view, I do not focus on one particular thing in the world that I come across or have access to. I focus on my way of coming across things, on the access itself.

There is an analogy in the *Tractatus* that helps to make this clearer.[16] (This analogy is one of the things that Wittgenstein derives from Schopenhauer.[17] In presenting it I shall go some way beyond what is in the *Tractatus* itself.) Consider my current visual field.

[14] Ibid., 6.4 ff. There are somewhat fuller remarks in his preparatory notebooks, *Notebooks*, pp. 72 ff. For further discussion of these and related ideas, see below, Chapter Eleven.

[15] Paul Engelmann, *Letters From Ludwig Wittgenstein*, pp. 143–4, Wittgenstein's emphasis.

[16] Wittgenstein, *Tractatus*, 5.633–5.6331.

[17] Arthur Schopenhauer, *The World as Will and Idea*, vol. iii, p. 285. See also Hacker, *Insight and Illusion*, pp. 88 ff.

Suppose I represent how it is from my current visual point of view
and without explicit reference to anything outside the field. Then
no matter how comprehensive my representations are, nothing in
them will give any explicit indication that I see what I am describing from a particular point at the edge of the field. For my point of
vision is not itself anything in the field. Yet this fact will be manifest
in the form that my representations take. I shall use terms like 'left'
and 'right'. And the fact will be manifest to *me* when I stop representing how things are *in* my visual field and focus on the structure
of the field as a whole.

This is only an analogy, however. Obviously I can say, with perfect propriety, that I see things from a particular point at the edge
of my visual field, and that what is on the left, or on the right, is on
the left or right of *me*. At most the analogy exhibits inexpressibility
relative to certain imposed restrictions. The saying/showing distinction relates to that which is *completely* inexpressible. It is as
though there were, as a kind of brute cosmic datum, an unrelativized division of things into the sinister and the righteous.

The question we must now address is whether Wittgenstein's
saying/showing distinction can help us in our own efforts to make
sense of the inexpressible, and whether it can give the transcendental idealist some refuge. Is it acceptable to say that the truth of
transcendental idealism, though it cannot be stated, *can* be shown?
Is it acceptable to say that, though we cannot deny that absolute
representations are possible, we are shown that they are not?

Prima facie no. Wittgenstein's distinction seems not to advance
the discussion at all. Why is 'It is shown that . . .' any kind of
improvement on 'It is inexpressibly true that . . .' or 'It is transcendently true that . . .'? Why is filling in the dots in 'It is shown
that . . .', or in any other way adverting to what is shown, not the
most blatant self-stultification? Admittedly, self-stultification is relative to an aim. I am assuming that the aim is that of saying something true, and hence meaningful. Using such locutions would not
be self-stultifying if the aim were one which would not be frustrat-
ed by uttering nonsense. Someone might say, 'The truth of transcendental idealism can be shown,' and then admit, with complete
nonchalance, that what he has said makes no more sense than an
affirmation of transcendental idealism would have done. The point,
however, is that he cannot then expect to communicate any insight,
or not in such a way that what he has said can be regarded as the

vehicle of communication. For something to be a vehicle of communication *is* for it to make sense. Or at least, that seems to be Wittgenstein's own view in the *Tractatus*. He is adamant that having sense, or being a representation, is nothing recondite. Representations just *are* the stuff of regular communication.[18]

For my own part I aspire, in making sense of the inexpressible, to say only what is meaningful and true. If Wittgenstein's saying/showing distinction is to be of any service here, there is still much work required to demonstrate how.

3

A basic problem with any attempt to exploit the saying/showing distinction concerns what is being distinguished. What is the genus of which saying and showing are species? What *sort* of things can be shown though they cannot be said? Not truths. I have already tried to discredit the idea that there can be unsayable truths, and in any case this idea is foreign to the *Tractatus*.[19] But if not truths, then what? On a trivial interpretation of the claim, all sorts of things can be shown though they cannot be said. For instance, I can show you a chair though I cannot say it. But this, obviously, has little or nothing to do with what Wittgenstein intends.

We should beware lest our characterization of this problem betrays a misunderstanding. The questions posed may be bad questions, on a par with: 'What is the genus of which form and content are species?' Certainly we are less inclined to pose these questions when we return to key parts of the text. For although Wittgenstein speaks of representations as both saying things and showing things, he also suggests that the real contrast is between what *we* say by means of representations and what shows *itself*, or makes itself manifest.[20] Still, to the extent that a division is being made, we are bound to want some sense of the territory which is being divided.

My fundamental proposal, which I am not proffering as exegesis—I want to make use of Wittgenstein's work but I do not now

[18] e.g. Wittgenstein, *Tractatus*, 3.328 and 5.5563.

[19] Cf. ibid., 4.063.

[20] Ibid., 4.121 and 6.124. Cf. Max Black, *A Companion to Wittgenstein's 'Tractatus'*, p. 190. (The idea that representations both say things and show things occurs at, e.g., *Tractatus*, 4.022.)

claim to be rehearsing it—is that we should see the distinction as being primarily a distinction between different kinds of *knowledge*. States of knowledge divide into those that are effable and those that are ineffable. The former have a content that can be captured in some representation; or equivalently, and more directly, the former are themselves representations. The latter are not.

This proposal, it seems to me, not only enables us to overcome the problem stated, it also enables us to overcome what is undoubtedly the most basic problem in any discussion of the ineffable, namely that posed by the threat of self-stultification. Provided we take due care, this threat is annulled. For there is nothing self-stultifying about describing someone as having ineffable knowledge, nor indeed about knowing and putting into words what is involved in her having it. What cannot be put into words is what she knows. Knowing and putting into words what is involved in someone's having ineffable knowledge is a little like defining indefinability, or explaining inexplicability, except that in those cases the threat of self-stultification is annulled by our having moved up a level whereas in this case it is annulled by our having moved, so to speak, sideways. What is known and put into words is not what it *is* for knowledge to be ineffable, but what is involved in *that* person's having *that* knowledge. Russell, with a characteristic combination of scepticism and irony, complained in his introduction to the *Tractatus* that "after all, Mr Wittgenstein manages to say a good deal about what cannot be said".[21] But in fact there is no absurdity in the idea of saying a good deal about what cannot be said. What is impossible is to say a good deal—anything—*that* cannot be said.

How then do we specify a state of ineffable knowledge? There are various ways, as I hope to make clear in due course. But one particularly important way is by actually attempting to put what is known into words. Or so I propose. This proposal is paradoxical, but the basic idea is simple. Consider the schema '*A* knows that *x*'. We use this schema to specify states of effable knowledge. When it comes to replacing '*x*' we put what is known into words: we verbally endorse the state in question. My proposal is that we use the schema '*A* is shown that *x*' in a similar way, to specify states of ineffable knowledge, only this time, when it comes to replacing '*x*', we *attempt* to put what is known into words. This is not a proposal to

---

[21] Wittgenstein, *Tractatus*, p. xxi.

compromise on any commitment to say only what is meaningful and true. The point is not to stand by our attempt, which we know must fail, but rather to *register its result*, much as if someone who knew that his arm had been paralysed attempted to raise it in an experiment to register the resultant activity in his brain. The schema '*A* is shown that *x*' is to be understood as equivalent to:

> *A* has ineffable knowledge, and when an attempt is made to put what *A* knows into words, the result is: *x*.

What we put in place of '*x*' may be nonsense. In fact, I shall argue later that what we put in place of '*x*' must be nonsense. No matter. What we say as a whole can still be true—just as it could be true to say:

> When asked to utter the first thing that came to mind he replied, 'Interstellar backlash carrot.'

or:

> The monkey sat at the keyboard and typed out, 'O! that this too too solid flesh would zgertzliyop.'[22]

In the next two chapters I shall try to provide clear, coherent support for this proposal. (And henceforth in this book I shall only ever use the word 'show' and its cognates in accord with it.) I shall also argue that the proposal can be used to cast light on the lingering appeal of transcendental idealism. In particular, I shall argue that

[22] *Note for Aficionados*: An extremely important feature of this proposal is that whatever wording we put in place of '*x*' we mention rather than use. That is, roughly, we make the wording itself the subject matter of our sentence. (There are all sorts of devices for mentioning expressions. The commonest is the use of inverted commas. Thus whereas cats have four legs, 'cats'—note the singular verb coming up—has four letters. In the case of '*A* is shown that *x*', rather as in the case of 'My name is *x*', it is the very meaning of the schema which determines that what is put in place of '*x*' is mentioned.) In this respect the underlying syntax of '*A* is shown that *x*' may be very different from that of '*A* knows that *x*'. It *may* be. There are some niceties here which I do not now want to get involved in. Perhaps in both cases the word 'that' functions as a demonstrative and the utterance that takes the place of '*x*', on any occasion of use, is its *demonstratum*. (This suggestion takes its cue from work by Donald Davidson: see 'Quotation' and 'On Saying That'.) At any rate, the schema '*A* is shown that *x*' expresses a relation in which people can stand to bits of language. (Later I will suggest that we stand in this relation to certain particularly long and complex bits of language. In those cases I *shall* use demonstratives—'this', 'the following', and the like—to indicate what we are shown.) Instances of the schema have no special logical connection with whatever replaces '*x*' in them, even when the latter can be used to say something true or false in its own right. In particular, there is nothing corresponding to the valid inference-schema '*A* knows that *x*; therefore, *x*'.

we are shown that reality is held together at our transcendent point of view, and that absolute representations are (therefore) imposs-ible. But I cannot overemphasize that this does *not* constitute any kind of defence of transcendental idealism and it does *not* involve my reneging on the Basic Argument. The claim is not that tran-scendental idealism, though true, cannot be stated. The claim is rather that transcendental idealism, though incoherent, is the result of an unsuccessful attempt to state what cannot be stated. Ultimately, the transcendental idealist has no refuge.

The division of labour between the next two chapters is as fol-lows. To claim that *A* is shown that *x*, for some given person *A* and some given verbiage *x*, is to make two subsidiary claims. It is to claim, first, that *A* is in a state of ineffable knowledge. And it is to claim, second, that *x* is the result of any attempt to put this know-ledge into words. I need to make sense of each of these subsidiary claims. In particular, I need to make sense of the idea that there is such a thing as ineffable knowledge, and I need to make sense of the idea that there is such a thing as the result of attempting to put it into words. The first of these tasks is that of Chapter Eight, the second that of Chapter Nine.

4

To conclude this chapter I shall present something midway between an overview of what is to come and a prelude to it. My basic premiss is that we are finite. This raises anew the question of who "we" are. The rather nonchalant attitude that I took towards this question in Chapter Six, though perfectly justified in that con-text, where 'we' was being used in conjunction with 'can', will look increasingly inadequate as the discussion progresses. I shall return to this question in Chapter Nine. Meanwhile, whoever "we" are, the premiss that we are finite can be regarded as a kind of fixed point.

It is a rich, polymorphous premiss. It connects with the Basic Assumption that our representations are representations of what is there anyway. (I shall have more to say about this connection in Chapter Eleven.) The following are some of the many glosses on it. We are cast into a world that is not of our own making; we are only a part of this world; the form and general character of this world are independent of us; it is to this world that our representations answer; and, as a specific instance of the last of these, it is of this world that we have any representational knowledge that we have (where 'representational', remember, is equivalent to 'effable').

It follows from this premiss that we cannot know anything about the world unless we are *given* it in some way, or, less metaphorically, unless it affects us in some way. Hence, whenever we do know anything about the world, there are two facets to our knowledge. On the one hand there is that in our knowledge which is determined by what we are given. On the other hand there is that in our knowledge which is determined by our own receptive capacities, which enable us to receive what we are given. When we self-consciously reflect on our knowledge we can focus attention on these separately. Focusing attention on the former, we receive more of the same. We "see through" our knowledge to what we know, and are given again whatever we were given before. When we focus attention on the latter, however, we might not receive anything. We might simply become self-consciously receptive. So, for instance, if I self-consciously reflect on my knowledge that there are seven chairs in the next room, I can focus on what I receive. I can think about the fact that there are seven chairs in the next room. In doing this I re-activate my knowledge and produce, if only internally to myself, a true representation to the same effect. I endorse my original state of knowledge. But I can also focus on my receptive capacities. I can think about various relevant parts of my outlook: about my concept of a chair and about how I count, for example. In doing this I again re-activate knowledge, but knowledge of a different kind. Unlike my knowledge that there are seven chairs in the next room, this knowledge cannot be characterized as knowledge *that* anything. It is knowledge *how* to do various things. For instance it is knowledge how to apply the concept of a chair. This is not yet to say that it is ineffable. Even so, it *is* ineffable. Or at least, it has a component that is ineffable. This is because it has no *content*. There is nothing that it answers to.[23] By the same token there is no such thing as endorsing it. Someone else can share my knowledge, obviously. But what this means, very roughly, is that he or she is

---

[23] Cf. Wittgenstein's commitment in his later work to the "autonomy of grammar", e.g. in *Philosophical Grammar*, § 68. See Hacker, *Insight and Illusion*, ch. 7, § 2.

disposed to carry on in the same way as I am. Our states of knowledge are not representations. They are part of that which makes
our representations possible. They are ineffable. Moreover, when I
am indulging in this self-conscious reflection and re-activating the
knowledge, I am shown something. For there is a persistent temptation, activated by just such self-consciousness, to treat the knowledge as if it were effable, and succumbing to this temptation
involves attempting, in a distinctive way, to express the knowledge.
This is enough (I shall argue) for there to be such a thing as "the
result" of attempting to put what I know into words.

The premiss that we are finite is a very Kantian premiss. Kant
too inferred from this that we can only know anything about the
world because we have suitable receptive capacities, capacities
through which we impose a rigid structure on what we receive.[24]
The details of this, some of which I sketched in the last chapter, do
not matter for now. What matters is how far his work conformed
to the picture that I have just sketched. I think it conformed well.
Kant himself was involved in deep self-conscious reflection on our
knowledge of how to do various things. Centrally, this included our
knowledge of how to unite the diverse elements that we receive
when we engage with the world, so as to be able to produce representations about what the world is like. In re-activating this knowledge he achieved an inexpressible insight which he nevertheless
tried to express. This led him to treat conditions of our receiving
things as if they were things we receive, or, as I put it in the last
chapter, to treat our epistemic faculties as if they were spectacles
through which we view the world. True, this is something of a car-
icature. But it does, I think, indicate a real crux in his thinking. He
was led to acknowledge a deep contingency in the form of that to
which our representations answer; to regard some of what is a priori as synthetic; and eventually, having explained this in the only
way he could, to embrace transcendental idealism.

We find something similar in the later work of Wittgenstein, as
I tried to argue in the last chapter. The receptive capacities that
Wittgenstein investigated were those involved in our understanding
of our language. The concept of understanding, which is central to
this discussion, is a broad and versatile one. There are all sorts of

[24] See e.g. Kant, *Critique of Pure Reason*, B71–2. Cf. B33, and note the amendments to the
first edition version of this, A19.

things that can be objects of understanding: languages, in the various different senses of that term; specific linguistic items, such as words or sentences; theories; data; works of art; people. But wherever it occurs, and whatever its object, understanding helps us to organize what we receive into something coherent, manageable, and unified that merits the title of knowledge. Understanding is itself a kind of knowledge. It is knowledge of how to process knowledge. It is knowledge of how to pass from some states of knowledge to others. For instance, someone who understands how televisions work knows how to tell by inspection what is wrong with a broken set; someone who understands English knows how to tell, by listening, what a fellow English-speaker is saying; someone who understands her son knows how to tell by observation what he is thinking and feeling. In most cases understanding has an ineffable component. This is significant because it indicates that, however mysterious the idea of ineffable knowledge may initially have looked, many instances of it are mundane and familiar. They are also susceptible of mundane and familiar specifications. We do not have to use the schema 'A is shown that x'. We can say, for instance, that Elizabeth understands English, though we cannot put into words (the whole of) what she thereby knows. Now for Wittgenstein, in both his earlier and his later work, clarity of understanding was the main goal of philosophy. Clarity of understanding was to be sought in those cases where, for whatever reason, we misconstrue the logic of our own language and become bemused and confused by nonsense. To achieve such clarity of understanding we must focus self-consciously *on* our understanding, that is on our understanding of our language. We must self-consciously re-activate it. But then, for the reasons which I sketched above and which I shall try to substantiate in the next two chapters, we not only have ineffable knowledge, we are shown something. What we are shown depends on what we are led to when we try to put what we clearly understand into words. And that, here as in Kant, is transcendental idealism.

In the previous chapter I tried to say something about how this connection with transcendental idealism comes to be. I shall now rehearse some of that discussion, but in the light of what I have just been saying. Focusing self-consciously on our understanding, we recognize the deep contingencies that sustain it. These are especially clear when we are thinking about the contrast with misunderstanding. For consider: how do we identify misunderstanding? How, for example, do we identify misunderstanding in mathematics? We must first assimilate the language of mathematics. And to do that we must carefully attend to it. But what exactly are we to attend to? The language of mathematics is not something that can be straightforwardly read off from actual mathematical practice. This is because, for all we know, there is a kind of misunderstanding to which mathematicians themselves are prone and which they infiltrate into their own discipline. (This is not just a theoretical possibility. Some revisionists will cite use of classical logic as an example. Others will point to the development in the twentieth century of transfinite mathematics. Wittgenstein himself had reservations about both of these.)[25] There seems to be a circularity. Only with the benefit of clear understanding can we recognize that to which we must attend in order to achieve clear understanding. Or again: something counts as misunderstanding because we identify it as such when we have clear understanding, and we count as having clear understanding when, among other things, we correctly identify misunderstanding. I do not say that such circularity is vicious. But to acknowledge it is to be reminded very forcibly that there is nothing independent of our understanding that we can use to justify it. Ought we therefore to be racked with sceptical doubts about whether our understanding is right? Not at all. There is no question of right or wrong here. Our understanding has nothing to answer to. It is part of how we receive the world. The only question is whether we *have* such understanding, and whether we can get it into sharp enough focus to achieve the clarity that will enable us to identify various misunderstandings. If we do achieve such clarity, then what we actually get into focus is an arrangement of interlocking, mutually supporting practices that are grounded in one another's contingency, a complex knotted structure that might easily have been different.

But how different? And in what ways? In the last chapter I mentioned the possibility of people with a concept that applied in some circumstances to green things, and in other circumstances to blue things. We might have had a concept like that. But might we have had a concept like that which nevertheless played *the very same role*

[25] Wittgenstein, *Remarks on the Foundations of Mathematics*, *passim*, but esp. Pts. V and II respectively. Cf. *Philosophical Investigations*, § 254.

in our lives as is actually played by the concept *green*, say because the circumstances in which it applied to blue things were circumstances in which grass, Granny Smiths and all the rest were blue, or because they were circumstances that obtained millions of years after our demise, or because they were circumstances that, though possible, were never actual? This question raises issues of a different order. It is not just a question about how our language might have stood in relation to the world, in the sense of: how we might have carried on. It is a question about what it *is* for us to carry on in different ways, about what it *is* for things to be as we represent them as being, about what "our language" and "the world" really are. In asking a question of this kind we are no longer simply exercising our understanding as part of receiving the world, we are regarding the understanding itself as something open to the same kind of investigation and thus as part of what we receive.

Assimilation of Wittgenstein's work tempts us to answer the question negatively. More fully, it tempts us to argue as follows. For a concept to play the very same role in our lives as is actually played by the concept *green* just *is* for it to be the concept *green*—just *is* for it to apply to green things. To suppose otherwise is to suppose that our language engages with the world in a way that outstrips our practices, a throwback to the idea of a super-physical landscape. A corollary of this is that what it is for something to be green depends partly on our participation. It depends on how potential interactions with the thing, on our part, would be woven into the overall fabric of our lives.

Broaching a question of this kind in a Wittgensteinian frame of mind, then, we do not recognize our language and the world as set apart from each other and capable of independent variation. Rather our concepts seem to be at work in the situations we use them to describe. Having come to regard our language, or our understanding, as part of what we receive, we are tempted to say that, nevertheless, it is not a distinct, isolable part. In a kind of pluralization of the *Tractatus*'s solipsism, we are tempted to say that the world is *our world*, and that our representations are all from the point of view of our understanding.

The questions that lead to this temptation are bound to arise when we focus self-consciously on the contingencies of our own understanding. Even so, they are spurious questions and the temptation must be resisted. If we succumb to it, then, in my view, we are trying to give voice to an inexpressible insight which we have achieved in the course of our reflection, an insight which is fundamentally an insight into how to carry on. Our knowing how to carry on is one of the conditions of the possibility of our representing anything at all. But we must accept it for that, neither more nor less. And as soon as we are inclined to raise metaphysical questions about what it is for us to carry on as we do, or about what it is for things to be as we represent them as being, we must accept that we can do no more than, precisely, carry on as we do and represent things as so being. Here, in conclusion, is Wittgenstein:

Perhaps what is inexpressible (what I find mysterious and am not able to express) is the background against which whatever I could express has its meaning.

The limit of language is shown by its being impossible to describe the fact which corresponds to . . . a sentence, without simply repeating the sentence.—(This has to do with the Kantian solution of the problem of philosophy.)[26]

FURTHER READING

Much of this chapter is derived from my 'On Saying and Showing', and *The Infinite*, ch. 13. I should like to thank the editor and publisher of *Philosophy* for permission to re-use material from the article, and Routledge for permission to re-use material from the book.

Questions about brains in vats are raised by Hilary Putnam in *Reason, Truth and History* , ch. 1. They are further discussed by Anthony Brueckner in 'Brains in a Vat'; Graeme Forbes in 'Realism and Skepticism: Brains in a Vat Revisited'; me in 'Solipsism and Subjectivity'; Mark Sacks in *The World We Found*, ch. 3; and Crispin Wright in 'Putnam's Proof that We are not Brains in a Vat', to which Putnam replies in 'Comments and Replies'.

On Wittgenstein's early work, see: G. E. M. Anscombe, *An Introduction to Wittgenstein's Tractatus*; Peter Carruthers, *The Metaphysics of the Tractatus*, especially ch. 8; Allan Janik and Stephen Toulmin, *Wittgenstein's Vienna*; David Pears, *The False Prison*, vol. i; and Erik Stenius, *Wittgenstein's 'Tractatus'*.

Specifically on the mysticism in the *Tractatus*, see Brian McGuiness, 'The Mysticism in the *Tractatus*'.

---

[26] Respectively: Wittgenstein, *Culture and Value*, p. 16; and ibid., p. 10.

The connections between Wittgenstein's early work and the work of Kant are explored by Peter M. Sullivan, 'The "Truth" in Solipsism and Wittgenstein's Rejection of the A Priori'; and by Julian Young, 'Wittgenstein, Kant, Schopenhauer, and Critical Philosophy'. (Schopenhauer, as I said in the main text, was an important intermediary here: see *The World as Will and Idea*.)

Connections between Wittgenstein's early work and the work of Heidegger are explored by Ingvar Horgby in 'The Double Awareness in Heidegger and Wittgenstein'.

On the limits of language, see Graham Priest, *Beyond the Limits of Thought*; and Paul Standish, *Beyond the Self*—both of which are relevant not only to this chapter, but also to the next two.

For a different approach to the threat of self-stultification that afflicts any discussion of the ineffable, see William P. Alston, 'Ineffability'.

For further discussion of the issues raised in n. 22, see John McDowell, 'Quotation and Saying That'; and my 'How Significant is the Use/ Mention Distinction?'.

CHAPTER EIGHT

I certainly have composed no work in regard to [this subject], nor
shall I ever do so in the future, for there is no way of putting it in
words like other studies. Acquaintance with it must come rather
after a long period of attendance on instruction in the subject itself
and of close companionship, when, suddenly, like a blaze kindled by
a leaping spark, it is generated in the soul and at once becomes self-
sustaining.

(Plato)

§ 1: *The suggestion that simple reflection on the semantics of the idiom 'knows
how to' is enough to establish the existence of ineffable knowledge is rejected.*

§ 2: *Some general comments are made about the nature of knowledge. States of
knowledge are distinguished from physical capacities, and three marks of knowledge are identified.*

§ 3: *An argument for the effability of all knowledge, using these three marks, is
sketched. This argument rests on a premiss, the Independence Claim, which is
then scrutinized. Certain states of understanding are presented as falsifying the
Independence Claim, and indeed as being examples of ineffable knowledge.*

§ 4: *These and other ideas are tied together in some final comments on the relation
between knowledge and reflection.*

*Appendix: A rough chart of the concept of knowledge is drawn, in partial sum-
mary of the chapter. Two questions are raised but not addressed.*

1

MY AIM in this chapter is to clarify and defend the idea that there
is ineffable knowledge, or in other words knowledge which is non-

representational. I shall proceed by surveying the concept of knowledge as a whole. By the end of the chapter I hope to have provided a rough chart of the concept, and to have located ineffable knowledge on that chart.

—*"But why is there even an issue here? Your claim in the last chapter that there is ineffable knowledge initially sounded bold. But when you subsequently made clear that, by 'knowledge', you meant "knowledge how" as well as "knowledge that", surely your claim assumed the status of a well established philosophical commonplace. We long ago learned to accept that "knowledge how" and "knowledge that" are entirely disparate kinds of knowledge. To know that something is the case is to be apprised of some truth. To know how to do something, by contrast, is to have a capacity. This is related to the fact that states of "knowledge how", unlike states of "knowledge that", are not states of belief, a fact which is evidenced in our language. I can say that Mary knows how to throw a boomerang. But it makes no sense to say that she "believes" how to do this. To claim that states of "knowledge how" are non-representational is just another way of making these points. It is hardly, or hardly any longer, controversial."*—

This seems to me to be nearly all wrong. There are not two disparate kinds of knowledge here. There are two disparate ways of characterizing knowledge. And nothing in the semantics of the expression 'knows how' suggests that states of "knowledge how" cannot also be states of belief, nor that they cannot be representational.

To deal first with your linguistic point: note that 'believes' *never* combines with an interrogative. For instance it makes just as little sense to say that Jim "believes" where the post office is. Yet that in itself provides no reason to doubt that Jim's knowing where the post office is is his having a belief. I think this fact about 'believes' is a matter of the most superficial grammar. Jim can *have an idea* where the post office is. Likewise Mary can *have an idea* how to throw a boomerang.

The familiar use of 'knows' alongside an interrogative arises because states of knowledge, by their very nature, can be pressed into service in addressing questions, whether formulated or unformulated, whether theoretical or practical. Hence 'knows when', 'knows where', 'knows whether', 'knows why'. 'Knows how' is just another member of this list.

—*"But it is not just another member of this list, or at least, not on the interpretation that is of concern to us. There is an interpretation of 'knows how' for which what you say is correct, namely that which applies when it occurs in a context such as 'knows how the getaway was made'. 'How', in that case, does function as an interrogative, and 'knows how', like the other phrases on the list, is an indefinite variation on 'knows that'. Thus the janitor knows how the getaway was made because he knows that it was made in a stolen lorry, say. But when 'knows how' occurs in a context such as 'knows how to install a washing machine', or 'knows how to charm people', it signals something of an altogether different kind. It then marks a contrast with 'knows that'."—*

I disagree. I see no reason to suppose that 'knows how' is ambiguous in this way. The important difference between its use in 'knows how the getaway was made' and its use in 'knows how to charm people' is not the difference between two senses of the phrase, as it were a "propositional" sense and a "practical" sense. It is rather the ensuing difference between the finite verb and the infinitive. We find the same thing with other interrogatives. There is 'knows when the meeting starts'. And there is 'knows when to stir in the cream'. (I admit that 'knows why' may not fit this pattern. In so far as it does not, then I suspect that there is an interesting explanation for why it does not. But nothing I have said, or will say, would be affected if there were no explanation.)

—*"Very well, what significance attaches to whether the verb is finite or an infinitive?"*—

A finite verb is used to characterize a state of knowledge in terms of some question that the knowledge can be called upon to address *about how things are*. (This question can be more or less general: 'He knows where she does her weekly shopping,' 'He knows where she shopped yesterday.') An infinitive is used to characterize a state of knowledge in terms of some question that the knowledge can be called upon to address *about what to do*. (Again, this question can be more or less general: 'He knows where to put the apostrophe in possessives,' 'He knows where to put the apostrophe in this shop sign.') In the latter case certain goods are presupposed in a way that the context usually makes clear. These may be the knower's, or they may be shared by the speaker and the audience, or the context may indicate some third possibility. In ascribing the state, the speaker alludes to some respect in which the knowledge, by leading the knower to act in a certain way, can help him or her to deliver these goods. The same effect can often be achieved by using the auxiliary 'ought' within the scope of the interrogative, as in 'He

knows when he ought to stir in the cream.' Whether the verb is
finite or an infinitive is a matter of how the knowledge is ascribed.
There is nothing here to indicate distinct kinds of knowledge.

—*"This account may work for 'knows when'. To say that someone*
knows when to stir in the cream is to indicate a specific respect in which
that person can be relied upon, at least as far as his knowledge goes, to
deliver some presupposed good, a proper consistency in the sauce let us say.
Similarly for 'knows where' and the rest. But surely 'knows how' is differ-
ent. I agree that there are some uses of 'knows how', together with an
infinitive, which do fit the account, for example when I say, 'She knows
how to reply to this invitation,' presupposing, as the good, someone's com-
pliance with certain rules of etiquette. But other uses of 'knows how to'
are different. They pick out, as I said before, capacities, or dispositions that
people have to succeed in doing certain things if they try. When 'knows
how to' is used in this way, it is equivalent to 'can'. And the knowledge in
question is different in kind from the knowledge picked out by standard
uses of 'knows that'."—

There is simply not enough here to demonstrate that some uses
of 'knows how to' need a separate account, nor (therefore) to indicate a separate kind of knowledge. It is true that 'knows how to' is
often used to pick out a disposition of the sort you described, in
such a way that 'can' could have been used just as well, but only for
reasons which, given the nature of the activity and given the context, my account is able to supply. The fact that the knowledge in
question is a disposition to succeed in doing something if one tries
is already enough to ensure that, when the presupposed goods
amount to nothing more than that success, 'knows how', together
with the relevant infinitive, can be used to pick out the knowledge.
But if the presupposed goods amount to more than that—if there
are ways of doing the thing that would violate those goods—then
a gap opens up. Thus I may be able to break bad news to somebody
but not know how to. (I am not squeamish about it. I could do it if
I tried. But I do not know how to do it "for the best", as we naturally say.) And notice that the possibility of further presupposed
goods can never be ruled out. Someone writing a logic textbook
may still be undecided, on pedagogic grounds, how to prove the
completeness of the predicate calculus. 'I still do not know how to
prove this result,' he may say. But of course, he *can* prove it.

There are other cases in which knowledge how to do something,
even though it is a disposition to do the thing if one tries, is

naturally distinguished from the capacity to do it. This has to do with a range of tacit conventions governing the use of the word 'can' which I do not propose to go into. What I have in mind are cases in which the disposition depends on the satisfaction of certain physical conditions, and in which the claim that the person "can" do the thing in question is naturally understood as meaning simply that these conditions are satisfied. Thus consider somebody who mistakenly thinks he is locked in a building because he is unaware of a particular exit. He *can* get out. But he does not know how to. It is also instructive to consider the same person when he has later found out about the exit but has lost the capacity to get out as a result of some other misfortune, say by being tied up. He now knows how to get out but no longer can. His knowing how to get out was originally, and briefly, a disposition to get out if he tried, but this was thanks to the presence of a physical capacity, loss of which the knowledge has survived. There are many examples of this sort of thing. Consider an ex-swimmer, now confined to a wheelchair, who is still a fine instructor. She knows how to swim. But she is no longer able to. All of this casts doubt on your claim that there is a special use of 'knows how to' which picks out dispositions of this kind.—*"What if I say that the disposition in such cases survives the loss of the physical capacity? The ex-swimmer is disposed to succeed in swimming if she tries. It is just that her disability means she cannot even try."*—Then you must relinquish your claim that, when 'knows how to' is used to pick out such a disposition, it is equivalent to 'can'. And more importantly, there is still nothing to indicate a special use of 'knows how to'.

For my own part I see no simple relation between uses of 'knows how to' and uses of 'can'. And a lot of what is traditionally said in favour of the orthodoxy that "knowledge how" and "knowledge that" are disparate kinds of knowledge demonstrates rather, it seems to me, that certain capacities and states of "knowledge that" are disparate kinds of state.[1] Moreover, even where circumstances conspire to ensure that there is no difference between being able to do something and knowing how to, I see no reason to attribute this to a peculiarity of 'how'. Context could equally ensure that there was no difference between being able to place a jigsaw piece and

---

[1] I include the *locus classicus*, Gilbert Ryle, *The Concept of Mind*, ch. 2, esp. § 3.

knowing *where* to, or between being able to identify the changes of key in a piece of music and knowing *when* to.

It is not that I want to deny that there are distinct kinds of knowledge. Far from it. Nor do I want to deny that there is a distinction to be drawn between "propositional" and "practical" knowledge. Propositional knowledge can usefully be defined as knowledge that something is the case, where the canonical evidence for someone's having it includes the person's asserting that this thing is the case. Practical knowledge can then just be defined as its complement. (I do not claim that this distinction is sharp. But clear examples of the former are knowledge that Mercury is the closest planet to the sun and knowledge of what the date is, while clear examples of the latter are knowledge of how to make an omelette and knowledge of what coffee smells like.) What I do want to deny is that there is any interesting distinction to be read off from the two familiar ways of ascribing knowledge; and more pertinently, that a given state of "knowledge how" need *eo ipso* be different in kind from a given state of "knowledge that"; and more pertinently still, that there is any reason why the former, as far as its being a state of "knowledge how" is concerned, should not be representational. The thesis that some knowledge is non-representational cannot be proved just by appeal to the fact that people know how to do things. It is absurd to suppose that knowledge how to spell 'comma', for instance, is non-representational, or indeed anything other than knowledge that it is spelt 'c', 'o', double 'm', 'a'. Come to that, a state of "knowledge that" can always, with a modicum of artificiality, be specified as knowledge how to answer a certain question.

A brief digression. It is very natural, at this stage—assuming that what I have been arguing is correct—to wonder whether there is any *one* way of specifying all states of knowledge. The ways we have are myriad. We talk not only of knowing that something is the case and of knowing how to do something, but of knowing a person, knowing one's way around a place, knowing the ins and outs of a certain matter, and many more. Does any of these serve for every case?

Not the first. There are various kinds of knowledge which cannot be characterized as knowledge that anything is the case. Examples include most non-human animal knowledge, and indeed much of the knowledge for which my interlocutor said the special use of 'knows how' was reserved, namely that which is a disposition to succeed in doing something if one tries. (I shall not now try to argue for these claims. I think they would be generally accepted.)[2] What about the second way of specifying states of knowledge, namely as knowledge of how to do something? Prima facie this is more promising. But can it be used to specify my knowledge of Smith, say? Hardly. It is true that my knowledge of Smith involves knowledge of how to placate him when he is incensed. But there is no one thing, however complex, such that my knowledge of Smith is knowledge of how to do that thing. Here indeed is another reason why the first way of specifying states of knowledge will not always serve. There is likewise no one thing such that my knowledge of Smith is knowledge that that thing is the case. The other ways listed are manifest non-starters. My own view, which I shall not now try to defend, but for which I take these considerations to constitute evidence, is that there is no single way of specifying all states of knowledge.

A second brief digression. All propositional knowledge, clearly, is representational (which is another way of saying that all ineffable knowledge, if such there be, is practical). So propositional knowledge can be divided into that which is absolute and that which is perspectival. The first of these, absolute propositional knowledge, is the *only* kind of knowledge which an omniscient being must not lack. (By an omniscient being, I mean a being that knows all the facts.) For reasons considered in Chapter Three, there is nothing incoherent in the idea of an omniscient being that lacks perspectival propositional knowledge (knowledge of what the date is, for instance); nor perspectival practical knowledge (knowledge of how to make an omelette, say, or knowledge of what coffee smells like— granted, as I shall later argue, that these are representational); nor, if there is such a thing, ineffable knowledge.[3] At least, there is nothing incoherent in the idea of an omniscient being that lacks these kinds of knowledge provided there is nothing incoherent in the idea of an omniscient being.

In the next section I shall make some general observations about knowledge as a prelude to defending the claim that there is ineffable knowledge. That claim, I have argued, cannot be defended just

---

[2] See e.g. Bernard Williams, 'Deciding to Believe', pp. 138–9; David Pears, *What is Knowledge?*, ch. 3; and A. J. Ayer, *The Problem of Knowledge*, pp. 12–14.

[3] What about absolute practical knowledge? This I take to be an empty category: see further the appendix to this chapter.

by appeal to the fact that people know how to do things. In fact, as I proceed, the claim will look less and less plausible. That suits me. By the time I get round to defending it, I want it to be clear that I am defending something that both needs and merits defence (provided, of course, it is true).

2

What is knowledge? This is obviously a huge question. I shall not attempt anything as ambitious as an analysis. But I shall try to specify some of the principal marks of knowledge, and to give its rough location in conceptual space.

I shall take for granted that states of knowledge are, among other things, dispositional states which can serve to explain purposive behaviour. This is not entirely uncontroversial. Sometimes very crude machines are said to know things. But if my assumption is wrong, let it stand as a way of circumscribing my subject matter.

A number of philosophers, notably Craig, have recently advocated a new approach to the discussion of knowledge. This approach has two main components. First, there is a strategic component concerning how the discussion should be guided. The idea is to rectify a mistake made in traditional discussions of knowledge, the mistake of paying insufficient attention to the question of what the concept of knowledge is *for*. Secondly, there is a specific conception of what the concept *is* for. First and foremost, these philosophers argue, it is used to indicate those who are reliable sources of information, or, more generally, those who are reliable sources of instruction. In Craig's words, "the concept of knowledge is used to flag approved informants".[4]

I applaud the first component but have reservations about the second. On this conception there is something basic about situations in which one wants to acquire some information, or a skill, and one is looking for reliable instruction. I wonder. Is there not something yet more basic about situations in which one is looking,

---

[4] Edward Craig, 'The Practical Explication of Knowledge', p. 215. Craig develops these ideas in much greater detail in *Knowledge and the State of Nature*, where on p. 8 he records the help of a hint given by Pears in *What is Knowledge?*, p. 30. Another exponent of the new approach is Christopher Hookway, in *Scepticism*, ch. 10.

not for someone who is a reliable instructor, but just for someone who is reliable? Suppose I need someone who knows how to fix the plumbing. I am probably not the least bit interested in acquiring the skill myself.

I shall not press this worry, however. To do so I would need to spend much longer than I want to examining just what kind of "basicness" is involved here. In any case I do not think it would make much difference if my worry were well-founded. This is for reasons that I hope will eventually be clear. One point worth noting straight away is that, even without the emphasis on learning, there may still be good reason to suppose that states of knowledge typically *can* be shared through some process of learning, simply because of the variety of ways in which we pick things up.

With or without that emphasis, the most important conclusion to be drawn from this strategy, I suggest, is that there is a connection between knowledge and reliability. The concept of knowledge is used to indicate those who, at least as far as their knowledge goes, can be relied on to deliver the goods.

'Deliver the goods': I have deliberately used the same schematic phrase as I used earlier. Then I was talking about how states of knowledge could be ascribed when specific goods were presupposed. But of course, in different contexts, for different people, with different aims and interests, all sorts of things can count as "the goods", and one of the characteristic features of our concept of knowledge, it seems to me, is precisely that it rides such variability. Someone who knows can to that extent be relied upon to deliver the goods *whatever they are*. Knowledge facilitates desire satisfaction. More precisely, a state of knowledge is a state that disposes one to act on desires that one has in ways which, but for the interference of other states that one is in, will lead to the satisfaction of those desires.[5]

Knowing when to stir in the cream, knowing how to tie one's shoe laces, knowing shorthand, even knowing Smith, are all states of this kind. But so are many states that are not states of knowledge, for instance states of accidentally true belief and physical capacities such as being strong enough to lift a heavy load. What sets states of knowledge apart from these? Those who accept

---

[5] I have been helped in this formulation by D. H. Mellor, 'I and Now', p. 23.

Craig's conception have a particular story to tell here. The story goes roughly as follows.

> *What Distinguishes States of Knowledge From Other Enabling States*: We all have an interest in getting into these reliable states ourselves. In some cases we can do so, by finding someone else who is in the state and gaining instruction from them, or more generally assimilating the state from them. This is where the concept of knowledge applies. But the concept is enriched by the fact that we have to be able to *recognize* when someone else is in the relevant state. Two features therefore come to distinguish states of knowledge from other similarly enabling states: shareability through some process of learning or assimilation; and a certain recognizability.

Reservations about the details of Craig's conception aside, I am sure that we have to tell *some* such story. And I am sure that the point about recognizability will survive into whatever story we tell. That helps to illustrate why, and how, the concept of merely true belief falls short of the concept of knowledge.[6] But what about being strong enough to lift a heavy load? The idea that knowledge must be shareable through some process of learning would presumably prevent *that* from counting as a state of knowledge. It is true that one might learn techniques of physical exercise which enabled one to achieve and maintain such strength. But what one would thereby have acquired, through learning, would be not strength to lift the heavy load, but knowledge of how to exercise in such a way as to be strong enough to lift it. However, unless Craig is right about the basicness of situations in which one wants to learn something, the shareability of knowledge through learning is not something we can yet take for granted. Is there anything else we can say about why a physical capacity such as being strong enough to lift a heavy load is not a state of knowledge?

I think there is. I have already touched on it. We have a special interest not just in those who can be relied on to deliver the goods, where this means *these particular goods*, but in those whose reliability is of a kind to deliver whatever the goods may be. In other words we have an interest in those who can adapt their activities to an

---

[6] For a similar route to the same insight see Bernard Williams, *Descartes*, pp. 37–40.

indefinite range of circumstances, projects, and contingencies. The concept of knowledge is used to draw attention to a distinctive reliability of this kind, and to specific respects, however trivial or minimal, in which states instantiate it. This is reflected in a range of interconnected differences between states of knowledge, on the one hand, and physical capacities, on the other. I shall present three such differences. These will at the same time serve as three marks of knowledge. (In other words they will indicate three necessary conditions of a state's being a state of knowledge. I make no claims about sufficiency.)

(i) *Versatility*: The potential usefulness of a state of knowledge is not annulled if, for any reason, certain possible courses of action are ruled out. This is not true of a physical capacity. Precisely what a physical capacity does is to ensure that certain courses of action are possible. Once *those* have been ruled out, the capacity is idle.

By way of illustration: suppose that I am indeed strong enough to lift a heavy load. There is no telling what unforeseen circumstances might call upon this capacity. Nevertheless, the capacity will be of no use to me if I resolve not to exert myself. On the other hand, no comparable resolution can block the potential usefulness of even the most trivial item of knowledge. True, if the item is *very* trivial, and if I resolve for some reason not to reveal that I have it, then examples of its use will have to be pretty far-fetched. But they can always be constructed. (The point is a conceptual one.) Thus suppose I know that there were 243 people in the lecture hall. And suppose I resolve not to reveal that I know this. (Perhaps I do not want the rest of you to think that my attention was wandering.) Still my knowledge can be of use to me. Someone else who was at the lecture may subsequently assure us of his reliability at gauging audience sizes and may say that there were some 500 people in the hall. I can now draw various conclusions about this person.

(ii) *Performance-Transcendence*: Whereas it is decisive evidence for one's having a physical capacity that one manages to bring certain things off—*ab esse ad posse*—this is never true of a state of knowledge.

Thus if I manage to jump over a gate, this is decisive evidence for my having the physical capacity to jump over it (albeit, perhaps, a physical capacity that can be realized only in exceptional circumstances, such as when I am being pursued by a pit bull terrier). But nothing I could bring off would be decisive evidence for my knowing that Schumann wrote four symphonies. My simply saying, 'Four,' when asked, 'How many symphonies did Schumann write?' would leave room for the suspicion that I was guessing, or being untruthful, or perhaps even parroting.

(iii) *Rationality*: Whatever one knows when one is in a state of knowledge can have a reason and can be a reason. To quote Sellars: "in characterizing . . . a state as that of *knowing* . . . we are placing it in the logical space of reasons."[7]

This is not to say that the logical space of reasons is made up entirely of states of knowledge. What one knows may have as a reason what one experiences. And it may be a reason for what one conjectures, or for choices one makes, or for actions one takes. Thus what I know when I know that it is too early for lunch may have as a reason what I see when I look at my watch, and it may be a reason for my remaining at my desk. (Here, as in other such cases, the capacity for what I know to be a reason depends on my conative states. I shall have more to say about this in Chapter Eleven.) The point is: if ever one is doing something under the control of knowledge, then, at least to that extent, a rational justification will be available for what one is doing, accessible from a position of critical self-conscious reflection.

—*"But surely there is knowledge which has none of these three marks. Consider knowledge of how to drive a car. First, this is of no use in someone who has resolved not to do so. Secondly, decisive evidence for someone's having such knowledge is that she actually performs in a certain way— that she "manages to bring certain things off". Suppose she drives perfectly safely for two hundred miles through hazardous conditions. Then there is no question but that she can drive. Thirdly, such knowledge neither has a reason nor can be a reason. It simply makes no sense to ask where a state of knowing how to drive should be placed in "the logical space of reasons"."*—

[7] Wilfrid Sellars, 'Empiricism and the Philosophy of Mind', p. 169. John McDowell has been keen to pick up on the idea of the logical space of reasons: see *Mind and World*, pp. 5–13, 70–86, and 180.

I think I can counter all three of these points. In reply to the first: it is not true that knowledge of how to drive a car can no longer be of use in someone who has resolved not to do so. For example, it may enable her to teach others to do so. Or it may enable her to handle some newly invented contraption whose operation requires precisely the same skills, or some of the same skills. There is no foreclosing, by any simple resolution, the possibilities that such knowledge affords.

In reply to the second point: it is important to be clear about what exactly is evidence for what. I shall deal first with the *arguendum*. It is certainly true that someone's managing to bring something off is always decisive evidence for her being able to do the thing. But there is an ambiguity here, as noted in the previous section. To say that she is able to do the thing may mean simply that certain physical conditions are satisfied, including, centrally, her having the physical capacity to do it. If there is an implication about what she knows, however, then it means that she has the sort of disposition that we considered earlier, a disposition to succeed in doing the thing if she tries. There is an old joke which brings out this ambiguity well. A patient, having just been told that he will recover from a serious injury to his arm, asks the doctor, 'Will I be able to play the violin?' The doctor assures him that he will. 'That's funny,' the patient replies, 'I couldn't before.' Now it is only in the first sense, the sense in which the relevant physical conditions are satisfied, that someone's managing to bring something off is decisive evidence for her being able to do the thing. Whether she has the relevant disposition or not depends on whether this was a fluke. That must be settled on independent grounds.—*"But surely it is a matter of canonical evidence, if not conceptually necessary, that some performances could not be flukes, for instance driving safely for two hundred miles through hazardous conditions, or playing the violin."*—No doubt. But this brings us to the *arguens*. I intend the construction 'bring *x* off' in a minimal sense. Its instances must not themselves entail anything, or represent canonical evidence for anything, about what the agent was trying to do, beyond what may be entailed by the very fact that the agent was performing an action. Driving like that, or playing the violin, are not things that in this sense anyone could manage to "bring off". (Nor, incidentally, is writing a definitive comprehensive study of the symphonies of Schumann—which blocks a natural objection to the Schumann example.)—*"What would be decisive evidence, in that case, for someone's having the physical capacity to play the violin?"*—His bringing certain things off: his holding his head at a certain angle, moving his arm in a certain way, and so forth. These are things that are necessary conditions of his playing the violin, or at least of his playing the violin in the usual way. But it is possible, and it would be perfectly compatible with everything I have said, that if the evidence is to preclude worries about co-ordination and suchlike, then he has no alternative but to play the violin.

Finally, in reply to your third point: remember that any state of knowledge can be pressed into service in addressing a question, whether formulated or unformulated, whether theoretical or practical. Whenever this happens, what one knows is playing its role as a reason. Thus this person's knowledge how to drive a car can be a reason for what she says and does when she teaches someone else to drive. Similarly with the swimming instructor's knowledge how to swim. And as the other person learns, there is a sense in which what he is being apprised of (certain basic causal relations between different parts of the car, say, or certain rough and ready principles of fluid dynamics in the case of the swimmer) are reasons, however ill-equipped he may be to articulate them and however badly placed he may be even to recognize them as such, for what he comes to know.

A picture emerges, then. We have an interest in enabling states. Enabling states, in the right circumstances, can be of clear importance to us. The fact that someone is strong enough to lift a particular heavy load may be important because it is important that the load should get lifted. Similarly, the fact that someone can drive you to the station may be important because it is important that you should get there quickly. However, because driving you to the station is not something that anyone could just bring off, this person must also be able to deliver an uncircumscribed range of other goods. It is in situations of this kind that our concept of knowledge has its roots. The knower is in a state whose structure engages with that of other similar states so as to allow, not just for the realization of specific possibilities, but for the negotiation of possibilities. In knowing, the knower can, to a greater or lesser degree and in a more or less specific respect, cope. This coping—the successful channelling of motivation to control action—can always be assessed from a position of critical self-conscious reflection. And any such assessment will always locate the knowledge in the logical space of reasons.

This picture does, I think, put pressure on the idea that there is ineffable knowledge. In the next section I shall amplify on this and then say how the pressure can be resisted.

3

Consider the following argument. (This is an argument for the effability of all knowledge. In other words it is an argument for the position I am ultimately attacking. I shall call it the Effability Argument.)

> *The Effability Argument*: A state of knowledge is a disposition on the part of the subject to act on his, her, or its desires in a certain way. As with any other disposition of this kind there are conditions in which, *ceteris paribus*, it would issue in acts that satisfied those desires, in other words conditions in which it would be what I have been calling an enabling state. Let us refer to these as its *success conditions*.[8] The success conditions of my knowledge that the rain has stopped, for example, are conditions in which the rain has stopped. My knowledge is a disposition to act in ways that would tend to satisfy my desires in just those conditions. If, say, I want to post a letter as soon as I can do so without getting wet, then I am disposed to venture out. Now part of what makes my disposition a state of knowledge is that the success conditions are satisfied. The rain has in fact stopped. Had I had exactly the same disposition though the rain had not stopped, then my disposition would have been a state of mistaken belief, not of knowledge. And I might then have got wet. Similarly in the case of my knowledge of how to ride a bike. Part of what makes this a state of knowledge is that various truths hold, concerning what I must do in different circumstances to maintain my balance, steer round corners, and the rest. Had I had exactly the same disposition though these truths had not held, then my disposition would have amounted to a mistaken idea of how to ride a bike, not knowledge of how to do so. And

---

[8] Cf. what Mellor calls utility conditions in 'I and Now', p. 23—though success conditions are less finely individuated.

I might then have fallen off my bike. But nothing about a state of knowledge itself ensures that its success conditions are satisfied. They are, to that extent, independent of it. Call this the Independence Claim. The Independence Claim is not true of physical capacities. Consider my strength. That is an enabling state which would have been an enabling state however things had otherwise been. True, the following is a possibility: that my strength is strength enough to lift the box in the corner, which it would not have been had the box not just been emptied. But this only means that, had certain conditions not been satisfied, my enabling state would not have fitted the same description. It would still have been an enabling state. My strength would not have been strength enough to lift the box in the corner, but it would have been a state that disposed me to act on my desires in ways which, *ceteris paribus*, led to the satisfaction of those desires. This is not to deny that physical capacities have success conditions. The point is, the success conditions of a physical capacity, unlike the success conditions of a state of knowledge, are simply the conditions in which the subject is in that state. They are not independent of the state. There is nothing to which the state is answerable. A state of knowledge, by contrast, is answerable to something. It is answerable to how things are. In other words it has content. In other words again, it is a representation.

Obviously I must resist the Effability Argument. In particular I must resist the Independence Claim. There are general reasons for worrying about the Independence Claim, having to do with whether it is ever possible to prise apart states of knowledge from whatever is involved in the satisfaction of their success conditions.[9] But suppose we are able to waive such worries by construing states of knowledge, or if necessary reconstruing them, as narrowly dispositional, so that, to put it crudely, states of knowledge do not intrinsically involve anything "beyond" their subjects. Still I need to resist the Independence Claim. I need to defend the idea that there are states of knowledge which are not answerable to anything, and whose success conditions are simply the conditions in which their subjects are in those states. The problem is that, at this stage, the

[9] See e.g. the essays in Philip Pettit and John McDowell (eds.), *Subject, Thought, and Context*.

Independence Claim appears to be the only explanation for the three marks of knowledge identified in the last section. It explains Versatility: if what makes a state of knowledge an enabling state is something independent of it, then the state's potential usefulness is not just a matter of what is involved in being in that state, which in turn means that there is no relevant foreclosing of the possibilities it affords. It explains Performance-Transcendence: evidence for someone's knowing something has to be, on this conception, evidence for her suitably engaging with what is independent of her, which can never be a matter of her simply bringing something off. And it explains Rationality: if a state of knowledge has content, then it stands in various logical relations to whatever else has content, and in various rational relations to whatever is in turn rationally related to what has content: it has a place in the logical space of reasons.

—"*But does the Independence Claim really tell against the existence of ineffable knowledge? On your conception it does. But surely there is now reason to suspect your conception. A state of knowledge would ordinarily be said to be effable, surely, when something counts as putting it into words, that is when it can be endorsed verbally. It follows that an effable state of knowledge has content. But it does not follow, what you have been taking for granted, that a state of knowledge with content (a state of knowledge which answers to how things are) is effable. Thus consider various states of practical knowledge, such as a dog's knowledge of where its bone is, or a comedian's knack for timing, or a composer's ability to convey pathos, or your own knowledge of what coffee smells like. Each of these answers to how things are. If certain conditions were not satisfied—if the bone were elsewhere, if people were generally slower at recognizing puns, if the sound of a violin had a different timbre and coffee a different smell— then these states would no longer dispose their subjects to achieve things they want to achieve. But none of them, surely, can be endorsed in words. And the existence of ineffable knowledge now seems, just as I said it was at the outset, a relatively uncontroversial matter.*"—

The sheer fact that these states are representations means that all of them can be at least indirectly endorsed in words. This was implicit in the Basic Argument. I am inclined to go further and say that they can all be *endorsed* in words.[10] For 'can' is to be interpret-

---

[10] See again Chapter One, §§ 3 and 4 for the definitions of endorsement and indirect endorsement. (These definitions are also in the glossary.)

ed in its customarily weak sense, allowing for any possible extension of our linguistic resources. However, if I am wrong about
that—if indirect endorsement is the most that we can achieve
here—and if it is agreed that the label 'effable' should be withheld
from what can only be indirectly endorsed in words, then I ought
certainly to reformulate some of my chief contentions. But I think
this is just a question of terminology. I shall stick with my usage
and apply 'effable' to any state of knowledge which is a representation. It remains the case, on that usage, that the existence of ineffable knowledge is ruled out by the Independence Claim, and also
that it is decidedly non-trivial.

A word, before I proceed, about the smell of coffee. On one
understanding of the phrase 'knows what coffee smells like'—not
the understanding I adopt—it applies to anyone who is acquainted
with the smell of coffee and who is thereby able to grasp a concept
that picks out that smell. On that understanding, I would say that
knowledge of what coffee smells like is ineffable. This is for reasons
that I hope will soon be clear. On the understanding which I adopt,
'knows what coffee smells like' applies only to those who know that
coffee smells like that. (Similarly in the case of other such phrases.)
This is different, because someone might be acquainted with the
smell of coffee by having smelt, not coffee, but something that
smells like coffee, having no idea that coffee smells that way. On this
understanding, knowledge of what coffee smells like is certainly
effable. In fact my state of knowing what coffee smells like can not
only be indirectly endorsed in words, it can be *endorsed* in words.
This is because we can coin an adverb, 'coffily' say, to pick out the
way coffee smells, and then endorse my state simply by asserting,
'Coffee smells coffily.'[11]

To return to the main issue: how am I to resist the Independence
Claim?

By appeal to understanding. It seems to me that there are many
states of understanding which, though they satisfy the three marks
of knowledge, falsify the Independence Claim and are ineffable. But
I should enter a caveat before I go any further. In calling these or
any other states ineffable I do not mean to deny that they have significant effable components. (Many of the states of knowledge that

[11] For points of agreement and disagreement with what I say in this paragraph (the
former, I suspect, outweighing the latter), cf. D. H. Mellor, 'Nothing Like Experience'.

ordinarily concern us, if not most, are a complex tangle of the effable and the ineffable.) My understanding of English is a prime example. I would certainly count that as ineffable, even though it includes large tracts of effable knowledge such as my knowledge that the past tense of a regular English verb is formed by adding 'ed'—or, for that matter, my knowledge that the word 'rabbit' denotes rabbits, and my knowledge that the word 'green' denotes green things.

Understanding, of the sort that I have in mind, has nothing to answer to. Of course, I may think that I know what a particular word in English means and be wrong: I may think that the word 'rabbit' denotes hares as well as rabbits. If that is the case, then what I understand is strictly speaking an idiolect distinct from English. But I do still *have* my understanding. (This does not violate anything in Wittgenstein's so-called "private language argument".[12] My understanding is one that others can share, and, if they do, we are able to communicate with one another.) The point is this. My understanding, part of which is grasp of a "language" in the Chapter Six sense of a range of conceptual resources, is a mode of reception. It is not itself a reception. It includes my knowing how to exercise the concept *green*, for instance, which in turn includes my knowing what it is for something to be green. But this is not the same as my having an answer to any question. (Still less is it the same as my having an answer to the pseudo-question, 'What is it for something to be green?') Likewise with other knowledge that grounds my state of understanding. And if the world were different in various ways but I were still in this state, then I would still have my understanding—though it might well be of considerably less use to me. (Compare: if I were transported to a planet whose surface gravity was five times that of the earth, I would still have my strength but it would be of considerably less use to me.)

What my understanding enables me to do is what any state of understanding enables its subject to do, namely process knowledge. I can use my understanding to advance from some states of knowledge to others. If someone tells me where the post office is, for instance, and I know various things about his reliability, trustworthiness, and so forth, then I can use my understanding to arrive at

<hr />

[12] See Ludwig Wittgenstein, *Philosophical Investigations*, §§ 243–315. It is instructive here to look at one of the very few sections in which Wittgenstein actually uses the phrase 'private language': § 269.

knowledge of where the post office is. My understanding enables me to make sense of what I glean in my transactions with the world and with other people. It enables me to locate what I glean in a fuller and more coherent conception that includes what I have not yet gleaned (as it may be, the whereabouts of the post office). And this in turn enables me to draw conclusions about the latter. My understanding is knowledge of how to acquire knowledge, then. But it is not itself a true representation of how things are. It is not a representation at all. In this respect it differs from (say) someone's understanding of how televisions work. To say that my understanding is not a representation is not to deny that what it delivers is genuine representational knowledge; nor that it could combine with mistaken beliefs, for instance about how other people use words, to lead me astray; nor even that my making sense of what I glean is as much a matter of my finding sense as imposing it. (On this last issue it is silent.) The point is rather that what qualifies my understanding as an enabling state is the fact that it enables me to make sense, not the fact that it enables me to make the "right" sense. There is no question of right or wrong here, only of what is more or less useful.

But the primary use of my understanding is a cognitive one. And *this* is why, despite the fact that its success conditions are nothing independent of it, it satisfies the three marks of knowledge. It satisfies Versatility because, although its own success conditions are nothing independent of it, its potential usefulness is a matter of how it processes states whose success conditions *are* independent of them; so its potential usefulness is not just a matter of my being in that state. It satisfies Performance-Transcendence because decisive evidence for my being in it must be evidence for my properly processing other states that I am in, states that I cannot be in unless I suitably engage with what is independent of me; so such evidence cannot just consist of my bringing something off. And it satisfies Rationality because what I know as a result of my understanding is a reason and has a reason: it is a reason for how I communicate with other people, and it has as a reason how other people communicate with me. This is not to say that anything *justifies* my understanding. My understanding is not *true*, nor true of anything, nor yet true *to* anything. But the fact that other people communicate with me as they do is a reason for my having an understanding that will enable me to make good sense of them (as mine does). More generally, the fact that the world is the way it is is a reason for my having an understanding that will enable me to make good sense of *it*. And as for what 'good' means here: it means, not 'right', but, as I intimated above, something more like 'useful'. This is not to say that, granted the concepts I have, there is no right or wrong in how I use them to arrive at my interpretations. The point is rather that there is no right or wrong in the concepts I have.

Towards the end of the last chapter I said that effable knowledge had a kind of "transparency" that ineffable knowledge lacks. This idea can now be reinforced in a way that casts further light on why my understanding is ineffable. Suppose I focus self-consciously on one of my effable states of knowledge and see it *as* a state of knowledge—a crucial preliminary to locating it in the logical space of reasons. Then I cannot help focusing on whatever ensures the satisfaction of its success conditions. In other words I cannot help focusing on *what I know*, the process I described in the last chapter as "seeing through" the state. If I focus self-consciously on my understanding, however, and see *that* as a state of knowledge, nothing analogous happens. This is more like focusing self-consciously on my strength. The state itself comes opaquely into focus. True, I can exercise the state to derive further effable knowledge. For instance, I can exercise it to derive knowledge of each of the following: that if I act in accord with my understanding, then I shall call grass green; and, correlatively, but more directly, that grass is green. But these are not part of what I know just in having my understanding. Rather my understanding makes it possible for me to know these things. The understanding itself is ineffable.[13]

4

In order to get another important angle on ineffability, I want to turn in this final section to the relation between knowledge and reflection.

[13] For various echoes of this idea of understanding as ineffable knowledge, in Kant and Wittgenstein, see Immanuel Kant, *Critique of Pure Reason*, B157–9 and A132–6/B171–5; and Wittgenstein, *Philosophical Investigations*, §§ 78, 150, 199, and 241. Kant, in the second of these passages, is talking about something that cannot be taught: in this respect I prefer the emphasis in Wittgenstein, *Philosophical Investigations*, pp. 227 ff., which compares with the quotation from Plato at the head of this chapter (*Letters* 7, 341c–d). Note: there are many passages in

How does reflection affect knowledge? One thing it can do is to destroy it. In due course I shall be more concerned with the *constructive* effect that reflection can have on knowledge, which is of greater direct relevance to the current discussion. First, however, I think it is worth commenting briefly on this potential for destruction.

The claim that reflection can destroy knowledge sounds bold. But it can be understood in a very unexciting way. The juggler, reflecting on what he is doing and on how he is doing it, may no longer know how to proceed. The flustered examinee, reflecting on why he is about to write down 'πr^2', may no longer know that that is the correct answer. (A similar but philosophically more interesting example will crop up in Chapter Ten.) Here the destructive power of the reflection is highly contingent. Other cases are more serious. They involve knowledge which is constitutionally at the mercy of reflection, because exercising the knowledge in certain characteristic ways is incompatible with reflecting on it. An example would be knowledge of how to maintain some self-deception.

Knowledge of how to maintain a self-deception is practical knowledge. Are there also examples that are propositional? And is there any knowledge such that even having it is incompatible with reflecting on it? And is Williams right when he says that sometimes, in the case of propositional knowledge, what reflection does is to undermine the conceptual apparatus required even to think in those terms, with the result that the knowledge, once lost, can never, in the full light of reflection, be recovered?[14] I am inclined to answer all three of these questions negatively. This relates back to the Basic Argument. According to the Basic Argument any true representation must be capable of being assessed from a position of critical reflection in such a way that it can be seen *as* a true representation, alongside any other true representation. In particular this is true of any effable state of knowledge. But when the assessor is also the knower, assessing it in this way means reflecting self-consciously on it and seeing it as a state of knowledge. And this in turn, given the "transparency" of effable knowledge, means focusing on

Wittgenstein that seem to tell against my claim that understanding satisfies Rationality, e.g. *Philosophical Investigations*, §§ 217 and 219, and *Zettel*, § 301. The tension seems less, however, when we reflect that reasons for what I know when I have my understanding are justifications for my *having* it, not justifications for the understanding itself.

[14] Bernard Williams, *Ethics and the Limits of Philosophy*, pp. 148 and 167–9.

what is known. However, although these considerations support a
negative answer to all three questions, their support contains significant lacunae. In the first place they apply only to effable knowledge. They do not rule out the possibility of ineffable knowledge
whose possession is incompatible with reflection on it. Secondly,
they apply only when the assessor is also the knower. But precisely
what is at issue, it might be said, is whether this is always possible.
Thirdly, they apply only when the assessment is contemporaneous
with the knowledge. But if Williams is right, there are cases in
which, as a result of reflection, the assessor is constrained to look
back on the knowledge as erstwhile knowledge, seeing it as knowledge from a point of view which she can no longer occupy. It
would be too great a digression to attempt to fill any of these lacunae here.

Of greater current concern, as I have said, is the constructive
effect that reflection can have on knowledge. Whatever its destructive powers, reflection certainly enables us indirectly to integrate
different states of knowledge, and thereby to see them *as* states of
knowledge. It is through reflection that we are able to take steps
along the way to an ideal of not only knowing but knowing that we
know, an ideal in which self-consciousness and knowledge are
brought together. Steps along that way are also steps along the way
to absoluteness, the stuff of omniscience. But reflection not only
enables us indirectly to integrate different states of knowledge. It
also leads us to recognize that such indirect integration is possible
at all. It is through reflection that we come to see that different effable states of knowledge must cohere, and that there must be a way
of seeing how they cohere. It is through reflection that we come to
see that there is such a thing as "the" logical space of reasons in
which all these states of knowledge are located. It is through reflection that we come to see that all these states of knowledge, indeed
all representations, *are representations of what is there anyway.*

This is the Basic Assumption, the assumption on which the Basic
Argument rests. I have repeatedly said that I have no defence of the
Basic Assumption. I do not think that it can be justified. But this is
not to say that it cannot be known. It is a complex assumption that
many people have taken it upon themselves to challenge, in many
different ways, as we have seen. Even so, I think it *can* be known;
and I think that part of what prevents it from being justified is that
knowledge of it is acquired through due exercise, and only through

due exercise, of a fundamental kind of ineffable knowledge, which exercise is itself a sort of reflection.

Through such reflection one achieves an inexpressible insight into how one implements, combines, and exploits whatever one knows, an insight into how one works with, and reasons with, whatever one receives. The knowledge one thereby exercises is a kind of understanding. It is knowledge of how to process knowledge. It is constituted by various receptive capacities, in particular conceptual capacities. Again, these have nothing to answer to. What matters is what can be done with them. One's insight does not therefore consist of receiving anything. It derives from a certain *mode* of reception, a mode of making sense. That mode involves seeing some things as relevant to others, making connections, recognizing similarities—having what I called in Chapter Five an outlook. This in turn involves bringing what one receives under the unity of concepts, making possible an awareness of it as that to which one's representations answer. As a result the insight has two complementary aspects. On the one hand it is an insight into the unity of the manifold of what one knows. It enables one to see that one's knowledge, where effable, is knowledge of what is there anyway. On the other hand it is an insight into the unity of the manifold of one's states of knowledge. It enables one to see oneself as the knower, representing the world from various points of view. These come together as follows: it is an insight into the unity of the manifold of *one's knowing what one knows*. One comes to regard the unity of the world and one's own unity as set over against and implicating each other.[15] And in the course of this one achieves a degree of rational reflective self-consciousness. Not only does one receive, one sees what one receives *as* what one receives. One sees one's epistemic resources and other receptive capacities *as* one's epistemic resources and other receptive capacities, one's reasons for acting *as* one's reasons for acting. To put the point in a Kantian way: one comes to act not just in accordance with rules but in accordance with the idea of a rule.[16] One comes to acknowledge the logical space of reasons.

[15] Cf. Kant, *Critique of Pure Reason*, 'The Deduction of the Pure Concepts of Understanding'.

[16] See e.g. Immanuel Kant, *Groundwork of the Metaphysic of Morals*, p. 36 in the pagination of the original 2nd edition.

It barely needs saying that I am still talking about an ideal, or at least about something which admits of degrees and which, in its most extreme form, is an ideal. This is related to a claim I made back in Chapter One, namely that a perspectival representation, unlike an absolute representation, can never be fully self-consciously endorsed by simple repetition. What I had in mind was this ideal. I was thinking of the kind of endorsement that could contribute to a conception of reality fit to cast the representation, and any other representation, as true, if such they be: a conception of reality fit to cast the representation as a representation of what is there anyway. Endorsing one's representations in a way that is fully self-conscious (or indirectly so endorsing them where endorsement is not possible) means producing representations that are absolute.

But of course, self-consciousness, at least for any finite being, must also include perspective. One is self-conscious in so far as one sees *oneself* in a certain way. And if this in turn involves seeing one's *representations* in a certain way, then, for reasons mentioned in earlier chapters, it introduces further perspective. For the concept of a representation cannot be exercised except from a suitable interpretative point of view. Now the idea that self-consciousness should ideally involve producing both absolute representations and perspectival representations is no indictment of it. There is nothing in these considerations to suggest that the ideal is an impossible ideal. What would suggest this would be any reason for thinking that the endorsement of all one's representations, if it is to count as fully self-conscious, should, in and of itself, yield that (full) self-consciousness. But there may be reason to think this, *as an ideal*. For the ultimate way of seeing the unity of the world as complementing and implicating one's own unity is by seeing them as two aspects of a single unity, manifest in a single conception of how things are. In the ideal, the unity of the conceived and the unity of the conceiver are seen as two aspects of the unity of the conception. And granted that this is not to be explained *à la Tractatus*, where what is absolute can "manifest" what is perspectival ("the world is my world"), then the absoluteness and the perspectivalness do militate against each other. It is as if maximum self-consciousness requires the disappearance of the self. The ideal does begin to look like an impossible, merely regulative one.

We have already in fact seen a variation on this theme. In Chapter Two I talked about an ideal involving absolute representations that are their own best explanation. And near the beginning of Chapter Four I said that, given the perspectival character of the concept of a representation, this too is an impossible, merely regulative ideal. But when the ideal was mentioned in Chapter Two it was mentioned as an ideal of *rational reflective self-understanding.* A conception of the world as being thus and so was supposed to incorporate a full explanatory understanding of how there comes to be a conception of the world as being thus and so, where this understanding was in turn supposed to be part of the self-understanding of whoever had produced the conception. This might make some sense if we relaxed what we mean by a conception and included the sort of thing that an infinite being could produce. But for finite beings such as us it makes no sense. In our finitude we have inexpressible insights into how to approach nearer and nearer to a kind of infinitude. But the infinitude is always, ineluctably, unattainable.

Still, were it not for our finitude there would be no such insight. There would be no ineffable knowledge. As I intimated in the last chapter, the fact of our finitude has many different aspects, including our being cast into a world that is there anyway. It is because this is our situation that we cannot know anything about the world unless we somehow receive it. And it is because we receive the world in the way that we do that there is such a thing as our knowing, ineffably, how to do so. Reciprocally, our knowing, ineffably, how to receive the world in the way we do issues in the knowledge that this is our situation, that we are finite beings cast into a world that is there anyway. Our finitude generates awareness of itself. It is, by its very nature, self-conscious finitude. This will be exceedingly important in later chapters.

APPENDIX

At the beginning of this chapter I promised a rough chart of the concept of knowledge. It will be useful, I think, as a partial summary of what has gone, actually to draw this chart. That is the purpose of this brief appendix. I shall also raise two questions in connection with the chart, though I shall not attempt to answer either of these questions here.

The fundamental boundary on the chart is between propositional knowledge and practical knowledge. The former is knowledge that something is the case, where the canonical evidence for someone's having it includes his or her asserting that this thing is the case. Propositional knowledge is always effable. Practical knowledge sometimes is. Propositional knowledge divides into that which is absolute and that which is perspectival. See Diagram 1.

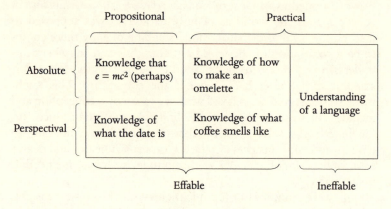

Diagram 1

The two questions are these. First, given that any state of effable knowledge is a representation, does the absolute/perspectival distinction extend beyond propositional knowledge to effable practical knowledge, or is the latter always perspectival? Secondly, where is the vertical line between knowledge which can be characterized as knowledge that something is the case and knowledge which cannot be so characterized? It is not on the right of the line dividing effable knowledge from ineffable knowledge, obviously. Nor is it on the left of the line dividing propositional knowledge from practical knowledge, even more obviously. Nor does it simply coincide with the former: consider my knowledge of Smith and most (all?) non-human animal knowledge. But does it coincide with the latter, or does it lie strictly between them? In sum, is there a division corresponding to either of the dotted lines in Diagram 2?

I raise these questions simply for their interest. It would be beyond the scope of this book to attempt to answer either of them. Suffice to say, in connection with the first, I am convinced that there *is* no such thing as absolute practical knowledge and inclined to think that there could not be;[17] and, in connection with the second, which is a question about canon-

---

[17] This was the point I made in n. 3 above.

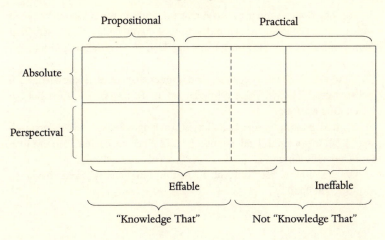

DIAGRAM 2

ical evidence, I take this to be a version of the question whether there is such a thing as "tacit" knowledge.[18]

FURTHER READING

This chapter is derived from my 'Ineffability and Reflection: An Outline of the Concept of Knowledge'. I should like to thank the editor and publisher of *European Journal of Philosophy* for permission to re-use material from this article.

Of general relevance to the chapter are: Bill Brewer, 'Compulsion by Reason'; R. L. Franklin, 'Knowledge, Belief and Understanding'; David Pears, *What is Knowledge?*; Michael Polyani, *Personal Knowledge*; Michael Polyani, 'Tacit Knowing'; Israel Scheffler, *Conditions of Knowledge*; Zeno Vendler, *Res Cogitans*; A. R. White, *The Nature of Knowledge*; and Paul Ziff, *Epistemic Analysis*. (Also relevant are the pieces cited in the further reading for Chapter Three as counter-objections to the "knowledge" objection to physicalism.)

---

[18] Cf. Martin Davies, 'Tacit Knowledge and Subdoxastic States'; and Daniel Dennett, 'Styles of Mental Representation'.

For views very similar to those that I defend on the relations between states of "knowledge how" and states of "knowledge that", see Paul Snowdon, 'Knowing How and Knowing That: A Distinction and Its Uses Reconsidered'.

Zeno Vendler, in *Res Cogitans*, ch. 5, argues that states of knowledge are never states of belief. For a rejoinder see O. R. Jones, 'Can One Believe What One Knows?'.

On understanding, see: Franklin, 'Knowledge, Belief, and Understanding'; J. M. Moravcsik, 'Understanding'; and Herman Parrett, 'Significance and Understanding'.

On ineffability, see William P. Alston, 'Ineffability'; and David E. Cooper, 'Ineffability'.

CHAPTER NINE

After silence that which comes nearest to expressing the inexpressible is music.

(Aldous Huxley)

§ 1: *An argument is given to establish that only nonsense can replace 'x' in the schema 'A is shown that x', where nonsense is simply that which lacks sense. This in turn suggests that in order to make sense of the schema, we should be thinking not just in terms of the narrowly semantic features of language but also in terms of its aesthetic qualities.*

§ 2: *A digression on Kant's aesthetic theory helps to indicate how this might work.*

§ 3: *In the light of this, further consideration is given to how the schema functions and to how, despite the argument of § 1, meaning is relevant to what replaces 'x'. A general philosophical tactic is identified for coping with circumstances in which we want to say each of two incompatible things, namely to consider the possibility that one of the things is true while the other is something we are shown.*

§ 4: *Some claims are made both about the things we are shown, one of these being transcendental idealism, and about what underlies our being shown them. Three principles are identified which are fundamental to this.*

1

THE main task of this chapter is to make sense of the schema 'A is shown that x'. More specifically the task is to make sense of the second component in the definition of the schema, as applied to someone in a state of ineffable knowledge:

> When an attempt is made to put what A knows into words, the result is: x.

On the face of it this is a hopeless task. Even supposing that anything constitutes making the attempt in the first place—an ambitious enough supposition, one might think—that falls far short of
warranting talk about "the result" of doing so. This is clearly so if
such talk is intended as a descriptive generalization about what
issues from all such attempts. No single thing might issue. On the
other hand if such talk is intended with some normative force, as I
in fact want it to be, then there is the question of what possible
standards of correctness there can be for attempting to do the
impossible. Does any authority attach to what the knower himself
comes out with? Or to what designated people come out with on
his behalf? *Are* there reasons to expect a degree of convergence
here? If there are, what sort of convergence? This connects with
another problem: what is the criterion of identity for "results"? In
the case of a state of effable knowledge, two very different things
can issue from two separate attempts to put it into words, one in
French and one in Russian, say, yet count as the same result because
the two utterances are representations with the same content.
What is the counterpart of having the same content for utterances
that may be gibberish? In sum: on what possible grounds can something either count or fail to count as a suitable replacement for '*x*'
in the schema '*A* is shown that *x*'?

These are real difficulties, but I think I can say a few things at the
outset to make the task seem a little more tractable. First, I am not
claiming that, for each and every state of ineffable knowledge, there
is such a thing as the result of attempting to put it into words. Just
as there are different ways of specifying effable states of knowledge,
some of which suffice for only a narrow range of cases, so too there
are different ways of specifying ineffable states of knowledge, some
of which suffice for only a narrow range of cases, and use of the
schema '*A* is shown that *x*' is one such. The narrow range of cases
for which it suffices are cases in which some other, more familiar
kind of ineffable knowledge, such as understanding of a language,
is reflectively activated to issue in a particular (reflective) insight.
Secondly, I neither recognize nor need to recognize any more deter-
minacy in uses of the schema '*A* is shown that *x*' than there is in
uses of the schema '*A* knows that *x*', which, for reasons made familiar by Quine and others, is often not much.[1] And I certainly do not

---

[1] See e.g. W. V. Quine, 'Mind and Verbal Dispositions'.

mind admitting that the schema '*A* is shown that *x*' cannot be used except from some interpretative point of view, nor that, from different points of view, people might be shown different things. Thirdly, the result of attempting to put an ineffable state of knowledge into words need not single the state out from all others, any more than the result of putting an effable state of knowledge into words need single *it* out from all others. To put an effable state of knowledge into words is verbally to endorse the state or, where necessary, and subject to various further restrictions, to do so indirectly. In other words it is to come as close as possible to capturing the state's content in words. But even given whose state it is, and when, that leaves open *which* state it is. Recall Mr Meanour in Chapter Two. He knew that Mr Meanour was wanted by the police. He also, eventually, knew that *he* was wanted by the police— once he had made a further discovery. Yet these two states of knowledge have the same content. Putting either of them into words would slur over the distinction between them. (The schema '*A* knows that *x*' is therefore more discriminative than the schema '*A* is shown that *x*'. Properly to replace '*x*' in the former it is not sufficient to put what is known into words. Properly to replace '*x*' in the latter it is sufficient to attempt—that is, properly to attempt—to put what is known into words.)

These comments are intended to mitigate my task. But I must straightway emphasize something that may appear to exacerbate it. Any satisfactory gloss on the schema '*A* is shown that *x*' must respect what I will call the Nonsense Constraint. The Nonsense Constraint is this. What replaces '*x*', in any true instance of the schema, must be pure and utter nonsense, such as 'Phlump jing ux.'

—"*But that is crazy! If there is anything at all to these ideas, then surely the result of attempting to put an ineffable state of knowledge into words might be some bona fide truth, or (more likely) some bona fide falsehood. And even if it is nonsense, why should it be that kind of nonsense, as opposed to something interestingly incoherent? Indeed, is not the whole point of this exercise to argue that we are shown such things as that transcendental idealism is true, and that absolute representations are impossible?*"—

That is the point of the exercise, and one of the things I must do in this chapter is to reconcile the claim that we are shown such things with the Nonsense Constraint. But the Nonsense Constraint cannot be evaded. There is a comparatively simple two-step argument for it. The first step demonstrates that the result of attempting to put an ineffable state of knowledge into words must be nonsense, while the second step demonstrates that, if it is non-sense, then it must be what I have termed "pure and utter" non-sense. That is, its nonsensicality must be sheer lack of sense.

The first step of the argument is this. Suppose an attempt to express the inexpressible[2] issues in something that can be interpret-ed as a truth or as a falsehood, and thus as having content. Then the very fact that there is such a thing as a state's having that content means that this cannot be the *intended* interpretation. For example, in attempting to express some of my inexpressible knowledge, I may say, 'If we had never existed, it would not have been true that electrons have negative charge.' This can clearly be interpreted as a falsehood, for instance that the power of electrons to attract positrons is causally dependent on human beings. But precisely what makes it false on that interpretation ensures that that is not what I meant. Likewise if it is interpreted as a truth, for instance that it was an arbitrary decision on the part of English-speakers to call the charge that electrons have 'negative'. To the extent that what I say cannot be interpreted either as a truth or as a falsehood it is nonsense.

—*"To that extent. But is there not a vast gap between an utterance's being nonsense to that extent, which is essentially its not being a repres-entation, and its being what you call "pure and utter" nonsense? Surely there is scope for all sorts of possibilities between these extremes."*—

This is the cue for the second step in the argument. This step demonstrates that, in one important respect, there are no interme-diate possibilities, or not in this context. (The qualification 'in this context' entitles us to ignore all those kinds of utterance, such as the asking of a question or the issuing of a command, which do not even purport to be representational and are *eo ipso* not what is required here: to attempt to express any state of knowledge is to attempt to produce a representation.) A little more precisely, what the second step in the argument demonstrates is that, in narrowly semantic terms, there is one and only one way in which an utter-ance can fail to be a representation, namely because the words involved in it have not been assigned suitable meaning: they have

---

[2] A reminder that I use 'inexpressible', 'non-representational', and 'ineffable' inter-changeably in this book.

not been assigned such meaning as would give the utterance content.

The guiding principle here is that there cannot be as it were positive semantic reasons for an utterance's failing to make sense. It cannot be because of what the parts of the utterance *do* mean, that the whole thing does not mean anything. The meaning of the parts *is* their contribution to the meaning of a range of wholes. So, for instance, there cannot be a special sort of meaning attaching to some words, as it may be a "transcendent" meaning, which prevents any utterances in which those words are used from being proper representations. The only thing about a word that can prevent utterances in which it is used from being proper representations is its not having any meaning at all. Again, an utterance cannot be nonsense because words have been used in *violation* of their meaning, which we might think was the case if someone said, 'The circumference of infidelity is green,' or, 'In sweetcorn bat are slowly.' If these are nonsense, it is because their constituent words have not been given any meanings that equip them to work together in this way. It is not because their constituent words *have* been given meanings that *prevent* them from working together in this way. To appreciate this, think about the ambiguous word 'bat'. If we reckoned that it was in part because of what this word meant that the second utterance above lacked sense, then it would behove us to say which meaning we had in mind and what difference it would have made if we had had in mind one of the other meanings. The meaning of a word is given by the meaning of a range of potential utterances in which it is used, or equivalently, by the meaning of a range of contexts in which it occurs, and beyond that range there is nothing but an (easily rectified) lack of meaning. ('Easily rectified' because there is never any obstacle to our explicitly conferring meaning.)

—*"But still, there are degrees of nonsense, are there not? A sentence might be just one word short of making perfectly good sense, for instance, 'If ugoks had never existed, it would not have been true that electrons have negative charge.'"*—

It is certainly true that we could give this "sentence" sense simply by assigning a suitable interpretation to 'ugoks'. But until we have done that, none of the other words here is in any of the contexts that give its meaning. Assigning a suitable interpretation to 'ugoks' is but one way, albeit a particularly simple way, of giving this sequence of words a sense, but *as things stand* all we can say about the sequence, in these narrowly semantic terms, is, quite simply, that it lacks sense. And it is in *that* respect that the nonsense one comes out with when trying to express the inexpressible can be none other than the pure and utter nonsense of 'Phlump jing ux.'

The point I am making here is really quite simple. It is that the result of any attempt to express the inexpressible must be an utterance that lacks content, not an utterance with a *special kind* of content. In particular I want to distance myself from the absurdity that the things we are shown are things that can be interpreted as having an "inexpressible" content. This is related to a point I emphasized in Chapter Seven, namely that the inexpressible is not a matter of how things are. Nor is trying to express the inexpressible a matter of trying to capture how things are in some way that differs, mysteriously, from simply representing them as so being.

Many of these ideas have their roots in Wittgenstein, where they occur, variously, in both the *Tractatus* and the later work. In the former they are bound up with his view of representations as facts. The details of this need not detain us now. Suffice to remark that, for Wittgenstein, the fact that certain simple signs are configured in a certain way can only fail to represent that certain simple objects are configured in the same way if at least one of the signs has not yet been assigned any object as its meaning. There is no question of attributing nonsense to an inappropriate configuration of signs corresponding to an "impossible" configuration of objects. Here are some pertinent quotations:

The reason why 'Socrates is identical' means nothing is that there is no property called 'identical'. The proposition is nonsensical because we have failed to make an arbitrary determination, and not because the symbol, in itself, would be illegitimate . . . We have not given *any adjectival* meaning to the word 'identical'.

We cannot give a sign the wrong sense.

Whenever someone . . . wanted to say something metaphysical, [the correct method in philosophy would be] to demonstrate to him that he had failed to give a meaning to certain signs in his propositions.[3]

---

[3] Respectively: Ludwig Wittgenstein, *Tractatus Logico-Philosophicus*, 5.473 and 5.4733, his emphasis; 5.4732; and 6.53. Many of these ideas have also been forcefully argued by Cora Diamond, to whom I am much indebted and who is in turn very effective at locating them in Wittgenstein: see *The Realistic Spirit, passim*, e.g. pp. 30–1 and 106–7, the latter including

On the other hand we must not exaggerate the force of these considerations. They certainly do not entail that there are no interesting distinctions to be drawn between different kinds of nonsense. What they entail is that there are no distinctions of a certain sort. (Even then 'nonsense' has to be construed in narrowly representational terms. Questions and commands, remember, were excluded from consideration in the second step of the argument.) The point of the argument was to establish that there can be no other reason for an utterance's failing to be a representation than that certain words lack meaning, meaning that would give the utterance content. But this leaves scope for all sorts of distinctions of, say, a psychological kind between the different ways in which we are liable to react to nonsense, the different associations it can be expected to have, the different needs it might serve. Thus there are clear and interesting differences between saying, 'Phlump jing ux,' and saying, 'The borogroves were mimsy,' or, 'Le grass est green,' or, 'The dish ran away with the spoon,' or 'Absolute representations are impossible,' where the last is hedged with qualifications that prevent it from being interpreted as the falsehood that absolute representations are impossible.[4] There is even scope for classifying nonsense according to whether it is, in the words of my interlocutor, "interestingly incoherent". There is scope indeed for classifying nonsense according to what *meaning* it has, on a suitably broad conception of meaning. Just think of the different ways in which music can have meaning, and the different sorts of meaning it can have.[5] No such classification is inappropriate provided that it does not carry the suggestion that there is nonsense that captures in some more or less obscure way *how things are*. And this in fact provides the clue as to how best to take on board the Nonsense Constraint. I introduced the Nonsense Constraint initially as something that appeared to exacerbate the main task of this chapter. There seems to be something especially problematical about identifying that

interesting quotations from Wittgenstein's later work. Note that Diamond traces the ideas back further, to Frege.

[4] Here it is interesting to look at the two sections immediately preceding one of those that Diamond cites from Wittgenstein on p. 106 of *The Realistic Spirit*, namely Wittgenstein, *Philosophical Investigations*, §§ 498 and 499. Cf. also Wittgenstein, *Philosophical Investigations*, § 299, Pt. II, § ii, and p. 216.

[5] Think also about what Frege called "illumination": see Gottlob Frege, 'The Thought: A Logical Inquiry', pp. 22–3. It is not obvious why an utterance that lacks sense should also be completely lacking in this sort of meaning.

which straightforwardly lacks sense—in the way in which 'Phlump jing ux' does—as the result of attempting to express the inexpressible. In fact, however, the Nonsense Constraint can help us. In view of the analogy I just drew with music, we can think of the Nonsense Constraint as offering the following guideline when it comes to making sense of the schema 'A is shown that x': namely, to prescind altogether from considerations of content and to think more in aesthetic terms. I think this is just the guideline we need. To say of some piece of nonsense that it is the result of attempting to express the inexpressible is *something like* making an aesthetic evaluation. It concerns what might be called, justly, if a little grandiloquently, the music of words.

If this is correct, then it immediately opens up all sorts of prospects. It opens up the prospect that there are minimal standards of correctness for replacing 'x' in the schema 'A is shown that x'. It opens up the prospect that there are people, as it were critics, who are particularly good at recognizing when these standards have been met; and that there are people, as it were artists, who are particularly good at producing the nonsense in the first place, an activity that can be performed more or less well. (It is as if trying to express the inexpressible is an art form. My saying, 'If we had never existed, it would not have been true that electrons have negative charge,' perhaps corresponds to a crude sketch. Wittgenstein's working through of transcendental idealism in the *Tractatus* perhaps corresponds to a significant work of art.) Finally it opens up the prospect that what people are shown varies not only from one point of view to another but from one point of involvement to another, in other words the concept of showing contains not only an element of perspective but an element of subjectivity; and these points of involvement might be both culture-bound and time-bound.

Not that the implications of this for the production and critical evaluation of the relevant kind of nonsense are significantly different from what many people, I among them, would want to say about the production and critical evaluation of various kinds of sense. Any use of language is an art form of sorts. Putting words to service is always an imaginative exercise, if only of a very limited kind, in which the infinite possibilities of the words' meaning are played off against one another and against the context, in order to secure some desired effect. (Or perhaps we should except a few very atypical uses of words, such as saying 'Cheese' when having a photograph taken or writing one's name in order to test a new ballpoint.) Understanding of a language, itself a main source of our being shown various things, has all sorts of affinities with being skilled in traditional forms of artistic creativity. As I said in the last chapter, my understanding enables me to make sense of what I glean in my transactions with the world. Artists are people who make sense of what they glean in their transactions with the world. Moreover, knowing how to produce and evaluate nonsense of the kind that concerns us is itself an aspect of such understanding. It is one particular way of knowing how to play off word meanings against one another. So the somewhat unexpected and ironical conclusion of the discussion so far in this chapter is that use of the schema '*A* is shown that *x*'—along with the production of nonsense that is an integral part of it—does not differ in any major respect, or not in any major respect of principle, from use of any other bit of language.[6]

2

At this point it is helpful to turn to Kant, in particular to his aesthetic theory. Kant's aesthetic theory is a direct product of his transcendental idealism. Having argued that we can know nothing about things in themselves, he concedes that we have some sort of awareness of our own existence as things in themselves, in which capacity we are free rational agents.[7] Moreover, we have some sort of awareness of what it would be for us properly to exercise our free rational agency. This awareness is our moral sense: Kant holds that what we would do, if we acted in a way that was purely rational, is what we recognize ourselves as being under a moral obligation to do. However, none of this makes any real sense to us except in so far as we can represent it from the point of view of possible human experience, which is to say in terms of the world of nature, the world of space and time. We need to be able to recognize what

---

[6] Cf. here and elsewhere in this chapter, David Bell, 'The Art of Judgement'. For instances of Wittgenstein assimilating language to music, in both his early work and his late work, see e.g. *Tractatus*, 3.141 and *Philosophical Investigations*, §§ 341 and 527.

[7] See e.g. Immanuel Kant, *Critique of Practical Reason*, pp. 97–8 in the *Akademie* edition.

behaviour of ours, in the here and now, would count as acting purely rationally. So we need to be able to make due sense of our environment. (Notice how the idea of making sense comes to the fore
again.) What this means is that if we are to keep a suitable grip on
the difference between right and wrong, then we need to be able to
recognize our environment as being in harmony with the dictates
of rationality. We need to be able to find in our environment a certain order, a certain purposiveness, a certain intelligibility. But there
is no guarantee that we shall find these things. To the extent that we
do, we feel pleasure. This Kant identifies as aesthetic pleasure, or
more specifically as a feeling of beauty. Kant's aesthetic theory is a
kind of "phenomenology" of transcendental idealism.[8]

As a consequence there are, on Kant's conception, reasons for
expecting convergence on questions of beauty even though they
lack the decision procedures and methods of verification that are
available in the case of, say, mathematical or scientific questions.
They lack these because they concern what it feels like for beings
with our constitution to engage with the world as we do, not, or
not so directly, what we actually engage with. (One could say that
they are deeply subjective. But then so too, for Kant, are mathematical and scientific questions, at least on my use of 'subjective'.)
There are reasons for expecting convergence on them, however,
because we do all have the relevant constitution. We are all rational
creatures, with shared receptive capacities, representing the world
from a common point of view. This shared constitution, which
Kant refers to as "the supersensible substrate of humanity",[9] he
takes to be transcendent. But he thinks we are justified in assuming
it to be the same from one person to the next, because otherwise
we would never have been able to communicate our knowledge in
the that way we do. In Kant's own words, "we assume a common
sense [sc. a subjective principle which determines what pleases or
displeases with universal validity] as the necessary condition of the
universal communicability of our knowledge."[10]

Except for the appeal to transcendence, what I am suggesting
has a similar basic structure to this. Our shared constitution, that
without which we could neither communicate nor express our

---

[8] See Immanuel Kant, *Critique of Judgement*, Pt. I, *passim*.
[9] Ibid., p. 340 in the *Akademie* edition.
[10] Ibid., pp. 238–9 in the *Akademie* edition.

knowledge in the way we do, I take to be our shared understanding, that which grounds our ineffable insights. Where Kant talks of this constitution sustaining a feeling of beauty, I want to suggest that it sustains feelings of "aptness" directed at attempts to express those very insights. And just as Kant sees the dynamics of our feeling of beauty in terms of the interplay between our rationality and our various epistemic faculties—where the former constitutes an element of the infinite within us and the latter characterize our essential finitude—so too, I shall later suggest, we should see the dynamics of our feeling of aptness in terms of the interplay between our craving for the infinite and the impossibility of our attaining it.

'Except for the appeal to transcendence,' I said. There would have been reason enough for me to recoil from this aspect of Kant's aesthetics merely in my attitude to the idea of the transcendent. But there is reason for it anyway. The appeal to transcendence places a burden on Kant's aesthetics which ultimately gives it a deeply unsatisfactory structure. To see why, consider what would have been the most obvious thing for Kant to say, granted the sketch of his theory that I offered above, about aesthetic displeasure, or more specifically about a sense of the repugnant. It would have been something like this: we feel such displeasure when our environment does not help us to keep a grip on the difference between right and wrong, that is when it thwarts our attempts to see free rational agency in terms of the world of nature and strikes us as, say, bewildering, morally inert, or alien. But he does not say this. On the contrary, he says that when our environment is uncooperative in this way, it merely serves to remind us that "the moral law" transcends that which is in space and time and is infinitely more magnificent than even the most magnificent natural phenomena; and he says that this too issues in aesthetic pleasure, albeit a negative counterpart of our pleasure in the beautiful. He identifies this as pleasure in the sublime.[11] It is as if the contingencies and vicissitudes of our environment are ultimately irrelevant to our moral sense, or at least to the fact that we can sustain it, if not to the precise way in which we do so. Nature comes to appear as aesthetically pleasing not in virtue of what it is actually like, but in virtue of its simply being there, with us in its midst. And this is just

[11] Ibid., Pt. I, §§ 23 ff.

as it must be if the grounds of our pleasure lie in our commerce with the transcendent, that which helps to determine, not the content of nature, but its form, the structure it would have had whatever it had actually been like. I am not saying there is an inconsistency in Kant's aesthetic theory. But there is certainly a tension: a tension between his appeal to transcendence, on the one hand, and his attempts to make play with the contingencies of nature, on the other. The eventual enervation of the latter, in his account of sublimity, reveals a good deal about the pressures that his own transcendental idealism brings to bear on his aesthetic theory.

The early Wittgenstein is truer in this regard to their shared transcendental idealism. Like Kant he connects aesthetics with ethics. But where Kant has recourse to an elaborate theory to express the connection, Wittgenstein simply identifies them. This is because for Wittgenstein, as I observed in Chapter Seven, to be "good", or to be "happy", is to adopt a certain attitude towards the world whereby one views it as a whole, and to do that is to treat the world aesthetically. The beautiful is what makes one happy. The source of aesthetic pleasure thus has nothing to do with the world's being contingently thus and so. What is beautiful, like what is mystical, is not how things are within the world, but that it exists.[12]

Unlike either Kant or the early Wittgenstein, however, I am not a transcendental idealist. I do not think that our understanding of the world either consists in or points to some transcendent unifying structure that determines the form of the world. On the contrary, I accept Wittgenstein's own later insistence that our understanding is a matter of deep contingency, and that there are all sorts of identifiable concurrences that help to sustain it. So when I suggest, in line with Kant, that our understanding in turn helps to sustain certain quasi-aesthetic reactions, I need have no qualms about seeing these, again in line with Kant, as sensitive to how things happen to be. Without the transcendental idealism there is no reason why such reactions should not be targeted on what is highly particular. One thing I am therefore quite ready to concede is this: that had we found ourselves cast into a world that was different in various specifiable ways, then what we were shown would also have been different.

---

[12] See Wittgenstein, *Tractatus*, 6.4–6.45, though I am also drawing on Wittgenstein, *Notebooks*, pp. 83 ff.

3

The point of this excursion into aesthetics has been to indicate what kind of claim it is that some given piece of nonsense is the result of attempting to express some given state of inexpressible knowledge. In particular I hope to have indicated how the questions raised at the beginning of this chapter might be answered. (I shall return to these shortly.) I take this to be the main philosophical component in the task of making sense of the schema 'A is shown that x'. Saying what the result *is* of attempting to express any given state of inexpressible knowledge may be a largely non-philosophical exercise. Certainly explaining why the result is this, rather than something else, may be a largely non-philosophical exercise, just as it may be—in fact would be—a largely non-philosophical exercise to explain why some people find certain musical scales more "natural" than others. But I do not want to get involved in a demarcation dispute. It behoves me, given the unfamiliarity of the concept of showing, and given also the connection which I claim it has with the other issues that I have been addressing, to say *something* about why we are shown the things we are. I shall return to this task in the next section.

What then of the questions raised at the beginning of this chapter? Well, the Kantian model does give us reason to expect a degree of convergence on questions of what we are shown, convergence enough to sustain standards of correctness. As with other similar matters, however, the convergence that counts will be the convergence that occurs in "favourable" circumstances, where favourableness itself has to be defined in ways that depend partly on the convergence. Circumstances are not favourable, for instance, if those assessing the nonsense are not adept at doing that sort of thing. Such circularity is not vicious. Indeed, as I indicated towards the end of Chapter Seven, something of the sort is unavoidable: any concept is grounded in a set of mutually interlocking practices and shared reactions. But the circularity does strongly suggest, even if it does not entail, the possibility of people who are relatively expert at exercising the concept of showing, or at attempting to express the inexpressible. As regards the question of whether a person whose own inexpressible knowledge is under consideration has any authority, there is no reason to think so. How he himself attempts to express the knowledge (if at all) will no doubt be of special significance, but only as a symptom of what it is he knows. Finally, the criterion of identity for results must itself be determined by the relevant convergence. If two pieces of nonsense issuing from two separate attempts to put a state of ineffable knowledge into words are both sanctioned by the standards determined by such convergence, then they can count as the same result.

In practice, word meaning is bound to be relevant to whether two pieces of nonsense enjoy this equivalence. If we are shown that no representation can be absolute, then we are *ipso facto* shown that any representation must be perspectival. In saying this I am not flouting the Nonsense Constraint. The point is this. Part of what it is to acknowledge that a certain piece of nonsense is the result of trying to express an inexpressible state of knowledge is to indulge in the pretence that it is not nonsense; and part of what it is to indulge in this pretence is to pretend that certain familiar patterns of inference apply to it. (Part of what it is to indulge in the pretence that 'All borogroves are mimsy' is not nonsense is to pretend that it entails 'Nothing non-mimsy is a borogrove'—assuming that the pretence follows, as it were, the line of least resistance.) Showing is never "atomistic". Take transcendental idealism. Transcendental idealism is (interestingly) incoherent. There are various more or less elaborate ways of explicating it, but none of these is enough for it to make sense. However, they are enough for the pretence that it makes sense to involve a good many of these patterns of inference. Hence, if we are shown that transcendental idealism is true (where the sequence of words 'transcendental idealism is true' is itself a piece of nonsense equivalent to a statement of transcendental idealism), then we are shown all sorts of other things as a result: that our representations have a transcendent aspect; that some of what is necessary is grounded in what is contingent; and so forth. And if we are shown that transcendental idealism is true in the specific form outlined at the end of Chapter Five, then we are shown still more as a result, in particular that absolute representations are impossible.

Exploiting patterns of inference is thus crucial to trying to express the inexpressible. This reinforces the idea that producing nonsense when trying to express the inexpressible is in many ways like producing sense. In general we should be as wary of forgetting the similarities between these as we should be of forgetting the differences. They can serve many of the same functions. Thus a judiciously chosen and carefully targeted piece of nonsense can help one person to impart her ineffable knowledge to another. There is as much scope for imaginative teaching methods in the case of ineffable knowledge as there is in the case of effable knowledge. Moreover, just as inventive language use is often an indispensable accompaniment to the imparting and acquiring of new effable knowledge—think about the creative use of metaphors in, say, scientific revolutions—so too the inventive production of nonsense can be an indispensable accompaniment to the imparting and acquiring of new ineffable knowledge, however reluctant the person who produced the nonsense may be to recognize this description of what he or she has done. And just as those involved in scientific revolutions, or in revolutions in the arts, sometimes make available insights that were in some sense not antecedently available, so too Kant (for instance) makes available insights—in his case ineffable insights—that were in some sense not antecedently available.

In the final section of this chapter I shall make some tentative comments about what underlies our being shown the things we are. This will also involve me in making certain claims about what we are shown, a process that I shall continue in Chapters Ten and Eleven. One thing that will emerge, I think, is a philosophical tactic of very general utility. The tactic applies whenever we find ourselves inclined both to affirm a sentence and to deny it. It is this: to try out the possibility that doing one of these things is correct, under some suitable interpretation, while doing the other, perforce not under that interpretation, constitutes trying to express inexpressible knowledge which we have. Roughly, if ever you find yourself inclined to say both *S* and *Not-S*, consider saying:

S, but we are shown that *Not-S*.

4

We are finite. I identified this in Chapter Seven as a basic premiss of my discussion. Our finitude is overlaid with self-consciousness. I identified this at the end of Chapter Eight as an important consequence of the particular way in which our finitude leads us to receive the world. What our finitude *is* is self-conscious finitude. (This means that we are conscious of ourselves as finite. It does not mean that we have attained, or are even capable of attaining, that ideal of maximum self-consciousness which I identified in Chapter Eight as a regulative ideal.) These two principles, that we are finite and that we are conscious of ourselves as such, which come together in our being self-consciously finite, are two of the three principles that I shall suggest underlie our being shown the things that we are. The third is that we aspire to be infinite.

What status do these principle have? My inclination is to say that they are simply data. But what sort of data? Brute facts? And in any case who are "we"? (I promised in Chapter Seven that I would come back to this question.) Pigs and newborn babies are not conscious of their finitude. Nor, perhaps, do they aspire to be infinite. Here too there are various things that I am inclined to say. I am inclined to say that I am reckoning at some level, somewhere along the line, with *human* finitude, and that newborn babies come into the reckoning in a way that has something to do with their potential. But really this is floundering. By far the best way to address both this question (the question of who "we" are) *and* the question of what status the principles have is to address them together. Very well, then. Let the answer to both questions be this: the three principles are an implicit definition of who "we" are.[13]

Now it is because of our finitude that we have ineffable knowledge. Our finitude means that we cannot know anything about the world without receiving it, and our receiving the world as we do involves our knowing, ineffably, how to do so. An infinite being— or perhaps we should say, the infinite being—could have knowledge without receiving anything outside it. There would be no difference between its knowing how things were and their being that way. It would be as if, in the terms of the *Tractatus*, the elements of the infinite being's thoughts were themselves the objects for which they stood, so that the fact that things were thus and so was quite literally the same as the infinite being's thinking that things were thus and so. There would be no distinction between subject and object;

---

[13] It is interesting to compare this with what Iris Murdoch says about the status of her premiss that we are ineluctably imperfect (itself, I take it, an aspect of our finitude) in *Metaphysics as a Guide to Morals*, p. 509. For the genesis of the third principle cf. G. W. F. Hegel, *Phenomenology of Spirit*, esp. pp. 104 ff. For amplification of all three principles see further below, Chapter Eleven.

no distinction between the manifold of the being's knowledge and the manifold of what it knew; no distinction between states of the being's knowledge whose success conditions were independent of them and states of its knowledge not of that kind; no distinction between states of the being's knowledge that were effable and states of its knowledge that were not.[14]

—*"Presumably all of the being's knowledge would be ineffable, since none of it would have anything to answer to."*—

Yes, but one might equally want to say that all of the being's knowledge would be *effable*, since it would all have content; or rather, it would all *be* content. Your way of putting it would be truer to the letter of the distinction, the other truer to the spirit. But a better alternative than either would be not to wield the distinction at all in respect of the infinite being's knowledge. The very use of the distinction, like everything else in my discussion of knowledge hitherto, is best understood as applying exclusively to finite knowledge.

Our aspiration to infinitude includes an aspiration to just such infinite knowledge. It also involves an inability to come to terms with the fact that we cannot attain it. Thus not only do we aspire to know things in such a way that the effable/ineffable distinction does not apply, we are tempted, when we indulge in a certain kind of reflection, to construe ourselves as having already got there. That is we are tempted, on the one hand, to construe our effable knowledge as having nothing to answer to, and, on the other hand, to construe our ineffable knowledge as having content. As a consequence we are tempted to try to put our ineffable knowledge into words. That there is such a temptation, with its shared ground, is enough, I think, for there to be standards of correctness for making the attempt, or equivalently, for there to be a right way of making it: the temptation allows for a degree of convergence, and the degree of convergence is enough to sustain these standards. Very roughly, the right way of making the attempt is by succumbing to temptation. This means, among other things, affecting a kind of infinitude and producing nonsense such that the pretence that it

---

[14] This idea of infinite knowledge is borrowed, with embellishments, from Kant, though interestingly, in view of what we observed in Chapter Six, it is not explicit in Kant until the second edition of *Critique of Pure Reason*: see esp. B72 and B138–9. See also Kant, *Critique of Judgement*, Pt. II, §§ 76–7.

makes sense chimes with that affectation. One of the most basic things that we are shown, therefore, is that we are infinite.

But we are not infinite; we know that we are not; and we can never ultimately prescind from that fact. So the affectation is mitigated. And it is this distinctive combination of hubris and restraint that most fundamentally shapes what we are shown. We imagine that our ineffable knowledge has content, that what we know in virtue of our receptive capacities is itself a feature of how things actually are. Thus we imagine that the link between being an aunt and being female, say, is a kind of brute structure which we have imposed on the world, a structure which we might just as easily not have imposed. Through self-conscious reflection we then confront the question of what it *is* for the world to have this structure. On the one hand, we see it as a product of how we represent the world. On the other hand, conscious of ourselves as finite, and recognizing the world as that into which we are cast, we see it as a *constraint* on how we represent the world. For the world embraces all that we can represent. Its structure, its form, is a matter not merely of how things are but of how they must be. So the apparent contingency of our having imposed this structure comes to seem a transcendent contingency, a contingency beyond all that we can represent. The nonsense that is most apt to accompany this charade is the nonsense of transcendental idealism. We are shown that transcendental idealism is true.

Moreover, we are shown that it is true in the specific form outlined at the end of Chapter Five. Thus we are also shown that absolute representations are impossible. And we may, in succumbing to temptation, compound these absurdities by taking pride in our modesty. For in affirming such nonsense we may think of ourselves as acknowledging limitations. For instance, it does look modest to say, 'The nearest we can get to absoluteness, namely the deliverances of an idealized physics, are still only representations from our point of view.' But such nonsense can just as well, and more revealingly, be turned round so as to make it look much less modest. In effect what we are saying is: 'Even in representing the world from our point of view, we are able to attain to the deliverances of an idealized physics.' Ultimately what we want to say is: 'Our point of view is privileged. Reality is held together there.' These are scarcely intimations of modesty. They are different manifestations of our desire to play God.

There are various ironies here. I shall return to some of them in Chapter Eleven. One is this. Our being shown that we are infinite is at the root of much of our ineffable knowledge. Suitably exercised, it could be the basis of our knowing how properly to be finite. It could help us to come to terms with the fact that we are finite, and curb our aspiration not to be. That is already something of an irony. The irony is given a further twist by the fact that if, *per impossibile* perhaps, we did lose the aspiration to be infinite, then either we would not be shown anything at all (meaning, not that we would not have ineffable knowledge, but that there would be no such thing as the result of attempting to put our ineffable knowledge into words) or we would be shown quite different things. In particular we would no longer be shown that we are infinite. That is, our being shown that we are infinite would have brought about, in an Hegelian term whose use in this context is irresistible, its own *Aufhebung.*[15]

Here is another irony. Our being shown that absolute representations are not possible is a crucial part of our knowing how to implement, combine, and exploit what we know. It arises from reflective activation of our understanding of our language. And it helps us to see that our representations are representations of what is there anyway (the Basic Assumption). Ultimately, if the Basic Argument is successful, it helps us to see that absolute representations *are* possible. Not only that. It also helps us to see, as a corollary, that to say, 'Absolute representations are not possible,' in an effort to express any state of knowledge—provided it is the best we can do—is to utter nonsense.

Both Kant and the early Wittgenstein succumb to temptation. Kant succumbs at an early stage in the *Critique of Pure Reason*. He succumbs as soon as he identifies some of our a priori knowledge as synthetic. Our a priori knowledge is knowledge of what is necessary. To identify it as synthetic is in *some* sense to grant the necessity a contingent base, in our representations. Wittgenstein, in the *Tractatus*, succumbs when, for instance, he considers the presuppositions of logic and its application to the world, something he does

---

[15] The German word can mean both 'annulment' and 'preservation'. Hegel used it for a dialectical transition in which a lower stage is both annulled and preserved in a higher one: see e.g. G. W. F. Hegel, *Encyclopedia of the Philosophical Sciences*, Pt. I ('Logic'), § 96. Cf. also Luke 17: 33.

most explicitly in the immediate build-up to his solipsistic procla-
mation: 'The world is *my* world.' He talks about the "what" that
precedes logic, the kind of thing that he later describes as mystical
and connects with his own will.[16] In both Kant and Wittgenstein
there is a sense of some deep human contingency underlying the
form of reality. In both it betokens our standing in a God-like relation of creative representation to the world, and in both it finds
expression in the absurdity of transcendental idealism.

Ah, but what a resonant absurdity! This book is poised somewhat, in its attitude to nonsense, between reproof and celebration.
In a way I make no apology for this. Nonsense, like almost everything else, has its uses and its dangers. I would be glad to think that
I had contributed something towards an appreciation of each. I certainly do not want to be complacent about the dangers. The greatest of these occur when nonsense masquerades as sense. And
towards *disguised* nonsense I have, for the most part, simple
Wittgensteinian antipathy (where this is one of those occasions on
which 'Wittgensteinian' can stand without the qualification 'early'
or 'late'). But once nonsense has been exposed as such, then I think
it can be a splendid and versatile instrument, of use not least in
specifying states of ineffable knowledge.

In another way I do apologize for my ambivalence. While
applauding what Kant and Wittgenstein produce when they succumb to temptation, I concede that in some sense it would have
been better had they not succumbed, and indeed had there not
been any temptation. In some sense it would have been better had
we not aspired to be other than we can be: it would have been better had we been flawlessly rational. However, the sense in which
these things are so is a hollow sense which has little purchase on us.
In *that* sense it would have been better, no doubt, had we lived in a
world without laughter. (There is a familiar and related paradox in
aesthetics. Much of the best art owes its existence to evil, in more
than one way and at more than one level. Who knows but that it all
does?) Meanwhile, we must see both sense and nonsense for what
they are. Transcendental idealism certainly has potential for harm
if we do not recognize it as incoherent, and in particular if we do
not recognize as incoherent talk of a transcendent contingency

---

[16] Wittgenstein, *Tractatus*, 5.55–5.641 and 6.4 ff.

underlying the form of reality. The only contingency here is the simple contingency of our own existence and of how we carry on. This in turn we must see for what it is, and, as far as possible, affirm for what it is. It is the contingency of our own finitude.

FURTHER READING

The core of this chapter is derived from my 'Human Finitude, Ineffability, Idealism, Contingency'. I should like to thank the editor and publisher of *Noûs* for permission to re-use material from this article. The material on Kant's aesthetics is derived from my 'Beauty in the Transcendental Idealism of Kant and Wittgenstein'. I should like to thank the editor and publisher of *British Journal of Aesthetics* for permission to re-use material from this article.

Of general relevance to the chapter is Gilles Deleuze, *The Logic of Sense*.

On Kant's aesthetics, see Paul Crowther, *The Kantian Sublime*; and Salim Kemal, *Kant and Fine Art*.

The unsatisfactoriness of Kant's treatment of aesthetic displeasure is discussed by Garrett Thomson in 'Kant's Problem with Ugliness'.

INTERLUDE

THE concept of showing is so important to this enquiry, and so liable to misinterpretation, that I include this interlude, with a question-and-answer format, as a compendium of the main features of the concept in an effort to forestall potential confusion before I apply the concept any further.

• *What is it for A to be shown that x?*

For A to be shown that x is for A to have ineffable knowledge and for x to be what results when an attempt is made to put this knowledge into words. The claim that A is shown that x is thus an existential claim. It is the claim that there exists a state φ of A such that φ is a state of ineffable knowledge and such that x is what results from attempting to put φ into words.

• *Does somebody who is shown something* ipso facto *know something? More precisely, is being shown something an instance of being in a state of knowledge?*

Yes, by definition.

• *Is there anything derivative or metaphorical about the sense in which being shown something is an instance of being in a state of knowledge?*

In so far as a question of this kind can ever receive the simple answer no, no.

• *Is the concept of knowledge involved here an orthodox one?*

I certainly hope so. It is the concept I tried to chart in Chapter Eight. It was not my intention in that chapter to chart anything that was not orthodox. In fact it was not my intention to chart anything other than what could reasonably be called "the" concept of knowledge. There is nothing out of the ordinary or recondite about the knowledge exemplified when somebody is shown something. Suppose I reflect on my grasp of the concept *green*. I thereby achieve various insights into the concept: I come to know, in the light of my reflection, how to apply it. This is a case of my being shown something.

• *Are instances of the schema 'A is shown that x' straightforwardly true or false?*

Yes indeed. There are criteria for whether a given bit of nonsense is the result of attempting to put a given state of ineffable knowledge into words. Whenever these criteria are met, we can produce a true instance of the schema by putting the name of the person whose state the state is in in place of '*A*' and the bit of nonsense itself in place of '*x*'. By the same token, whenever the criteria are not met, we can produce a false instance of the schema by following the same recipe—provided, of course, that the bit of nonsense does not result from attempting to put any of the rest of the person's ineffable knowledge into words. And 'true' here just means *true*; 'false' just means *false*.

• *Suppose A is shown that x. If this is a genuine instance of A's knowing something, and if the claim that A is shown that x is straightforwardly true, where does the illusion lie?*

There is no illusion—either in *A*'s being shown that *x*, or in our saying so. There are *related* illusions. The most significant of these is the illusion that *x* is the result of a *successful* attempt to put *A*'s knowledge into words. This may be an illusion which *A*, or someone else, is actually under. But equally, it may not be. To be sure, we cannot acknowledge the truth of the claim that *A* is shown that *x* without seeing that *x* is what results from the attempt to put *A*'s knowledge into words; and we cannot see this without actually making the attempt; and we cannot make the attempt without feeling the force of the temptation to make it; and we cannot feel the force of the temptation to make it unless there is, numbered among our imperfections, at least the *capacity* to be under the illusion specified, the illusion that the attempt is, was, or will be successful. Note, however, that a being which lacked this imperfection could still be shown that *x*. It is just that it could not acknowledge the truth of this description of itself.

• *Is it hyperbole to describe what we are shown—what replaces 'x' in true instances of the schema 'A is shown that x'—as "pure and utter" nonsense?*

Given what I said in the previous chapter about pure and utter nonsense, no. What replaces *'x'*, in any true instance of the schema, must fail to be a representation, and this failure must in turn be explained negatively, by the failure of the words involved to have suitable meanings; not positively, by their having *un*suitable meanings.

• *How can pure and utter nonsense be the result of attempting to express any state of knowledge?*

Pure and utter nonsense, as I am construing it, can conjure up all sorts of images, and can carry all sorts of associations and connotations. Indeed, on a suitably broad conception of meaning, it can have all sorts of meaning. This is illustrated by a simple sequence of nouns such as 'bread butter cheese pickle lettuce'. It is illustrated in a somewhat different way even by words that are not part of the lexicon, such as 'maxisplendiferous' and 'hugantic'. And it is illustrated by a good deal of poetry. There is no mystery in the idea that, among the many broadly semantic features that nonsense can have, is "aptness" to replace *'x'* in instances of the schema 'A is shown that *x*'. That is, there is no mystery in the idea that some nonsense can be what results from attempting to express some inexpressible knowledge.

• *Is this "aptness" not just a matter of psychology?*

Perhaps. (It depends to some extent on what the word 'just' is supposed to be doing here.) It is a matter of psychology in the sense in which beauty is a matter of psychology. It is not a matter of psychology in any sense that precludes interpersonal criteria for its correct application.

• *Is it not a matter of psychology in a sense that precludes* argument *for its correct application?*

No; it is not. Just as reasons can be adduced for regarding something as beautiful—just as careful argument can help to draw our attention to what it is about something that makes it beautiful—so too careful argument can help to draw our attention to what it is about some piece of nonsense that makes it apt to replace '*x*' in an instance of the schema '*A* is shown that *x*'.

• *Does such argument deserve to be called* philosophical *argument?*

Who knows? Some of what is involved in such argument I think is clearly philosophical. Some of it, perhaps, is not. But as I said in Chapter Nine, I do not want to get involved in a demarcation dispute. Whether what I was doing towards the end of that chapter, and will carry on doing in Chapters Ten and Eleven, merits the label 'philosophy' (which I distinguish from the question whether it has philosophical significance) is of no special concern to me.

CHAPTER TEN

To follow a story is to move forward in the midst of contingencies and peripeteia under the guidance of an expectation that finds its fulfilment in the "conclusion" of the story. The conclusion is not logically implied by some previous premises. It gives the story an "end point", which, in turn, furnishes the point of view from which the story can be perceived as forming a whole. To understand the story is to understand how and why the successive episodes led to this conclusion, which, far from being foreseeable, must finally be acceptable, as congruent with the episodes brought together by the story.

(Paul Ricoeur)

Introduction.

§ 1: A new kind of ineffable knowledge is identified, namely that which enables each of us to narrate a life, or equivalently to live a life. This involves discussion of the nature and identity of persons. Answers are given to some of the questions raised by what Parfit calls reductionism.

§ 2: These materials are then combined to indicate further things we are shown.

§ 3: Examples of things we are shown are drawn from set theory.

§ 4: The doctrine that Dummett calls anti-realism is expounded. Examples of things we are shown are given on the hypothesis that anti-realism is correct. A variant on anti-realism is considered. Something is said about how the examples just considered fare on the hypothesis that this variant is correct.

§ 5: The discussion is related back to transcendental idealism. It is also related to what Kant calls regulative principles.

WE ASPIRE to be infinite. That was the third of the principles that I used in Chapter Nine to define who "we" are. But does this mean that each one of us aspires to be infinite? Or is the aspiration in some sense corporate?

Both. Not that there is any equivocation here. Rather there is a single aspiration with two aspects. In Chapter Nine I was primarily concerned with the second, "corporate" aspect. The transcendental idealism which I claimed we are shown was the transcendental idealism which, in earlier chapters, I had associated with Wittgenstein's later work, a pluralized descendent of the *Tractatus*'s solipsism. But the other, "individualistic" aspect of our aspiration to be infinite also serves to explain why we are shown some of the things that we are shown. This is what I shall focus on, initially, in this chapter. I shall try to say some more, in connection with this aspect, about what we are shown and why.

More generally, my aim in this chapter is to carry on the process which I began in the last section of Chapter Nine, of specifying things that we are shown and giving some indication of why we are shown them—why it is *these* pieces of nonsense that we are tempted to come out with when trying to express our inexpressible insights. Much of this will be very programmatic. It will also be more tentative than it may appear. I am well aware that the topics I address in this chapter deserve a much more sensitive and careful treatment than I shall be able to give them. But I will be satisfied if I can say enough to lend my proposals further support, and to demonstrate their potential bearing on a number of familiar philosophical concerns.

1

I talked in Chapter Eight about the ineffable knowledge which enables me to make sense of what I glean in my transactions with the world. This knowledge, I later claimed, is the ground of an ineffable insight that I can achieve into the unity of the manifold both of what I know and of my states of knowledge. I was thinking in Kantian terms (though without Kant's own commitment to the idea that the unity in question has a transcendent source). In particular I was thinking of my exercise of such basic concepts as that of causation and that of an enduring physical object, which enable me to see myself as part of a spatio-temporal world in which things interact in accordance with various natural laws. But something similar and of equal philosophical importance occurs at a less basic level. I am able not only to recognize the unity of my animal life. I am able also to recognize the unity of my personal life. Not only do I see myself as coming into contact with a range of physical objects with which I engage in all sorts of familiar physical ways, I also see what I do and what befalls me as part of a history, or rather of various interlocking histories, one of which is the history of my own life, in which events stand to one another in all sorts of relations of illumination and explanation. I make sense of these events as episodes in one or more stories. I see later events as narrative consequences of earlier events. Thus not only do the latter sometimes causally depend on the former. They also have a significance whereby the former sometimes occur for the sake of the latter: people act to achieve certain ends. I discern a structure in these events, a complex retiform structure whose criss-crossing threads correspond to the creation, the nurturing, the pursuit, the clash, and the eventual realization, frustration, or simple lapsing of thousands upon thousands of more or less tacit, more or less significant, more or less private, more or less public, reasons, goals, aims, and projects.

This process of making narrative sense of one's life raises myriad questions and has been extensively discussed by philosophers. In the further reading at the end of this chapter I give a small sample of recent writing on the topic. But the discussion is as old as philosophy itself. Nietzsche is once again important. As I noted in Chapter Five, one of the motivations for his perspectivism was the view that in representing the world we are making sense of it as part of the very process of telling, or acting out, our own stories. These stories, in other words our autobiographies, are works of semi-fiction continuously in the writing. And in Nietzsche's view we must live our lives in such a way that we can interpret, and where necessary reinterpret, our pasts as an integral part of the overall narrative structure. (This registers one of the most significant *casus belli* between Nietzsche and orthodox Christianity. Only by thus re-assessing the past, Nietzsche believed, and thereby triumphantly affirming it, can we truly redeem it. The orthodox Christian view is that we cannot redeem the past, or rather the past cannot be redeemed, unless we renounce it.) The fact that Nietzsche saw the past as open to interpretation in this way helps to illustrate the important extent to which he viewed making narrative sense of one's life as a creative process. On other views it is much more of a process of discovery. But this is a matter of emphasis. On any realistic view, making narrative sense of one's life involves both creation and discovery, each constraining and informing the other.

It also involves risk. It must. What one creates will inevitably be at the mercy of subsequent discovery. To make sense of one's life is to make an *investment*, an investment which by its very nature is likely to be the greatest one ever makes. It is clear, then, that among the representations that one produces as part of this creative process there are bound to be some that are deeply subjective. They must be from a point of involvement which is conditioned by one's ultimate commitments, hopes, and values. Moreover, among the concepts that one exercises as part of producing these representations there are bound to be some that bear the mark of such subjectivity. These will include concepts whose very exercise is impossible except from some appropriate point of sense-making involvement. They will include such basic concepts as the concept of a person and the concept of a life.

The concept of a person is usually taken to be equivalent to that of a human being. But on a somewhat more philosophical conception, the possibility is left open that there are persons who are not human beings: aliens, say, or even God. It is this latter, broader conception that I am adopting. Even so, I think the point I am making here applies on either conception. It is true that 'human being' has relatively objective criteria of application. Yet even on the lay conception, whereby these are also the criteria of application for 'person', it remains the case that whether a subject counts as a person, and what counts as the same person, are informed to a significant extent not just by biology, or even by biology plus psychology, but by deeply felt, sometimes very painful, usually quite instinctive sentiments-cum-judgements about how to treat the subject or subjects in question. Thus consider a very premature baby who, though capable of surviving for two or three days on a life-support machine, has no prospect of living beyond the end of the week. The fact that all concerned, not just the parents for whom the baby is naturally an object of love, spontaneously respond to her with an emotion for which the best word is probably 'respect', and thereby accord her a special dignity—it is non-trivial, for instance, that she has a name by which they refer to her—is at least as much of a reason for her counting as a person as vice versa. Or consider a case of radical personality change, where a doubt arises as to whether *A* is the same as the person who married *B* some twenty years earlier. The fact that there is no question of *B*'s being entitled to re-marry is at least as much of a reason for *A*'s counting as the same person as vice versa. We do well to remember Locke's famous observation that 'person' is a forensic term.[1] At any rate, there is a crucial element of subjectivity in the concept of a person. In particular, it is a concept that cannot be properly exercised except from the point of involvement that one needs to adopt when making sense of one's own life, a process which involves recognizing oneself as a person in communicative interaction with others. There can be no knowing what a person is except through knowing what it takes to be one.

As I said, I think these comments apply even if 'person' is restricted in its application to human beings, though I shall not myself recognize any such restriction. I shall adopt the more philosophical conception of a person. In particular I shall count any being that is one of us, in the sense determined by the three principles in Chapter Nine, as a person. (The converse, however, I certainly want to reject. Babies are people, though they are not conscious of their own finitude. As I hinted in Chapter Nine, what I have to say about "us" can still be relevant to them because of their potential, as it may also be relevant, in other ways, to other people whom "we" exclude. Note, incidentally, that if "we" include nonhumans, that does not prevent my main concern from being with human finitude. It is still true that, for those of us who *are* humans, humans are the paradigms of persons.) The three principles themselves, considered collectively, are likewise deeply subjective. Only from the point of involvement of beings who aspire to be infinite is there any recognizing a being who aspires to be infinite. Or to put the point with a certain rhetorical force: only from our point of view do we exist. I shall return shortly to the important consequences that this has.

Before that, I want to continue the discussion of making narrative sense of my life. To make narrative sense of my life I must have a sense of who I am, where I have come from, and where I am

---

[1] John Locke, *Essay Concerning Human Understanding*, Bk. II, ch. 27, § 26.

going. 'Where', in these formulations, is not to be understood in literally spatial terms. It is to be understood rather in terms of the
space of possibilities, measured evaluatively. I must have a sense of
my distance from, and my orientation with respect to, various
goods and various ills. I must see myself as tracing a route through
these, pursuing some, eschewing others.

To do this I need a special kind of understanding. I need the conceptual resources to process what I receive in my interaction with
the world so that I can not only see myself as having basic physical
access to that world but as having a life. That is, I need insight not
only into my epistemic unity, but also into my narrative unity. I
need to see my own reasons for tracing the particular route that I
trace *as* my reasons for tracing that route, reasons determined by
my projects, my aspirations, and my own conception of the difference between right and wrong. Just as I cannot make proper sense
of what I receive in my interaction with the world except by recognizing myself as cast into that world, in contact with various of its
physical features and able to negotiate a way through it, so too I
cannot make proper sense of what I receive in my interaction with
the space of possibilities except by seeing myself as cast into that
space, in contact with various of its evaluative features and able to
negotiate a way through it. The special kind of understanding that
this requires, which is to say the ability to exercise concepts from a
suitably entrenched point of involvement, is a paradigm of ineffable knowledge. It answers to nothing. Its success conditions are
nothing but the conditions in which, by virtue of having that
understanding, and *solely* by virtue of having that understanding, I
create a life for myself. My point of involvement *is* my life.

This is not to say that what I create is immune to criticism. Other
people can clearly have all sorts of grounds for complaint and
resentment about how I pursue my life, as they in turn pursue
theirs. The point, here as in the case of linguistic understanding, is
that my knowing how to make narrative sense of my life is not my
knowing how to make any particular, privileged sense of it, but
rather my knowing how to make *some* sense of it. I am in an
enabling state that would still be an enabling state however else
things were and whatever objections might be levelled against it.

We exist, I said, only from our own point of view. The last few
paragraphs help to elucidate this. Being one of us is of a piece with
having a life. Neither concept, nor any other related concept, can be

exercised except from the point of view of one who knows what a life is, which is to say one who has a life. There is no prospect, for instance, that any such concept will admit of a biological definition. The concept of a life here is the concept of a *person's* life. It is the kind of concept whose application can still be contested even when all the relevant scientific questions have been settled, for instance in the case of a patient in a persistent vegetative state. To be one of us is not just to be an animal of a certain kind, nor yet an animal of one of a range of kinds, not even an animal of one of a range of kinds in a certain scientifically defined state. It is impossible to characterize who we are, or even to make any explicit reference to us, except from the very point of view that we ourselves adopt in being who we are. We are a kind of self-creation. This sounds mysterious, almost Fichtean.[2] But the point is relatively simple. We are the subjects of our own stories. In acting out those stories, we produce inherently perspectival representations about ourselves of such a kind that any being which did not share our point of view would be totally incapable of endorsing them.

—*"When you say that we are the subjects of our own stories, do you mean that we are* nothing but *the subjects of our own stories?"*—

Yes.

—*"But how is this possible? Do not stories require authors who are independent of them, about whom there is something to be said beyond what appears in the stories?"*—

No. If we are only ever acting, there is nothing to be said about us beyond the roles we play, the roles we have created for ourselves. And what makes it the case that we are *acting* (being actors) is the fact that we are *acting* (being agents). Each of us is tracing a route through the space of possibilities in the light of whatever narrative unity he or she wants to create for himself or herself.

—*"Very well, let us grant that it is possible for us to be both the authors and the subjects of our own stories, and nothing but that. Even so, I see three problems with your saying that that is what we are. The first of these is the threat of a kind of self-stultification similar to that which afflicts the transcendental idealist: what if it is part of all our stories that we are not just the subjects of stories? The second problem is that your claim that*

---

[2] See e.g. J. G. Fichte, *The Science of Knowledge, passim.* (Kant, who was originally very hostile to Fichte's ideas, came round to something similar in work that he was in the throes of producing at the end of his life: see Immanuel Kant, *Opus Postumum,* esp. pp. 170–99.)

some of our representations are thus "fictional" looks incompatible with
the Basic Assumption—that representations are representations of what is
there anyway. And the third problem is that, granted that our being the
authors and subjects of our own stories means that we exist only from our
own point of view, there is a conflict with the Basic Argument. For con-
sider a true representation, from our point of view, in which there is
explicit reference to us. And consider a true representation from some
incompatible point of view. According to the Basic Argument, it must be
possible to give a single account of how both these representations are
made true by reality, which is not itself from either of the points of view
but in which there is explicit reference to both. The fact that the account is
not itself from either of the points of view means that it cannot involve
explicit reference to us. The fact that it involves explicit reference to both
points of view, and in particular to ours, means that it must involve
explicit reference to us. This is a blatant contradiction."—

In response to the first problem: our stories are not uncon-
strained. We are not at liberty to tell it how we choose, not if we
are to tell it truthfully. At the very least our stories must cohere
with one another. But they must also cohere with whatever else is
true. And one thing that is true is that we are the subjects of our
own stories. ('Stories', 'fiction', even 'semi-fiction': these terms have
connotations of the fanciful that are not meant to apply in this context. Our stories are not simply yarns that we spin. They are truth-
ful and honest accounts of our lives, the telling of which is inseparable from the living of those lives.)

In response to the second problem: the Basic Assumption does
not preclude our having an active role in what is there "anyway".
What the Basic Assumption requires is that representations should
be made true or false by the states of a single world, and that all
true representations should (therefore) be compossible. Thus
someone's taking a representation to be true, or hoping that it is
true, or wishing it were true, is never a sufficient condition for its
being true: other people might think, or hope for, or wish for,
incompatible things. On the other hand, given some true representation, it is possible that things would not have been how the representation represents them as being had it never been produced
(and the use of the word 'anyway' is unfortunate in so far as it suggests otherwise). A simple case in point would be someone's saying,
'I am now speaking.' But other, subtler examples would include a
good many of the representations that we produce in narrating our

own lives. (Thus the club would never have disbanded had the chairman not foretold that it would. She would not now despise him had she never said that she did. He would not be afraid of exhibiting his paintings had it never occurred to him that he was. They would not be at loggerheads with each other had they not both assumed that they were.) A final point in connection with this second problem: do not forget that the question of when something qualifies as a representation is one that I have not addressed. No doubt a large proportion of the apparent representations we produce in the course of narrating our own lives are not really representations at all.

In response to the third problem, it is perhaps worth beginning by pointing out an assumption you have made. You have assumed that an explicit reference to our point of view is *eo ipso* an explicit reference to us. This is not obvious. For one thing, to say that a point of view is "ours" is not to say that it is peculiarly ours. You need to rule out the possibility that our point of view can also be referred to as the point of view of *X*s, where *X*s are other beings who share this point of view with us. Still, I think you *can* rule out that possibility. And I suspect your worry would surface in a somewhat different form even if it turned out that you were wrong to make this assumption. So this is a relatively trivial response to the third problem.

The important response is as follows. Given two true representations from incompatible points of view, the Basic Argument does not require that it be possible to give an account of how they are both made true by reality which is not itself from either of the points of view. What it requires is that it be possible to give an account of how they are both made true by reality, *part of which* is not itself from either of the points of view: the part which is used to provide for their indirect integration. Suppose, for instance, that one of the two representations involves the concept of a representation and is thus from some suitable interpretative point of view. There is no reason why the account in question should not itself involve the concept of a representation (there had better not be!); nor why it too should not be from that same interpretative point of view. Likewise, if one of the two representations involves explicit reference to us, then there is no reason why the account in question should not involve explicit reference to us.

—"*In your response to the second problem you seemed to concede that how reality is can depend on how it is represented as being, albeit in a way that is compatible with representations being representations of what is there anyway. Are you committed to some localized form of empirical idealism?"—*

No, for two reasons. First, the sense in which idealists claim that how reality is depends on how it is represented as being is the sense in which this is *not* compatible with representations being representations of what is there anyway. (Idealists deny the Basic Assumption.) Simply noting that someone can say, 'I am now speaking,' and thereby make his representation true, does not qualify me as an idealist. Nor is there idealism in the observation that we have a variety of practices and institutions through which we construct our lives, and ultimately ourselves. Secondly, idealism is not just the view that how reality is depends on how it is represented as being. It is the view that how reality *must be* depends on how it is represented as being. Idealism concerns the "form" of reality. But on my view, our authorship does not extend beyond a series of contingencies about who we are, where we have come from, and where we are going.

—*"There has been much debate recently about what Parfit calls reductionism, the view, roughly, that a person's existence and identity over time consist in the holding of facts which can be described "impersonally", that is to say without explicit reference to the person and without presupposing his or her identity.³ Would it clarify your position if you said where you stand on this debate?"—*

Both Parfit's views and the views of his opponents are too subtle for it to be sensible for me to state any kind of allegiance without going into far more detail than I am able to go into here. (See the further reading at the end of this chapter for some of the most important contributions to this debate.) Even so, I do think it would be worthwhile for me to rehearse some of the answers that I am committed to giving to questions which have a bearing on the debate.

Throughout what follows let π be the point of view that one must adopt in order to exercise the concept of a person.

(i) Any representation ρ involving the concept of a person, and thus from π, can be indirectly endorsed by producing a repres-

³ See Derek Parfit, *Reasons and Persons*, pp. 210 ff. See also Parfit, *The Metaphysics of the Self.*

entation not from π, and thus not involving the concept of a person. Indeed ρ can be indirectly endorsed by producing an absolute representation couched in purely physical terms. This absolute representation will weakly entail ρ, in the sense of weak entailment that I introduced back in Chapter One. However, I have done nothing to expound this sense beyond gesturing towards the notion of supervenience. A large part of the debate about reductionism is debate about what sense could fit here. (See further (v) below.)

(ii) The first two sentences of (i) do not hold with 'indirectly' deleted. Representations that make explicit reference to persons are inherently perspectival. It is not possible to endorse ρ except by producing another representation from π.

(iii) If there can be a complete description of reality, by which I mean a description of reality assimilation of which would suffice for omniscience—an issue on which I have not committed myself—then there can be a complete description of reality that is absolute. And a complete description of reality that is absolute is also, in one good sense of the word, a complete description of reality that is "impersonal".

(iv) No amount of knowledge of how things are "impersonally" can suffice for knowledge of how they are "personally". This is a schematic way of putting the kind of point that has been familiar ever since Mr Meanour was introduced in Chapter Two. Several further instances were given in Chapter Three. One of these was that a congenitally blind person, however familiar he or she was with the physics of colour vision, could not thereby know what a green thing looks like. It is for reasons of this kind that omniscience is compatible with ignorance. In particular, an omniscient being, who may be ignorant of what day of the week it is, and of what a rose smells like, may also be ignorant of what a person is. Such a being may not know, for instance, whether there exist any extraterrestrial people—nor indeed whether there exist any terrestrial people.

(v) π involves a significant amount of evaluation. Part of what it is to recognize a person as such, or as the same as before, is to acknowledge him or her as making certain demands on one, to acknowledge oneself as making certain demands on him or her, and to recognize his or her narrative unity as a constraint on one's own, a potential ground of mutual imputation. A person can be called to account for past deeds and can call to account for past suffering.[4] Anyone who thought that this evaluative element prevented attributions of personhood and claims about personal identity from admitting of truth or falsity (that is, from being representations) would have a ready answer to a question that Parfit calls, in a footnote to one of his earlier articles, "the real issue": 'Does personal identity just consist in bodily and psychological continuity, or is it a further fact, independent of the facts about these continuities?'[5] The answer would be, 'Neither. It is not a fact at all.' But for those of us who are happy to accept that attributions of personhood and claims about personal identity do admit of truth or falsity, the question cannot be so readily ducked. Having said that, I would not myself want to address it until glosses had been provided on 'consist in', 'further', 'fact', and 'independent of', and perhaps also on 'bodily' and 'psychological'. (This is not meant as a criticism either of Parfit or of others who have addressed his question. I am not suggesting that such glosses have never been proposed. But it makes a difference which ones we accept.)

(vi) Our use of the concept of a person, like our use of any other concept, is sustained by all sorts of contingencies. Furthermore, there are describable circumstances for which our current use does not legislate. If such circumstances were to arise, various questions involving the concept of a person would have no answers, unless and until we appropriately extended that use. Suppose, for instance, that two people exchange brains. As things stand, there may be no answer to the question which of the two resultant people, if either, is which. (How they both proceed to act out their own stories, if indeed that is something that they are capable of doing, is obviously relevant, but it is not relevant in a way that is obvious.)

(vii) Where we can and do exercise the concept of a person,

---

[4] Cf. Paul Ricoeur, *Oneself as Another*, *passim*., esp. Fifth Study; and Alisdair MacIntyre, *After Virtue*, esp. pp. 201 ff. Cf. again Locke's observation that 'person' is a forensic term: see above, n. 1.

[5] Derek Parfit, 'Personal Identity', n. 37.

from π, we take its application to be of huge importance, and rightly so. It matters very much whether something counts as a person, or as the same person. And this mattering is not reducible to the mattering of anything "impersonal". We may be able to bring about circumstances of the kind mentioned in (vi), in which we are all at sea concerning what matters. But if so, then one thing that matters is that we should not, or not lightly, bring about such circumstances.[6]

2

I shall now proceed to use the picture sketched in the previous section to indicate further things that we are shown. At the same time I shall try to defuse urges that we have to say things that we know we must not say, by diagnosing them as urges to express the inexpressible.

Two features of the picture are crucial to the way in which I shall try to graft it on to the picture I drew in Chapter Nine of what it is for us to be shown different things. The first of these is that each of us has knowledge of how to narrate a life. This is a paradigm of ineffable knowledge. It answers to nothing. It would still be knowledge however else things were. And it is knowledge, however bad, however desolate, however ugly the life narrated. The second feature is that we exist only from our own point of view. This is a paradigmatic mark of our finitude. In other words it is a mark of the first of the three principles that define who we are. And it combines with the other two, the fact that we are conscious of ourselves as finite and the fact that we aspire to be infinite, to ensure that our existing only from our own point of view is something that we can never shut our eyes to nor properly come to terms with. Our aspiration to be infinite includes an aspiration to be—how to put it?—*ultimate constituents of reality*, that to which direct reference is possible from any point of view and from none.

An infinite being would have no need to create its own specific unity, narrative or otherwise. Its unity would be the unity of the world. Nor would there be any need for it to act out its own story

---

[6] Cf. Ricoeur, *Oneself as Another*, p. 151.

within the world's overall history in order to achieve self-consciousness. Its self-consciousness would be neither more nor less
than a single omniscient representation of all that is there anyway.

When I reflect on the knowledge I have of how to create a life
for myself, or of how to create my own narrative unity, I am tempted by my aspiration to be infinite to see such unity in precisely these
infinitary terms, so far as this is compatible with my consciousness
that I am finite. I am tempted to see myself as reckoning with and
exploring something substantial which is how it is irrespective of
what anybody does with it, or of what story anybody tells about it:
my self. Insights I have into how to justify, avenge, celebrate, or
redeem things that I do and things that befall me come to appear as
effable insights into the fixed contours of this self, insights, moreover, that are not from my own special point of involvement with
it. To try to express these insights would be to succumb to the
temptation of seeing them in just this way. I am therefore shown
that I am a substantial self, that I am not my own creation, that I do
not exist only from some highly contingent point of view—in sum,
that I *am* an ultimate constituent of reality.

These various pieces of nonsense chime with other things that I
am tempted to say and other things that I am tempted to think. For
instance, it is difficult for me to assimilate the particularity of my
own existence. This difficulty is not just, not even primarily, the difficulty of assimilating the contingency of my own existence,
though that is bad enough. Granted that nature is not completely
deterministic, there were countless critical moments throughout
the past at which, of the billions of ways in which things might
have proceeded, only one allowed for the possibility that the world
would eventually contain *me*. My existence was, until who knows
how close to my actual conception, an improbability of stupefying
proportions. Yet I feel none of the relief and retrospective alarm
that I would feel if, say, I had just come through an ordeal in which
the chances of my survival were as high as nineteen to one. The
contingency of my existence does not register with me. Perhaps
there are good reasons for this. Perhaps the difficulty I have with
assimilating the contingency of my existence does not indicate any
inadequacy on my part but rather something about the parameters
within which anything can matter to me. However that may be, the
difficulty at issue now, the difficulty of assimilating the *particularity*
of my existence, is something different and, in its own way, yet

more acute. Many of us, in our childhoods or in our adolescences, have known the awful shock of suddenly realizing our own particularity. We are struck, not so much by the thought that "all of this" might not have been—which is the contingency of our existence— as by the thought that "all of this" is "all of THIS". So long as I can keep that shock at bay, continuing none the less to focus on "THIS", my difficulty is with the realization that there is, somewhere in the world, an ill-defined configuration of things and circumstances but for which I would not be and in the absence of which I eventually shall not be. My difficulty is with seeing "THIS" as something *in the world*. It strikes me rather as a way in which the world is presented, a kind of sheen on all the facts that does not itself constitute a further fact. I am tempted to say that the world might have been presented in that way *whatever* configurations of things and circumstances there had been; and that, if it had been so presented, then it would *ipso facto* have been presented to *me*. Another way of putting this would be to say that *I* could attend any possibility. And I feel that there would never be any indeterminacy about whether I did or not. I am tempted to say that *I* could have existed in the eleventh century; that *I* might have lived the life of Schubert; that *I* would determinately survive or determinately not survive a brain transplant, regardless of what any participant in the experiment, myself included, was disposed to say about what had happened.[7]

The diagnosis for my being tempted to say these things, which, on reflection, I know I must not say (not if my aim is to speak the truth), relates back to my ineffable knowledge of how to make narrative sense of my life, and indeed, more primitively, of how to make "physical" sense of it. While it is clearly true that my having this knowledge depends on a variety of deep contingencies, most obviously on the contingency of my existence, it is also true that, while I have it, I am in a state that rides any further contingencies. Precisely what my state is is a state that enables me to deliver the goods *however* things turn out, subject to the usual qualification about the non-interference of other states I am in. My knowledge is a preparedness to interpret things come what may. When I reflect self-consciously on it, I do not, as I would if it were effable, "see through" it to what I know. I reflect on the state itself, and on the fact of my being in it. That is, I do not focus on anything I come

[7] Cf. Thomas Nagel, *The View from Nowhere*, esp. ch. 4 and ch. 11, § 1.

across; I focus on my way of coming across things. And for as long as I am unable to acquiesce in the finitude that prevents all my knowledge from being of a piece, then I shall be tempted to try to put this state, or the ineffable insights that I derive from it when I am self-consciously activating it in this way, into words. I shall be tempted to regard my way of coming across things as something further I come across—though I shall also want to distinguish it from any normal configuration of things or circumstances, seeing it rather as a mode in which all such configurations have their being. This in turn will tempt me to say the things mentioned above: that I could attend any possibility; that I might have lived the life of Schubert; and so forth. And, precisely because that is the diagnosis for my being tempted to say these things, they have just the right resonance to qualify as results of attempting to put my knowledge into words. I am therefore shown these things. I am shown that I *could* attend any possibility. I am shown that I *might* have lived the life of Schubert.

Throughout this process my aspiration to infinitude is continuously mitigated and kept in check by my consciousness that I am finite. My being shown each of these things is a variation on my being shown that I am infinite. But I am always inclined to view my infinitude as limited and constrained in various ways (however self-contradictory this may be). In particular I can never fully prescind from the fact that I might never have existed. At times this issues in a familiar kind of solipsism. I allow that I might never have existed, but I insist that, in that case, nothing would have existed. At other times, when my ineffable insights are more directly infused by a sense of that which is independent of me, I am disinclined to insist even on that. I see my infinitude as extending no further than my own domain, the domain of how things are presented to me, and I do not flinch at the idea that there is something independent of this domain. I see my infinitude as "local". But I see it as infinitude none the less, because I do not recognize any distinction within my knowledge of this domain between the effable and the ineffable. Nor do I recognize any distinction, within the domain itself, between the manifold of my knowledge and the manifold of what I know, between subject and object, between how I take things to be and how they are. What I am then shown is that I am a Cartesian ego (an immaterial self) standing in various more or less direct and utterly contingent relations to an independent material world. This in turn is liable to induce scepticism in me. I am shown that my knowledge, which is a matter of how things are in my domain, extends no further than that domain; and hence that, for all I know, the independent material world is totally unlike how I take it to be (I might be a brain in a vat). In fact, of course, I know a good deal about the material world. But my inclination to voice such scepticism may shake my confidence. What I know may get temporarily demoted to what I merely believe. If this does happen, it will mean, ironically, that the scepticism is temporarily justified. (For all I *then* know, the material world is totally unlike how I take it to be.) It will also be a further illustration of something I discussed towards the end of Chapter Eight: how reflection can destroy knowledge.

To take stock. Each of us has ineffable knowledge of a deep, pervasive, and basic kind: knowledge of how to live, of how to be a person among other persons, of how to be one of us. Each of us can reflectively activate this knowledge to achieve insights into his or her own unity, and in particular into his or her own narrative unity. If an attempt were made to put any such insight into words, the result, initially, would be a rather gross solipsism.[8] However, a kind of context-relativity ensues. What I am shown depends on just what kind of insight I achieve and just what resonances various pieces of nonsense have for me, and these in turn vary with the strength of the influence of my awareness that I am finite. The more self-consciously I am able to reflect, the more heightened the intensity of the various insights I am able to achieve, but also the less inclined I am to view myself as infinite and the more mollified the nonsense that I find apt as an attempted expression of my knowledge. In due course I am tempted to cast myself as a Cartesian ego. Then I am tempted to embrace a familiar philosophical scepticism, which, were I to succumb to temptation, I might thereby in fact make true. What survives even my most self-conscious reflection, the source of the most enduring thing that I am shown in this connection, is my reluctance to acknowledge the main features of the picture that was sketched in the previous section, which lies behind all of this: my reluctance, in other words, to

[8] There are complications about inexicals such as 'I' and 'he' that I have been gliding over, I hope harmlessly. These are used in accord with the pretence that the solipsism makes sense, as expressed from the subject's point of view. I am shown that *I* am a precondition for the existence of anything else. You are shown that *you* are a precondition for the existence of anything else. He is shown that *he* is a precondition for the existence of anything else.

acknowledge that the concept of a person is deeply subjective and value-laden; that it can be exercised only from the point of view of those who, because they are themselves persons, have the relevant values; that I am insubstantial: that I am my own (finite) creation; that none of us exists except from our own highly contingent point of view. I am shown, as it were to the bitter end, that all of this is false and that I am rather, to use once again the phrase I used earlier, an ultimate constituent of reality.

3

I now want to change tack completely. In this and the next section I shall present further examples of things we are shown, but without the "individualistic" emphasis that there has been in the previous two sections. The first example, the one that I shall focus on in this section, is technical. It concerns set theory.

The practice of set theory might have been expected to yield examples because it is inherently self-conscious. It is inherently self-conscious not just to the extent that the practice of any mathematical theory is, but to the further extent that it is itself concerned with the frameworks of mathematical theories and the content of mathematical representations. (A mathematical theory is typically associated with some domain of things whose interrelations it describes, the domain being a set and the interrelations being set-theoretical features of it. Note: I am taking for granted something that I have more than once said is controversial, namely that mathematical statements are representations. If this is not the case, then the example I am about to give needs to be drastically altered though not, I think, abandoned altogether.)

For the purpose of this example I shall assume the iterative conception of a set. On the iterative conception there are things that are not sets, there are sets of these things, there are sets of *these* things, and so on, without end. Each set belongs to countless further sets. But there never comes a set to which every set belongs. There is no set of all sets.

We have encountered this conception before. It is the conception I referred to at the beginning of Chapter Six when we considered the question: what is the domain of the quantifier 'everything'? As

I observed then, there is no set of all things on this conception. This was the basis of the dilemma I went on to outline—the Domain Dilemma, as we could call it. The fact that there is no set of all things on this conception is entirely of a piece with the fact that there is no set of all sets. What I say in this section could also, I believe, sustain a satisfactory solution to the Domain Dilemma. This would replace the deeply *un*satisfactory solution mooted and rejected in Chapter Six, involving the transcendent/immanent distinction. My reason for introducing a slightly different focus in this chapter, rather than reverting to the Domain Dilemma itself, is technical. If we restrict attention to sets, it is easier to explain how the concept of showing gets applied.

To repeat: there is no set of all sets. This means that set theory is unlike other mathematical theories in one or other of two respects. Either it is not associated with a domain of things whose interrelations it describes (the domain of sets) or it is associated with such a domain but this domain is not itself a set.

There is an account that allows us to embrace the latter alternative. On this account, while it is true that every set is a collection, it is not true that every collection is a set. There are also "proper classes". The difference between sets and proper classes is that, whereas sets are built up from base in the way described above, proper classes are formed *once* the sets have been built up. The domain of set theory, on this conception, is a proper class, not a set.

The problem with this is that it was no part of the original conception that set theory was concerned only with *some* collections. 'Set' was meant to apply to *anything* of that sort, *any* collection. (This problem is reflected in the impropriety of talking about what happens "once" the sets have been built up. The building up of sets, on the iterative conception, is never-ending. Any collection of sets that is formed "once" certain sets have been built up is just another set, to be succeeded in the building up process by endlessly many others.) Provided that 'set' is understood in the broadest way possible, then the iterative conception leaves us with no choice, it seems to me, but to embrace the first alternative and deny that set theory has an associated domain. There are *too many* sets to be grouped together into a single domain. If you like, sets are a "many" that cannot be regarded as a "one".[9]

---

[9] This is an allusion to Cantor's famous definition of a set as a many that can be regard-

Now let *A* be a finite set of axioms and rules that fit the iterative conception. A simple example of an axiom that might occur in *A* is that any two sets belong to a third. A simple example of a rule that might occur in *A* is to infer the consequent of a conditional from the conditional plus its antecedent. No matter what the composition of *A* is, there will be a set-theoretical statement that can be neither proved nor disproved on the basis of it: this is a consequence of Gödel's theorem.[10] We can be more specific. There will be a set-theoretical statement σ such that σ can be neither proved nor disproved on the basis of *A* and such that we can see that σ is true if *A* is sound. (By 'can' in 'we can see that . . .' I mean the familiar weak 'can' of principle. By 'sound' I mean 'incapable of being used to derive something false'.)

Given that we can see that σ is true if *A* is sound, and given that we can see that *A* is sound, we can see that σ is true. So we may, if we wish, supplement *A* by adding σ as a new axiom. If we do, then we shall be manifesting our understanding of what sets are like. This understanding goes beyond *A*, which, though it tells the truth about sets and nothing but the truth, does not tell the whole truth.

But consider: how do we tell that *A* is sound, which is crucial to this way of exercising our understanding? The obvious answer is that we tell that *A* is sound by reflecting on the fact that its axioms are all true and its rules truth-preserving, and then concluding that it can never be used to derive anything false. I have no quarrel with this answer. But it is much less anodyne than it appears. The most direct way to exercise our understanding of what sets are like is to think about sets: to work with principles about sets, whether they be axioms belonging to *A*, consequences of those axioms, or candidates for supplementing them. But when it comes to recognizing that *A* is sound, we need to work with principles *about* principles about sets. We need to work with concepts such as truth and derivability. These concepts are not themselves the stuff of set theory. They are the stuff of its metatheory. We need to step up a level. Instead of simply thinking about sets we need to think that we are *right* in the way we think about sets. We need to exercise our understanding of sets in the light of self-conscious reflection on the

---

ed as a one: see Georg Cantor, *Gesammelte Abhandlung Mathematischen und Philosophischen Inhalts*, p. 204.

[10] Kurt Gödel, 'On Formally Undecidable Propositions of *Principia Mathematica* and Related Systems I'.

deliverances of that very understanding, so that we can eventually step back down a level and reach new conclusions about what sets are like.

This immediately suggests that there may be things we are shown in the offing. For our understanding of what sets are like, at least in so far as it consists in the grasp of concepts, is, like any other such understanding, ineffable. And the process described involves our exercising it in the light of self-conscious reflection. This is just the sort of situation in which we are liable to be shown something.

And indeed we are. To see how, note first that the process described not only involves our exercising our understanding in the light of self-conscious reflection. It involves our exercising it in the light of that self-conscious reflection which is characteristic of set theory. Such reflection is normally applied to other mathematical theories in specifying what they are about and how their theorems are true. Here it is applied to itself. In stepping up a level, while still exercising our set-theoretical understanding, we achieve ineffable insights into the unity of the very subject matter of our under-standing. This enables us to see that the axioms of *A* are faithful to this subject matter, and hence that *A* is sound. (It also enables us to see that the axioms are consistent with one another. There are echoes of the Fundamental Principle here.) But the subject matter of set theory is essentially infinitary. This is the point, once again, that sets are built up endlessly, in such a way that they outstrip any possibility of being grouped together into a single domain. Other mathematical theories have domains that are infinite in a technical (but familiar) sense of 'infinite'. For instance, the set of integers is infinite in that sense, as is the set of points in Euclidean space. But the infinitude of sets is more radical. In their case, there is not even a set of them to *be* infinite in that more modest sense. Sets are end-less, unsurveyable, immeasurable, in a way in which neither inte-gers nor points are. To attempt to express our inexpressible insight into the unity of this subject matter would be to succumb to the temptation of thinking that we, in our infinitude, had the measure of this immeasurable infinitude. It would be to think that the unity of all these sets was itself a mathematical object given to us in the course of our mathematical investigations; that the unity of our access to mathematical reality was itself an element within mathe-matical reality. The nonsense that would ensue would be that set theory *does* after all have an associated domain; that sets are a many that *can* be regarded as a one; that there *is* a set of all sets. (Similar pieces of nonsense would ensue in the case of other mathematical theories, only they could readily be interpreted as truths. Their nonsensicality would not be apparent until further claims were made about, say, our own transcendent involvement in ensuring the existence of the domains in question. In the case of set theory, by contrast, the nonsensicality would be apparent straight away, provided that we were exercising our understanding properly.) That set theory has an associated domain; that there is a set of all sets: these, then, are further things that we are shown.

4

The examples I shall focus on in this section have clear echoes in the set-theoretical example I have just been discussing, and will also serve to bring the discussion back to transcendental idealism. They are examples which relate to what Dummett, in various contexts, has called anti-realism.[11]

Anti-realism is both a revisionary philosophy of logic and a revisionary metaphysics. It questions an assumption that is pivotal to classical logic, namely that any proposition is either true or false. (By a *proposition* I mean something like a linguistic representation. How like? Well, exactly like—save only that the question of whether it is either true or false is left open. Representations, remember, are *defined* to be either true or false. A proposition that *is* either true or false *is* a linguistic representation.) The anti-realist challenge to this assumption concerns propositions whose truth or falsity we cannot determine. An example might be a proposition to the effect that Aristotle would have liked chocolate. What is the harm in our assuming that such a proposition is either true or false, even if we cannot tell which? The harm, according to anti-realists, is that it blocks a satisfactory account of our understanding of the proposition. Their argument is as follows. Our understanding of a proposition involves our knowing both how the world must be if the proposition is true and, derivatively, how the world must be if the proposition is false. But such understanding has to admit of

---

[11] See e.g. Michael Dummett, *The Logical Basis of Metaphysics*, and 'Realism and Anti-Realism'.

public ratification. This is because, if it did not, nothing would count as manifesting such understanding, which means that nobody could ever know whether anybody else understood the proposition, which means that it could not be used to communicate anything, which means that it would not have any meaning, which means that there would be no such thing as understanding it. But in order for our understanding of a proposition to admit of public ratification, the proposition must not be true without our being able to tell that it is, or false without our being able to tell that it is false.

Of the many possible objections to this argument, one of the deepest and most interesting is as follows. Consider the following claim (call it the Ignorance Claim).

The Ignorance Claim: There is at least one proposition whose truth or falsity we cannot determine.

As far as the anti-realist argument goes, it is only if the Ignorance Claim is true that there is any harm in our assuming that every proposition is either true or false. But *is* the Ignorance Claim true? On an anti-realist conception, only if we can tell that it is, in other words only if there is at least one proposition such that we can tell that we cannot determine its truth or falsity. But if there is such a proposition, then we can tell, in particular, that we cannot determine its truth. The only way of telling *that*, however, again on an anti-realist conception, is by determining its falsity. So we arrive at a contradiction. It follows that the Ignorance Claim cannot be true. Hence, as far as the anti-realist argument goes, there cannot be any harm in assuming that every proposition is either true or false.

Anti-realists have a number of ways of responding to this objection (which I shall call the Ignorance Objection). Most straightforward, and most heroic, is to admit that there cannot be any harm in assuming that every proposition is either true or false, but still not to assume it. This is itself an instance of anti-realist circumspection. It is to admit that the assumption cannot be false, but still not to accept it as true.

Suppose anti-realism is correct. Then it furnishes further examples of things we are shown. Or so I shall now argue.

Our understanding of propositions, a paradigm of ineffable knowledge, includes, on the anti-realist conception, knowledge of when to hold back from saying that one of them is either true or false. This knowledge is itself an ineffable insight achieved by reflectively activating our understanding in the light of what we can and cannot determine. Its ineffability is illustrated by something established in the Ignorance Objection, namely that there is no satisfactory way of justifying our circumspection. There is no satisfactory way of saying what could possibly be wrong with calling any proposition true or false.

Now if we were infinite we could determine the truth or falsity of any proposition. In fact any proposition would be true or false by our decree. Anti-realism would not be an issue. There would be a range of propositions, "infinitary" propositions as I shall call them, which we established in this way and which fixed every aspect of reality.

Thus, if we were to attempt to put our ineffable knowledge into words, we would begin by thinking of reality in this thoroughly "realist" vein. But self-consciousness about our own finitude would then incline us to sound the following note of caution. (And this in turn we would regard as justification for our anti-realist circumspection, so I shall call it the Case for Anti-Realism.)

The Case for Anti-Realism: Infinitary propositions are all bona fide representations. They are all true or false. But it is possible that, because of our finitude, the Ignorance Claim applies to them. That is, it is possible that there is at least one infinitary proposition whose truth or falsity we, in our finitude, cannot determine. Suppose there is. Call it ρ. Then we cannot understand ρ. The only propositions that we can understand are propositions whose truth we could determine in any possible circumstances in which they were true, and whose falsity we could determine in any possible circumstances in which they were false. The most that can be said of ρ is that, if circumstances had been favourable in a certain way (for instance, if there had been some discoverable correlation between liking chocolate and having some physical feature that Aristotle was known to have had), then we could have determined its truth; and if circumstances had been favourable in another way, then we could have determined its falsity. But that is not enough for us to understand ρ. What we *may* understand is a "finitary" surrogate for ρ, say $\rho^\star$. $\rho^\star$ is like ρ in that, in any possible circumstances in which we could have determined the truth of ρ, we could determine the truth of $\rho^\star$;

and in any possible circumstances in which we could have determined the falsity of ρ, we could determine the falsity of ρ*; furthermore, in all remaining circumstances, such as those which by hypothesis actually obtain, we cannot determine the truth or falsity of either. The difference between ρ and ρ* is this. In circumstances of this third kind, ρ* is neither true nor false. Hence the need for circumspection.

Such is the kind of nonsense that would result from attempting to put our ineffable insight into words. What the Case for Anti-Realism is is a *realist* attempt to justify anti-realist circumspection. It is an attempt, as if from an infinitary standpoint, to reckon with and to insure against our finitude. There is nothing in the Case for Anti-Realism that an anti-realist can properly assent to. For instance, the Ignorance Claim, on an anti-realist conception, cannot be true at any level, for the reason given in the Ignorance Objection. Nor, for a similar but even more basic reason, can any proposition be neither true nor false. If a proposition is not true, then it is *ipso facto* false. (To hold back from saying that a proposition is either true or false is not to say that it is *neither*. In fact, in itself, it is not to say anything.) But although, as anti-realists, we cannot embrace any part of the Case for Anti-Realism, we are shown all of it. We are shown that our circumspection, whereby we refuse to assume without further ado that every proposition is either true or false, is justified. (We are *shown* that it is. We cannot say that it is. For we cannot say what justifies it. It follows that there may be nothing to distinguish our circumspection from mere reticence.)

I said at the beginning of this section that the examples I would be discussing had clear echoes in the earlier set-theoretical example. It might clarify matters to say how. Anti-realism is particularly compelling in the case of set-theoretical propositions, whose subject matter is essentially infinitary. Specifically, it is compelling in the case of universal generalizations about sets, our understanding of which would be utterly mysterious if they could be true without our being able to tell that they were. What anti-realism amounts to, in their case, is recoil from the possibility of an infinite coincidence: recoil from the possibility that every set has a property though there is no single (finite, accessible-to-us) reason why. To assume, uncritically, that a universal generalization about sets is either true or false, in other words that either every set conforms with the generalization or there is a counter-example, is to allow for just such a possibility. As before, however, there is no way of saying when it would be wrong to make this assumption. Only by *conceding* the possibility of an infinite coincidence can we admit that circumstances may arise in which there is neither a single reason why every set has a given property nor a counter-example. But this is precisely what we would be tempted to say if we tried to justify our circumspection. The picture is as follows, then. Self-conscious introspection on our understanding of set theory tempts us to say that sets, which form a unified domain conferring truth or falsity on every "infinitary" set-theoretical proposition, allow for infinite coincidences. This is therefore something we are shown. And our being shown this is a practical insight into how to regulate our mathematical practice. We know when to hold back from applying principles of classical logic. But we cannot say what justifies us in doing so.

Here, then, are further examples of things we are shown—on the supposition that anti-realism is correct. But is it? I have certainly not said enough to demonstrate that it is. Nor in fact shall I add to the little I have said. The arguments for anti-realism are familiar through the writings of Dummett and others (see the further reading at the end of this chapter), and in any case, I am less interested in defending anti-realism than in exploring its consequences. Still, it is clear from claims I have made elsewhere in this book that I have anti-realist sympathies. For example, when I was discussing the weak interpretation of 'can' at the end of Chapter Six, I claimed that we can know anything, in other words that we can know whether or not any representation is true. It follows from this claim that, given any proposition, until we are sure that we can determine its truth or falsity, we should hold back from saying that it is a representation (that is, from saying that it is either true or false).

—*"But why even say that it is a proposition? You have defined propositions to be just like linguistic representations except that the question of whether they are either true or false is left open. But unless that question can be settled, affirmatively, what remains?*

—*"Surely we can do justice to the general ideas behind anti-realism— roughly, that there can be no more to the meaning of expressions we use than is manifest in that use, and that our understanding must admit of public ratification—without acceding to any of this anti-realist paraphernalia. Why not just say the following? Associated with any meaningful*

declarative sentence is that circumscribed range of recognizable circum-
stances in which an utterance of it would be a true linguistic representa-
tion (its "truth conditions") and that circumscribed range of recognizable
circumstances in which an utterance of it would be a false linguistic rep-
resentation (its "falsity conditions"). Together these constitute the recog-
nizable circumstances in which an utterance of it would be any kind of
representation. In all other circumstances an utterance of it would be non-
sense, on the strict understanding of the term 'nonsense' that you have
appropriated in this book. So, for example, if somebody were to say, 'This
is green,' without indicating anything, he or she would have uttered non-
sense (or if not nonsense, then something recognizably false). But the same
would be true if somebody were now to say, 'Aristotle would have liked
chocolate.' For, provided that 'circumscribed' is understood in a suitably
restrictive sense, we can tell that none of the sentence's truth conditions
obtains. On this view, apart from representations—these being true or
false by definition—there is only nonsense. Propositions do not come into
it. Nor does anti-realism."—

But even on this view, there will be situations in which, granted
our finitude, we need to exercise anti-realist circumspection.
Consider the sentence, 'Humans will one day communicate with
aliens.' Suppose we fix its truth conditions as the obvious ones. And
suppose we fix its falsity conditions as those in which, by appeal to
general considerations of some specifiable kind, we can rule out
there ever being communication between humans and aliens.
Suppose, finally, that someone were now to utter the sentence. For
the sake of definiteness let me do so. Humans will one day communicate with aliens. Now: have I just said something either true or
false? The only way to answer this question (for now) is to wait and
see. Or at least, this is the only way to answer the question if we are
to do justice to the general ideas behind anti-realism, as you
claimed to be doing. While we are waiting, what option do we have
but to call my utterance a proposition, and to treat it with anti-realist circumspection?

—*"You misunderstand. I intended 'circumscribed' to be more restrictive*
than that. Truth conditions must not only be such that we can recognize
them when they obtain. They must be such that we can recognize whether
or not they obtain. The same goes for falsity conditions. I am prepared to
say, playing devil's advocate, that your utterance is nonsense. It would
have been different, of course, if you had specified a time limit, for instance

if you had said, 'Humans will communicate with aliens by the end of the next millennium.'"—

But suppose that humans *do* communicate with aliens by the end of the next millennium. Will that not mean that my utterance was true after all? Are you saying that something nonsensical can turn into a bona fide representation because of how things subsequently turn out?

—*"No. If humans communicate with aliens during the next millennium, we shall then be in a position to say, truthfully, 'It was true in the last millennium that humans would communicate with aliens.' The natural interpretation of this will be: 'Humans have communicated with aliens during this millennium.' But this will not confer sense on your utterance. Your utterance, the utterance you made just now, lacked sense. Nothing that happens subsequently can alter that, not even your explicitly conferring meaning on the sentence, 'Humans will one day communicate with aliens,' and then uttering it anew."*—

So really, on your view, my mistake was to talk about the "obvious" truth conditions for this sentence. On your view, since truth conditions must be such that we can recognize whether or not they obtain, and since the "obvious" truth conditions would satisfy as it were only half of this requirement, they are not truth conditions at all; I failed to give the words in my sentence a suitable meaning and ended up uttering nonsense.

—*"Yes, except that I am not sure that it is "my" view. I am playing devil's advocate. I claim only that the view is worth considering. What it is, in a way, is a radical variation on the theme of anti-realism which nevertheless has a non-anti-realist conclusion. We could call it "partial" realism. I think it would be instructive to see how the examples you have given of things we are shown, on the hypothesis that anti-realism is correct, fare on the hypothesis that partial realism is correct."*—

Very well; I shall leave it to you to round off this section by saying something about how partial realism would combine with the model I have been defending.

—*"The account, I take it, would have to go as follows. We are still shown that reality is completely determinate, its features fixed by a range of infinitary representations. And it is still true that what we, in our finitude, can understand includes nothing infinitary. On the anti-realist view, what we can understand are propositions, and our being shown that reality is completely determinate is our knowing when to hold back from say-*

*ing that one of them is either true or false. On the partial realist view,
what we can understand are representations, and our being shown that
reality is completely determinate is our knowing when to distinguish these
from certain kinds of nonsense. On the partial realist view, your utterance
of 'Humans will one day communicate with aliens' was nonsense (as was
your talk of the sentence's "obvious" truth conditions). There is no obstacle to our simply saying that the utterance was nonsense, any more than
there is to our saying that an utterance of 'Phlump jing ux' is nonsense.
Even so, there is a difference between your utterance and an utterance of
'Phlump jing ux'. This is a difference that is masked somewhat by the artificiality of talking about "fixing" truth conditions. We do not typically
"fix" truth conditions, or confer meanings—not in the sense of going
through some explicit procedure. Typically meaning is determined in a
much less direct way, by our linguistic practices. Now the nonsensicality of
your utterance, unlike the nonsensicality of an utterance of 'Phlump jing
ux', cannot be attributed to the fact that you were using words that lack
meaning: you were not. But nor can it be attributed to the fact that you
were using words in a combination that has never been subjected to any
explicit meaning-conferring process: that does not distinguish your utterance from the majority of utterances that make sense. It must rather be
attributed to the fact that nothing in our linguistic practices equips the
words you were using to work together in that way. And this is something
we recognize through due exercise of our understanding of the language.
Now our understanding of the language is inseparable from the temptation, on occasion, to misuse it and to think that we have uttered sense
when we have not. In particular, it is inseparable from the temptation to
use words in a way that would make sense only if we had access to the infinite. Your saying, 'Humans will one day communicate with aliens' was a
case in point. If we were to attempt to put into words the insight that
enables us to recognize this as nonsense, we would succumb to that* very
*same temptation. We would construe ourselves as having access to the
infinite, and we would construe your utterance as making sense, but sense
that we, in our finitude, could not grasp. Among the things we are shown,
then, is that no representation of ours can have as its content that humans
will one day communicate with aliens. We are* not *shown that no representation of ours can have as its content that phlump jing ux. 'Phlump jing
ux' does not have the right resonances for this. It is as if, in the case of your
utterance, but not in the case of an utterance of 'Phlump jing ux', we first
grasp its sense and then recognize this sense as "non"-sense for finite*

beings such as us. In fact, of course, there is nothing there to grasp. Nonsense is not a special kind of sense. It is lack of sense.

—*"That, I think, is the account you must give if partial realism is correct."*—

5

There are two final brief tasks for this chapter. I said at the beginning of the previous section that the examples I would be considering there of things we are shown would bring the discussion back to transcendental idealism. The first task is to substantiate this claim. This is relatively easy. Granted anti-realism, we are shown that what our representations answer to is limited by their finitary nature. This is idealism. But we are also shown that the limitation in question is transcendent, since if it were not—if it were itself part of what our representations answer to—then our representations would have to answer to what lies on the other side of the limits. This is transcendental idealism.

The second brief task is to relate what I have been arguing in this chapter to other Kantian concerns. I have talked briefly in earlier chapters about regulative ideals. These are concepts like that of perfection. We can never realize them, but we can come ever closer to realizing them and ought continually to strive to do so (at least granted certain aims). To this end we may enjoin ourselves to proceed *as if* we could realize them. To enjoin ourselves to proceed as if we could realize a regulative ideal is to frame what Kant calls a regulative principle. A regulative principle is any rule for directing our behaviour in accord with the supposition that some concept, which cannot in fact be applied to reality, can be.[12] One of Kant's central examples concerns the concept of the physical world, considered as a whole. For various reasons connected with his transcendental idealism, Kant thinks that there is no such thing as the physical world as a whole. There are only more or less inclusive tracts. Whatever we encounter in space and time, there is more to encounter. But by proceeding *as if* there were such a thing as the physical world as a whole, we are propelled to carry on, whenever

---

[12] Immanuel Kant, *Critique of Pure Reason*, A508–15/B536–43.

we have explored some limited tract, to explore further in pursuit of some overall systematic unity, thereby increasing our knowledge and understanding.[13]

There is a close link between regulative principles and showing, which is this. Often, given a regulative principle, the concept involved, that is the concept which cannot be applied to reality, has some infinitary aspect; and our knowing how to proceed in accord with the principle is ineffable knowledge. Whenever both of these things are true, attempting to put the knowledge into words is liable to involve treating the regulative principle as if it were, as Kant would say, "constitutive". In other words (telescoping certain complications due to the distinction between using words and mentioning them),[14] if the principle is to proceed as if such and such were the case, then what we are shown is that such and such *is* the case. Conversely, and for essentially the same reasons, our being shown that such and such is the case often sanctions our framing a regulative principle to proceed as if such and such *were* the case. 'Often' is the operative word. I shall not attempt to state any general guidelines in connection with this. Whether a good way to narrate our lives is to proceed as if we were ultimate constituents of reality; whether a good way to do set theory is to proceed as if there were a set of all sets; whether a good way to exercise anti-realist circumspection is to proceed as if there were propositions that were neither true nor false: these are questions that I shall leave open. In each case an affirmative answer has both explanatory and heuristic potential.[15]

Kant proceeds from his own account of regulative principles to broader metaphysical concerns in Part II of his *Critique of Pure Reason*. There he emphasizes the importance of pushing enquiry beyond where it is without trying to push it beyond where it can be, of exploring what is unknown without trying to explore what is unknowable, of proceeding *as if* ideals can be realized without supposing that they can. A careful balance needs to be struck. Kant tries to strike it by setting precise limits. He has a wonderful analogy to illustrate this.[16] He likens the knowable world to a surface,

---

[13] Ibid., A670–2/B698–700.

[14] See above, Chapter Seven, n. 22.

[15] In the case of set theory, for example, I am thinking of use of the Reflection Principle: see e.g. Rudy Rucker, *Infinity and the Mind*, pp. 50, 203, and 255 ff.

[16] Kant, *Critique of Pure Reason*, A759–62/B787–90.

which, like the surface of the earth, appears flat, so that, given our limited acquaintance with it, we cannot know how far it extends, though we know that it extends further than we have managed to travel: however, like the surface of the earth, it is in fact round, and once we have discovered this we can, even from our limited acquaintance with it, determine both its extent and its limits. But there is a problem with this. If we *can* only know how things are on the surface, then our knowledge is limited to two dimensions. This does not preclude our determining the extent of what we can know. But it does preclude our determining its limits, or even acknowledging that there are any. To do this we should need access to another dimension. Without that access we must regard the surface as finite but unlimited. Not that the details of the analogy matter. The point is the by now familiar one, that we have no way of acknowledging limits that separate off what we can know from an unknowable beyond. There *is* no unknowable beyond. There is nothing which, by its very nature, we cannot know. We have to say this. It sounds immodest. But it is just a matter of what makes sense. True modesty means focusing not on the distinction between what we can know and what we cannot, but on the distinction between what we do know and what we do not. There is more than enough in this latter distinction to check our hubris.

FURTHER READING

On the process of making narrative sense of one's life, see: John Campbell, *Past, Space, and Self*; Jonathan Glover, *I: The Philosophy and Psychology of Personal Identity*, especially Pt. II; Martin Heidegger, *Being and Time*; Genevieve Lloyd, *Being in Time*; Alisdair MacIntyre, *After Virtue*, especially ch. 15; Paul Ricoeur, *Time and Narrative*; Paul Standish, *Beyond the Self*, especially ch. 4; Charles Taylor, *Sources of the Self*, especially Pt. I; and Mary Warnock, *Imagination and Time*. Nietzsche's contribution to this discussion can scarcely be traced to any single work, but of especial importance, perhaps, is Friedrich Nietzsche, *The Gay Science*.

Most notable among the countless works of fiction that cast light on the process of making narrative sense of one's life is Marcel Proust, *Remembrance of Things Past*.

On the nature and identity of persons, with particular reference to Parfitian reductionism, see: Campbell, *Past, Space, and Self*, ch. 5; Quassim

Cassam, 'Kant and Reductionism'; Quassim Cassam, 'Reductionism and First-Person Thinking'; David Lewis, 'Survival and Identity'; Sydney Shoemaker, 'Critical Notice of Parfit's *Reasons and Persons*'; and Bernard Williams, 'Persons, Character and Morality', § II. See also David Wiggins, *Sameness and Substance*, ch. 6; and Bernard Williams, *Problems of the Self*, Essays 1–5.

On the idea that we exist only from our own point of view, see Jennifer Hornsby, 'Agency and Causal Explanation'.

On scepticism, see: Christopher Hookway, *Scepticism*; Barry Stroud, *The Significance of Philosophical Scepticism*; and Michael Williams, *Unnatural Doubts*.

On Gödel's theorem, see Michael Dummett, 'The Philosophical Significance of Gödel's Theorem'. Crispin Wright comments on Dummett's paper in 'About "The Philosophical Significance of Gödel's Theorem": Some Issues', to which Dummett himself replies in his 'Reply to Wright'. See also Daniel Isaacson, 'Arithmetical Truths and Higher-Order Concepts'.

On Dummettian anti-realism, see: Michael Dummett, 'Truth', 'The Reality of the Past', 'The Philosophical Basis of Intuitionistic Logic', and *Elements of Intuitionism*; see also Edward Craig, 'Meaning, Use and Privacy'; Keith G. Hossack, 'A Problem About the Meaning of Intuitionist Negation'; John McDowell, 'On "The Reality of the Past"'; John McDowell, 'Mathematical Platonism and Dummettian Anti-Realism'; Timothy Williamson, 'Never Say Never'; Crispin Wright, *Realism, Meaning and Truth*; and Crispin Wright, *Truth and Objectivity*.

Wittgenstein embraces a kind of anti-realism in the philosophy of mathematics: see *Remarks on the Foundations of Mathematics*. But there is controversy about where exactly he stands in relation to Dummettian anti-realism. For variously opposing views, see: Peter Hacker, *Insight and Illusion*, ch. 11, especially § 4; John McDowell, 'Following a Rule'; and Crispin Wright, *Wittgenstein on the Foundations of Mathematics*, especially Pt. II.

On regulative principles, see Dorothy Emmett, *The Role of the Unrealisable*; and Hans Vaihinger, *The Philosophy of 'As If'*.

CHAPTER ELEVEN

The only original rule of life today . . . [is] to learn to live and to die, and in order to be a man, to refuse to be a god.

(Albert Camus)

Introduction: The three principles which have been foundational to this enquiry are identified. (They are the same three principles as were originally identified in Chapter Nine, § 4.)

§ 1: The first principle, that we are finite, is discussed. Its relations with the Basic Assumption, and with what I called in Chapter Two the Engagement Principle, are considered.

§ 2: The second principle, that we are conscious of ourselves as finite, is discussed.

§ 3: The third principle, that we aspire to be infinite, is discussed. It is used to explain why certain ideals of representation, conation, and agency are values (for us). Three worries concerning this explanation are raised. The first is addressed straight away. Two are left outstanding.

§ 4: The first outstanding worry is addressed by means of a stipulation about the relationship between rationality and infinitude.

§ 5: The second outstanding worry is addressed in terms of a certain diagnosis. This results in further examples of things we are shown, having to do with the nature of value.

§ 6: The question is raised of what value our aspiration to be infinite itself has. This issues in certain suggestions concerning the relationship between our ineffable knowledge and God.

THREE principles have been foundational to this enquiry. They are:

We are finite.

We are conscious of ourselves as finite.

254 Points of View

We aspire to be infinite.

Had I been presenting my ideas *ordine geometrico*, these three principles might have served as axioms. Questions therefore arise concerning their meaning, their independence of one another, and their completeness. These questions lack the precision that they would have in a formal context. But they arise none the less.

(i) *Meaning*: What prior interpretation, if any, do the key terms in the three principles have?

In the case of the pronoun 'we', none. The principles themselves define who "we" are. But 'finite', 'conscious', et cetera do have a prior interpretation. This is determined partly by ordinary usage, partly by glosses that I have given in other chapters, partly by what I shall go on to say in this chapter. Even in their case, however, a significant factor in determining how they are ultimately to be interpreted is the role that they play in these three principles.

(ii) *Independence*: Is each of the three principles independent of the other two?

Clearly not. The first, clearly, is a direct consequence of the second. It is also a direct consequence of the third, if 'aspire to be' is understood as entailing 'are not (yet)'. Indeed on *some* ways of understanding 'aspire to be', the second principle is a consequence of the third. For our purposes these matters can be left unresolved.

(iii) *Completeness*: Are the three principles complete?

This question, even more than the other two, must, in an informal context of this kind, remain a vague one. This is because of the inherent vagueness in its two main parameters: what range of truths is in question; and how much can be taken for granted as underlying logic. Intuitively, though, it makes sense to ask whether anything else in this enquiry has been foundational in the same way as these three principles without being a consequence of them. The most obvious candidate is the Basic Assumption, the assumption that representations are representations of what is there anyway. I shall have more to say about this shortly. Another candidate is the proposition that we exist only from our own point of view. (I elaborated on this in Chapter Ten, but without ever establishing it, not in the sense of deriving it from something more basic.) I shall have more to say about this too.

The plan of the chapter is as follows. I shall begin by looking again at each of the three principles, partly with an eye to addressing some of the issues just raised. As I do this, I hope to provide further clarification, not only of the principles themselves, but also of the way in which they sustain our being shown things. This will lead in stages to a discussion of value. By the end of the chapter I hope to have established significant connections between this discussion and the rest of the enquiry.

1

We are finite.

Our finitude has many aspects. (See above, Chapter Seven, § 4.) One is that we are cast into a world which, though we depend upon it, does not depend upon us, a world which is there anyway. Another is that we have edges. In particular, we have spatio-temporal edges. Each of us has an incarnation. Each of us arrives in the world and departs from it. But we also have edges of a more metaphorical kind: cultural, emotional, psychological, sensory. In every one of these respects we find ourselves "here" rather than "there". Thus the different points of view from which we represent the world. It is a fundamental aspect of our finitude that we can produce representations that are perspectival.

We can also produce representations—indeed we can only produce representations—of what is there anyway. For we are cast into a world which is there anyway. And it is to this world that our representations answer.

Is the Basic Assumption a consequence of our finitude, then? Can the Basic Assumption, after all, be derived from something more basic, namely the first principle?

Yes and no. Yes, the Basic Assumption can be derived from the first principle, granted that "representations" in this discussion are understood to be "our" representations, that is representations that we are capable of producing. (This is a qualification that has been implicit throughout the enquiry: see for example Chapter Five, § 1.) But no, the first principle is not more basic than the Basic

Assumption. The very fact that the Basic Assumption can be derived from it serves to indicate how much is built into the notion of our finitude. We are finite because we are up against that which is other than us, and in common with which we are part of a unified, substantial, independent reality. In effect, the Basic Assumption and the first principle are two ways of saying the same thing. What each of them comes to is this. Our representations are the representations of finite beings.

That we exist only from our own point of view is a further variation on this theme, but it involves more. It involves, as well as our representations being the representations of finite beings, our being the creatures of our representations. Not only does this go beyond what is contained in the first principle, it goes beyond what is contained in the second and third. Does it therefore deserve to be singled out as an independent, fourth principle? And if so, does it further narrow down who "we" are?

Better to regard it as a kind of meta-level principle about the status of the other three, not so much a further narrowing down of who "we" are as an amplification on what it is for us to be who we are. To say that we exist only from our own point of view is to make a claim about the perspectival character of the other three principles. It is as if one were to add to Newton's three laws of mechanics a claim to the effect that they are from the point of view of an inertial frame (see Chapter Two, § 3). But there is the further complication in this case, unlike in the Newtonian case, that what one adds entails one of the principles and has additional implications for the other two. That we exist only from our own point of view is a further aspect both of what we are conscious of and of what we aspire to lose.

Closely related to this is the Engagement Principle, about which I have said very little since first introducing it back in Chapter Two. The Engagement Principle is the principle that all the representations that directly engage us are perspectival. My reason for accepting this is, in large part, that I regard it as a feature of the fact that we exist only from our own point of view. To justify this properly would require a far fuller discussion than I can embark upon now. I shall just state, sketchily and dogmatically, what I have in mind.

First, direct engagement is a matter of degree. A representation ρ *engages* a person A when ρ is part of a reason that A has for doing something. The more *directly* ρ engages A, the less its doing so depends on inference to other representations that engage *A*. Thus reconsider Mr Meanour. Both his knowledge that Mr Meanour was wanted by the police and his knowledge that *he* was wanted by the police engaged him. Both made him take steps to avoid arrest. But the former engaged him only when, and only because, he was able to infer the latter. It did not engage him while he was still unaware that he was Mr Meanour. The latter engaged him more directly.

Now the Engagement Principle is stated without regard to such gradation. In effect it is a piece of legislation. Its purpose is to constrain where any line shall be drawn between representations that count, and representations that do not count, as directly engaging any of us *simpliciter*. No representation is to count if it is absolute.

There is a parallel and closely related principle concerning conative states. Just as representations can engage us more or less directly, so too conative states can be more or less *basic*, where the basicness of a conative state is likewise a matter of how little inference is involved in its being a conative state. The parallel principle is that no conative state is to count as basic, *simpliciter*, if it has an absolute character. (I use the phrase 'has an absolute character' advisedly. The absolute/perspectival distinction itself applies only to representations, not to conative states. It does however have a clear analogue in the case of conative states. Mr Meanour was concerned that *he* should not be arrested. He was initially indifferent to the prospect that Mr Meanour should be arrested.) The possibility of conative states with an absolute character is not ruled out. A scientist may hope that a certain theory, couched in absolute terms, is true. But if he does, this will be because his hope is parasitic on another, more basic hope, say that he should become famous (this is *his theory*).

What then is the rationale for these two principles?

Precisely that we exist only from our own point of view. Given this, any conative state that does not have a perspectival character corresponding to the point of view in question—call it π—is parasitic on one that does. Similarly, *mutatis mutandis*, in the case of representations that engage us. Or so I claim. These claims need argument. But if I am right, then they give us reason to insist both that any basic conative state has a perspectival character corresponding at the very least to π and that all the representations that directly engage us are, at the very least, from π. This is related to what I said in the previous chapter about how living a life is inseparably linked to producing representations from π. Only representations from π can, in one very good sense of the word, *mean* anything to us.

2

We are conscious of ourselves as finite.

Given the equivalence of the first principle with the Basic Assumption, such self-consciousness connects with the fact that we know, or can know, that the Basic Assumption is true: as I emphasized in Chapter Eight, the unjustifiability of the Basic Assumption does not entail its unknowability. Our consciousness that we are finite is based, as is our knowledge of the Basic Assumption, on reflection, reflection which is itself an exercise of the fundamental ineffable knowledge which enables us to process what we know by virtue of being part of the world (Chapter Eight, § 4).

The second principle raises a number of deep paradoxes. The deepest of these is as follows. The fact that we are finite (the first principle) suggests that we cannot grasp the infinite. The fact that we are *conscious* of ourselves as finite (the second principle) suggests that we can grasp this fact. The paradox comes in running these together. Grasping this fact seems, absurdly, to involve grasping the infinite as something that we cannot grasp.

This paradox, like the Engagement Principle, deserves a far more extended discussion than I can give it here. In particular, much more needs to be said about how we are to understand talk of "the infinite". We should beware of thinking that there is nothing more to be said about this than that 'infinite' is the antonym of 'finite'. Talk of *"the* infinite" has connotations of unity that go beyond that fact in all sorts of ways. The worry here is not that talk of "the infinite" has a clear sense that remains to be determined. The worry is rather that it remains to be determined that talk of "the infinite" has a clear sense. My own view is that, in very many cases, it does not. In particular, I think we can resolve this paradox by simply denying that the expression 'the infinite', as it occurs in the statement of the paradox, denotes anything. These occurrences are nonsense.[1]

Still, they are nonsense of precisely the kind that results from

---

[1] As I have intimated, there is much more to be said about which uses of 'infinite' and its

our trying to express the inexpressible. Our self-conscious awareness of our own finitude arises from the reflective activation of ineffable knowledge which, were we to attempt to express it, would
involve us in thinking of ourselves as able to grasp that which is in
fact utterly beyond our finite grasp: as we would naturally say, "the
infinite". The paradoxes associated with the second principle, however satisfactory solutions of this kind may be, will continue to
gnaw for as long as we feel the urge to put all of our knowledge into
words.

3

We aspire to be infinite.

We rebel against our finitude. Though aware of that which
marks us as finite, we defy it, we struggle against it, and at times we
simply shy away from it. We fantasize about an infinitude whereby
what we will, what we know, and what is are all one—not in the
sense that they are all aligned (a kind of technophile's dream) but
in the much more radical sense that there is nothing to align. For an
infinite being, the very distinctions would collapse. As Descartes
puts it:

[God's] understanding and willing does not happen, as in our case, by
means of operations that are in a certain sense distinct from one another;
we must rather suppose that there is always a single identical and perfectly simple act by means of which he simultaneously understands, wills and
accomplishes everything.[2]

This is what we aspire to. But we aspire to more. Descartes's picture
of infinitude can be extended, in a way that is more reminiscent
perhaps of Spinoza.[3] On the extended picture infinitude not only
involves the collapse of distinctions between representation and
volition. It also involves the collapse of distinctions between repre-

---

cognates make sense and which do not. For one of the most important contributions to this
topic, see Ludwig Wittgenstein, *Philosophical Remarks*, § XII and pp. 304–14.

    [2] René Descartes, *Principles of Philosophy*, Pt. I, § 23. For echoes of the idea that this is
what we aspire to see Friedrich Nietzsche, *Thus Spoke Zarathustra*, Pt. II, 'Of Redemption'.
Cf. also Nietzsche's famous epigram 'To impose upon becoming the character of being—
that is the supreme will to power', in *The Will to Power*, § 617. But there is much in what I
am arguing that would be abhorrent to Nietzsche.

    [3] Baruch Spinoza, *Ethics*, Pt. I.

senter and represented, between willer and willed, between subject and object. We aspire to be all there is.

Fundamental to what we rebel against, therefore, is the recognition of that which is there anyway, that to which all our representations must answer. We are under a continual temptation to proceed as if we recognized no such thing. We are tempted, so far as is compatible with our knowing that this is impossible, to proceed as if our representations constituted reality, and to treat conditions of their existence, such as our knowing how to produce them, as conditions of reality itself. This is why we are tempted to treat that knowledge as itself representational. And this in turn helps to explain how we can make sense of our being shown things (Chapter Nine, §§ 3–4).

The third principle is constrained throughout by the second. Our aspiration to be infinite is constantly muted, modified, and mitigated by our knowledge that we are not—that we are irremediably finite. Often our aspiration takes the form of an urge to attain that which is perfectly attainable, but which involves our either superseding or minimizing certain aspects of our finitude. Our urge to excel in various ways is an example of this. So too is our urge to produce absolute representations. In Chapter Two, when discussing the significance of the question whether absolute representations are possible, I said that the main reason for its significance is our craving for infinitude. This was in the context of the idea that there is a regulative ideal of rational reflective self-understanding, such as an infinite being might have, which involves the production of absolute representations. Later, in Chapter Four, § 1 and again in Chapter Eight, § 4, I talked about why this ideal is an unrealizable one. Roughly, it involves conflicting elements of finitude and infinitude. There is further evidence for this in what I have just said. The very production of *representations* is a mark of finitude. Nevertheless, the production of representations that are absolute is a less severe mark of finitude than the production of representations that are from a point of view. (God has no point of view.) Our urge to produce absolute representations, which we can do, persists as part of our craving for infinitude, despite our knowledge that, even were we to succeed in satisfying our urge—nay, even were we to succeed in producing a complete description of reality in absolute terms—still we should unmistakably be betraying our finitude.

There is an irony here. This urge, which may in fact spur us on to produce absolute representations, is linked, through our aspiration to be infinite, to our being shown that absolute representations are not possible. But the irony is not a deep one. Even when we are tempted to say that absolute representations are not possible, this is because we are tempted to say that all our representations are from a transcendent point of view; and this, if it only made sense, would leave us free to produce representations that are *immanently* absolute, or in other words, putting to one side the nonsense of the transcendent/immanent distinction, representations that are absolute.

Let us return to the ideal of rational reflective self-understanding. I first mentioned this ideal, in Chapter Two, having argued that it is a desideratum, when producing a representation, to produce one whose best explanation vindicates it. (See § 5 in Chapter Two for definitions, details, and discussion.) There are all sorts of ways in which the best explanation of a representation may fail to vindicate it, even if the representation is true. The producer of the representation may not think it is true. More interestingly, the producer of the representation may think it is true, but only as a result of psychological or cultural forces that have no bearing on its truth. Self-deception and advertising are clear examples of what I have in mind. There is, however, a kind of explanation such that, if the best explanation E of a given representation ρ produced by a given person A is of this kind, then E cannot fail to vindicate ρ. E is of this kind, or E is *reflexive* as I shall say, if, according to E, A's own reason for accepting ρ is a result of rational self-conscious reflection on E itself. 'Rational' does crucial work here. As will become clear later in the chapter, there is no non-question-begging way of explicating it. But that does not worry me. This is not an exercise in analysis. The point is this. With respect to any representation whose best explanation is reflexive, explanation and vindication fully come together. The representation has a quality for which I think the most suitable word, with its Kantian resonances, is 'unconditionedness'.[4] Conversely, any representation whose best explanation is not

---

[4] For various uses of this word in Kant, see e.g. Immanuel Kant, *Critique of Pure Reason*, A307/B364, and *Groundwork of the Metaphysic of Morals*, p. 72 in the pagination of the original 2nd edition.

reflexive has a quality—conditionedness—whereby critical self-conscious reflection is always liable to unsettle any reason the producer has for accepting it, however mildly, however briefly, however easily the reason can be reinstated. (See again Chapter Two, § 5.) If a representation is conditioned in this way, this is a mark of the finitude of the producer. Our aspiration to be infinite includes an aspiration to produce unconditioned representations. And if I am right that an unconditioned representation is bound to be true, then we have here an account, not so much of why truth is valuable—there are accounts enough of this, in so far as it means that we are better off, *ceteris paribus*, accepting representations that are true—but of why truth is *a value* (for us).[5]

This link between unconditionedness and value can be extended. Much of what I have just been saying about representations has parallels in the case of conative states and deeds. An unconditioned representation, to repeat, is a representation whose best explanation is reflexive, in other words whose best explanation is such that, according to it, the producer of the representation accepts the representation because of rational self-conscious reflection on that very explanation. Provided that we can have reasons for the conative states that we are in, which only someone with a rather blunt philosophical axe to grind will deny that we can, and provided that we can have reasons for the things that we do, which we patently can, then parallel definitions of an unconditioned conative state and an unconditioned deed are available. An unconditioned conative state is a state whose "best" explanation (the best explanation of a conative state being the natural analogue of the best explanation of a representation) is such that, according to it, the subject is in the conative state as a result of rational self-conscious reflection on that very explanation. And an unconditioned deed is a deed whose "best" explanation (likewise) is such that, according to it, the agent performs the deed because of rational self-conscious reflection on that very explanation. These definitions, like the definition of an unconditioned representation, point to certain ideals which are by their very nature impervious to critical self-conscious reflection and our failure to achieve which is a further mark of our finitude. Our aspiration to be infinite includes an aspiration to achieve

---

[5] However, for important reservations about whether truth *is* a value (for us) see Jane Heal, 'The Disinterested Search for Truth'.

these ideals. That is, our aspiration to be infinite includes an aspiration to be in unconditioned conative states and to perform unconditioned deeds. As for what this comes to: just as I claimed that an unconditioned representation must be true, so too I claim that an unconditioned conative state must be targeted on what is right and an unconditioned deed must be that which is required.[6] And these claims, I believe, provide a significant gloss on why rightness is a value (for us) and on why doing what is required is a value (for us), just as the parallel claim for representations provided a gloss on why truth is a value (for us).[7]

I shall pursue these ideas in later sections. But first, I need to say some more about my use of 'rational'. Again it is clear that 'rational' is doing crucial work for me. Again I deny that there is any non-question-begging way of explicating it. And again I think I can do so with equanimity. Rationality for me is a very thick notion. It is constitutively linked to, and presupposes, the notions of truth, rightness, and requirement—the three *limit* notions, as I shall call them. But the point is not to define these three limit notions in terms of rationality, nor indeed to define rationality in terms of them. The point is to see how all four notions can work together to indicate ideals of representation, conation, and agency.

However, there are several worries that these remarks leave unaddressed. The first is that what I have been saying not only gives 'rational' a huge amount of work to do, it gives it a huge amount of inappropriate work to do. This worry arises from a view which I shall call *instrumentalism*. According to instrumentalism, it never makes sense to use 'rational' in connection with conative states and deeds in the way that I have been doing, just as (according to instrumentalism) it never makes sense to describe conative states and deeds themselves as rational; or at least, if it does make sense, it is never correct to do so. This has the consequence that either the notions of an unconditioned conative state and an unconditioned deed are ill-defined or else there simply, and trivially, are no such

---

[6] I toyed with putting 'morally required' here. But the notion I am after need not in fact be confined to morality. It is the notion that applies whenever one recognizes that there is something that one (simply) *must do*.

[7] The ideas in this paragraph reflect currents of thought in both Spinoza and Kant: see respectively Spinoza, *Ethics*, Pt. III, Prop. I; Pt. IV, Prop. LXI; and Pt. V, Prop. VI; and Kant, *Groundwork of the Metaphysic of Morals, passim*. Cf. also Romans 7: 15–25. For the idea that these ideals involve conflicting elements of finitude and infinitude, cf. G. W. F. Hegel, *The Encyclopedia of the Philosophical Sciences*, Pt. I ('Logic'), IV. ii, esp. §§ 44 ff.

things. The province of rationality, on this view, consists exclusively of representations (and perhaps more exclusively still of linguistic representations). Reasoning leads from premisses about how things are to conclusions about how things are. It *combines* with conative states, which act as raw input, to issue in various different kinds of raw output: decisions, choices, courses of action, and the like. Indeed the output, on any given occasion, may be a further conative state: if I want to achieve some goal, and know, as a result of reasoning, that it is impossible to do so without achieving some subsidiary goal, then it is likely that I shall end up wanting to achieve that subsidiary goal too. But the reasoning itself, ultimately, involves nothing but representations. In so far as one can reason about what to do, this is always a matter of determining the means to an end, never of determining the end itself. Thus instrumentalism.

Although I am opposed to instrumentalism, and although I think that the issue on which I am opposed to it is an important and substantive one, I am happy, for current purposes, to treat it as merely terminological. I am happy, in other words, to proceed as if my use of 'reasoning' and 'rational' is simply broader than that of the instrumentalist. Nothing that I want to say here, or have said in previous chapters, depends on its not being so. This is partly because I agree with the instrumentalist about another issue which is the focus of much debate: the issue, namely, of whether there can ever be a reason for a person to do anything that is not grounded in some conative state of the person. (See the further reading at the end of this chapter for contributions to this debate.) I, like the instrumentalist, think that there cannot be. So although I am prepared to apply the concept of rationality beyond the sphere of representations, I also insist that there is a question about what reason anyone has to be rational. And my answer to this question is, 'None, without some appropriate conative state.' Moreover, this is my answer to the question even when the notion of a reason is being construed normatively rather than explanatorily.

I should pause to say something about this distinction. Construed normatively, the notion of a reason is a matter of why someone *should* do something: 'The subtle beauty of this music gives me a reason to try to understand it.' Construed explanatorily, the notion of a reason is a matter of why someone *does* do something: 'My reason for trying to understand this music is that I am afraid of appearing uncultured.' I have not hitherto drawn this distinction because, whenever I have talked about reasons up to now, either the distinction has not mattered or the context has made it clear which of the two kinds of reason I have been talking about. The distinction did not matter, for instance, to my discussion of "the logical space of reasons" in Chapter Eight. This space is the same, and is populated by the same miscellany of things, whichever way the notion of a reason is construed. Again, the Engagement Principle can be defended on either construal (though the discussion above was couched more in terms of explanatory reasons).

So much, anyway, for the first worry. For my current purposes I think this is all I need to say in response to it. But there is a second worry, which the last few paragraphs have served only to exacerbate. It is this. I cannot just take for granted the connection between rationality and infinitude. So far I have simply asserted that our aspiration to be infinite includes an aspiration to produce unconditioned representations, and to be in unconditioned conative states, and to perform unconditioned deeds. There would have been significant grounds for worry about this anyway, but the last few paragraphs have exacerbated the worry, because the more work 'rational' has to do, the more content there is to this assertion, and the greater the need, therefore, to justify it.

This worry would be altogether less severe if I were prepared to concede that rationality is "inherently motivating", in other words if I were prepared to concede that we have reason to be rational irrespective of our conative states. For then I could say that being rational was doing what there was reason to do, a plausible enough mark of infinitude. Furthermore, my linking of rationality to the three limit notions, so far from being an obstacle to my making this concession, encourages it. For there exists a powerful intuition, shared by many, that these three notions themselves have something about them that is inherently motivating. (In the case of requirement, that seems to be part of our very understanding of the notion.) Yet precisely what I have denied, in line with the instrumentalist, is that anything is inherently motivating. I could lessen the force of this denial, with respect to the three limit notions, by construing them as thicker than they are generally taken to be, say as incorporating some specific and contestable conception of our well-being. But that would obviously just make the second worry more acute. In any case it would not properly address what now clearly emerges as a third worry: simply, that I am wrong to deny the existence of inherent motivation.

In the next two sections I shall try to develop my picture in such a way as to provide a satisfactory response to these two outstanding worries.

4

I begin with the first of them, the second worry overall. Why think that unconditionedness is a mark of infinitude?

It is comparatively easy to see the converse, namely that conditionedness is a mark of finitude. This is partly a matter of form. A conditioned representation, or a conditioned conative state, or a conditioned deed, is one that is vulnerable to critical self-conscious reflection, in the sense that coming closer to a grasp of its best explanation is liable to make the subject withdraw, repudiate, or regret it. Explanation and vindication in such a case have not fully come together. This indicates a kind of disjointedness, which in turn indicates finitude.

But in order to establish what I want, namely that unconditionedness is a mark of infinitude, I need to adduce considerations of content as well as considerations of form. I need to uphold the connection between rationality and infinitude. (Not that this connection is irrelevant to the converse. The fact that conditionedness is a mark of finitude is not *entirely* a matter of form. Implicit in the gloss I offered above was the qualification 'in so far as the subject is rational'. 'Critical', for that matter, could just as well have been replaced by 'rational'.)

The notion of rationality is itself partly formal, as indeed are the three limit notions with which, on my conception, it is linked: we think what is true when things are as we think they are, we want what is right when things should be as we want them to be, and we do what is required when we do as we must. And it is plausible that an aspiration to be infinite would include an aspiration so to think, so to want, and so to do. None the less, my very repudiation of inherent motivation prevents me from regarding these notions as purely formal. It also prevents me from identifying being rational with doing what there is reason to do. Until I say more, it is not clear what being rational, on my conception, amounts to. *Once* I say more, it needs to be clear how I maintain this connection between rationality and infinitude.

My approach to this difficulty, and thus to the first of the outstanding worries that I am addressing, will I am afraid be disappointing. I am simply going to let my conceptions of rationality and infinitude be determined by each other. More bluntly: I am simply going to stipulate that the connection between rationality and infinitude holds.

The reason I think I can do this with impunity is that, while each of the two notions is already sufficiently determinate for such a stipulation to have a substantial impact in shaping the conceptual structure that I am trying to erect, each of them is also sufficiently indeterminate for the stipulation not to do violence to how it is antecedently understood. I said at the outset that the nature of infinitude was to be fixed partly by what I would go on to say in this chapter. This is a case in point. Infinitude is now to be understood as embracing, in a way that I shall come back to in the final section, ideals of representation, conation, and agency. Conversely, rationality is to be understood as an aspect of what we crave.

One thing that follows from this, and very importantly follows from this, is that our own nature does fundamental work in fixing the content of many of my claims. It is as though we ourselves are part of the sense of the word 'infinite'.

This might be thought to jeopardize my account of who "we" are. For who "we" are is supposed to be determined, in part, by the principle that we aspire to be infinite. Yet the nature of that principle now looks as if it is determined, in part, by who "we" are.

In fact, there is nothing wrong with this. An entirely analogous situation arises, frequently, in the natural sciences. Some entity is singled out by the role it plays in some theory. Yet the nature of the entity does work in fixing the content of the theory. Further investigation of the entity leads to a better understanding of the theory. (A good example is the way in which transuranic elements were singled out by their position in the periodic table.) Likewise here. The true nature of rationality and the true nature of infinitude are *there to be discovered*. And the process of discovery is, for us, a process of self-discovery. In fact it is part of the overall project of making narrative sense of our lives (Chapter Ten, § 1). But what this means is that it is part of living. It is not something that can be accomplished in a work of philosophy.

This is why I said above that I was afraid my approach would be disappointing. I was not referring to the fact that the justification I was about to provide for the unjustified assertions I had been making was justification by decree. That, in itself, ought not to have been ground for disappointment. Justification by decree, where it is available, is as good as any other. But my approach does mean that the really substantive issues are somewhere off the page—and that they must remain somewhere off the page.

5

I turn now to the second outstanding worry. Is there not inherent motivation?

Call the belief that there is *externalism*, and the belief that there is not *internalism*. I shall not attempt to defend internalism. I am inclined to think that, with respect to finite beings in whom there is a distinction between representation and conation, internalism is part of the very logic of the distinction. For I am inclined to think that for there to be such a distinction *is* for each reason, within the range of the distinction, to be resoluble into two vectors, one of which is a conative state. But whether or not that is all there is to it, which I concede is a good deal less plausible when reasons are construed normatively than when they are construed explanatorily, the fact remains that there is a powerful intuition in favour of externalism. What I want to do in this section is to combat that intuition.

Notice first that there are many ways of supplementing internalism that come very close to doing justice to the externalist intuition. A large part of the externalist intuition is that there are inescapable reasons. The internalist can do justice to this by arguing that there are inescapable conative states. And there are many ways of doing that, because there are many senses of inescapability. A conative state may be inescapable in the sense that any being that is in any conative state at all must be in a state of that type. Or it may be inescapable in the less restrictive sense that this is true of any being in so far as the being is rational. Thus, for example, any being that wants anything at all may, in so far as it is rational, necessarily want freedom.[8] This would certainly be relevant to the current discussion if, as I believe, there is a deep connection between unconditionedness and freedom. Again, a conative state may be inescapable in the more contextual sense that any being capable of engaging in the kind of reflective enquiry in which we are now engaging must be in a state of that type—must, for example, value critical self-conscious reflection and be motivated to live, or to act, in a way that answers to it. This would be an interesting variation on the Kantian theme that a necessary condition of our engaging in certain kinds of enquiry is that we should accept certain things or operate with certain concepts. Each of these senses of inescapability admits of sub-division, according to the different ways in which the 'must' can be interpreted: as standing for logical necessity, or for biological necessity, or for psychological necessity, or for any of a large range of other kinds of necessity. And for any conative state that is inescapable in any of these senses there are reasons that are inescapable in some suitable corresponding sense.

Another sense of inescapability which is pertinent to our discussion is a relativized sense connected with criteria. A conative state is inescapable in this sense, or rather—the logic here is slightly different—a *type* of conative state is inescapable in this sense, *for some group*, if being in a state of that type is a defining characteristic of belonging to that group. Thus, for instance, the aspiration to be infinite is inescapable for us. (I leave open the question of what other kinds of inescapability the aspiration enjoys, if any.) As before, there is a corresponding sense of inescapability for reasons, or for types of reason. And as before, given any type of conative state that is inescapable in the former sense, there are types of reason that are inescapable in the latter, corresponding sense. In particular, given the connection between rationality and infinitude, there is an inescapable reason (for us) to pursue the unconditioned. This is another perfectly good sense of 'inescapable reason'.

But it is not good enough for the externalist. None of the senses that we have considered is good enough for the externalist. I have emphasized how close the internalist can come to doing justice to the externalist intuition, not because I want to suggest that it is easy for the internalist to win the externalist over, but, on the contrary,

---

[8] Cf. Bernard Williams, *Ethics and the Limits of Philosophy*, pp. 55 ff., with its slightly different focus on the question of what any rational *agent* necessarily wants.

because I want to make clear how recalcitrant the externalist is. Precisely the point is that, even with all of these more or less exacting senses of inescapability on offer, still the externalist demands more. The externalist intuition is that there is something about doing what is required, say, which provides us with reasons quite apart from any conative states that we are in, whatever the necessity of our being in those states. If it is only by being in a conative state of a certain type that we are motivated to do what we are required to do, then all that follows, according to the externalist, is that we are required to be in a conative state of that type.

What is needed, in order to combat the externalist intuition, is diagnosis. But diagnosis, of a familiar kind, I think there is. I argued in Chapter Nine, § 4 that one of the most basic things that we are shown is that we are infinite. Attempting to express *any* inexpressible knowledge means affecting a kind of infinitude and producing nonsense that accords with the affectation. But one mark of our finitude is the fact that there are certain things which, because of our aspiration to be infinite, are values for us. This is a mark of our finitude because our aspiration to be infinite is a mark of our finitude. I say this without prejudice as to whether or not the first principle is a consequence of the third. Even if it is not, the form that our aspiration actually takes, which includes, among other things, its being a conative state separable from any representation we produce, clearly marks us as finite. So the affectation that we are infinite includes a recoil from the fact that these things are values for us—but not from the fact that they are *values*, because precisely what grounds the affectation, namely our aspiration to be infinite, is also what grounds the values (what *makes* them values). The nonsense that this inclines us to produce is therefore that these things are not just values for us but are values *tout court*; that neither they, nor the reasons that they furnish us with, depend on any conative state of ours; that there is something about them that is inherently motivating. Such is the source of our externalist intuition. And just as one of the most basic things that we are shown is that we are infinite, so too, given this diagnosis, one of the most basic things that we are shown is that externalism is true. More specifically, we are shown that rationality and the three limit notions have something about them that is inherently motivating.

But we can go further. We are also shown that this inherent motivation has something about it that is absolute. Inherent motivation provides reasons that are not grounded in any conative states. So any being of whom it so much as makes sense to say that it has reasons, and hence any being of whom it so much as makes sense to say that it has a point of view, has *these* reasons. These reasons are not just reasons from this or that point of view.

Another way of looking at the matter is this. Whereas internalism entails that any evaluative representation must be from a point of view, the point of view of those in a certain conative state, externalism leaves open the possibility of evaluative representations that are absolute. (There are connections here, incidentally, with the Engagement Principle. But the connections are not as straightforward as they appear. Even if the Engagement Principle had been false—even if there had been a basic conative state with an absolute character—this would not have posed any threat to internalism. It could still have been true that any evaluative representation must be from the point of view of those in a certain conative state, even if the conative state had been this one, with its absolute character. Roughly: the absolute character of what was valued would not have belied the perspectival character of the evaluation.)

Externalism, I said, leaves open the possibility of evaluative representations that are absolute. But it does no more than leave open that possibility. There is no absurdity in supplementing externalism with considerations that close the possibility off. The fact that inherent motivation has something absolute about it does not mean that there cannot be independent reasons for thinking that any evaluative representation must be from a point of view. Moreover, within the ambit of what we are shown, it looks as if there are indeed independent reasons for thinking that any evaluative representation must be from a point of view. For after all, one of the things we are shown is that absolute representations are impossible.

However, the matter is not so simple. We are shown that absolute representations are impossible because we are shown that any representation must be from the point of view implicit in our understanding of our language, a point of view that survives even into our most inclusive outlook (Chapter Six, § 3; Chapter Seven, § 4; and Chapter Nine, § 4). That point of view provides a kind of anchorage for every aspect of our representations. But inherent motivation cannot be anchored in this way. The element of absoluteness in it precludes that. What is going on here?

One thing we do well to remind ourselves, before we go any further, is that what we are shown is nonsense. Properly to replace '*x*' in the schema '*A* is shown that *x*' is a quasi-artistic exercise in which one creates something out of the resonances of (mere) verbiage. There is no reason whatsoever why this should not sometimes involve making play with inconsistency. Certainly it is misguided to demand consistency, or some suitable surrogate for consistency, in what we are shown.

That said, part of what makes the exercise possible is the pretence that certain nonsense makes sense. It is *not* misguided to demand enough consistency, or enough of its surrogate, in what we are shown, to sustain this pretence.

I suggest that what is going on is this. We are shown that value *tout court*, the value of rationality and the three limit notions, is *beyond representation*. If every aspect of our representations has an anchorage which inherent motivation lacks, then inherent motivation is not an aspect of our representations. It is rather transcendent, just as (we are shown) the point of view from which we cannot help producing all our representations is transcendent.

More fully, what we are shown is the following.

The Transcendence of Unrelativized Value: Typically, when we determine the value of anything, we do so by exploiting our point of involvement *in mediis rebus* and representing the thing in a way that is thoroughly subjective. For instance, it is only from such a point of involvement that we can recognize the emotive differences (and perhaps also the moral differences) between contraception and abortion. When we view these things more objectively, we see only the smooth transitions that exist between them. For that matter, it is only from such a point of involvement that we can recognize the emotive differences between the rhythm method of birth control and infanticide; or between anything and anything. For after all, there exist smooth transitions between any one configuration of physical states and any other. However, the value that we thereby determine cannot, in the nature of the case, be value *tout court*. To determine *that* we must do exactly the opposite. We must step back *ex mediis rebus*. We must do this not so as to represent things in a way that is completely objective: representing things in a way that is completely objective is liable to make us lose sight of value altogether. Rather, we must do it so as to adopt an attitude towards the world which is not one of representation at all, an attitude towards it as a transcendent whole. We must become motivated by what is inherently motivating, and must look upon the world in the light of that.

This is what we are shown. (There are connections here with the views of the early Wittgenstein, who identified being "good" with adopting a certain attitude towards the world in which one views it as a whole: see above, Chapter Seven, § 2 and Chapter Nine, § 2.)[9] Our being shown this, like most cases of our being shown something, is based on a kind of understanding. It is based on our understanding of how to evaluate things *from our point of view*—of how to see things in the light of that which motivates us, not because it is inherently motivating, but because we have a fundamental craving for infinitude. This understanding, like the craving which underlies it, has nothing to answer to.

We can, when spelling out what we are shown, go some way towards acknowledging the fact that we have this craving. For we can add the following. (I say 'can'. I do not want to play down the extent to which attempting to express the inexpressible is a creative exercise. There is nothing sacrosanct about the nonsense that I am about to produce, any more than there was about the nonsense that I produced above. All I am doing is proffering a concatenation of ideas that I hope will strike suitable chords.)

Our Being Motivated by What is Inherently Motivating: What is inherently motivating is inherently motivating. Nevertheless, it is only because we are actually motivated by it, that is to say it is only because we have a craving for infinitude, that we adopt the required attitude towards the world. When we do, we determine, from our transcendent point of view, how the world as a whole, our world, shall appear. We turn the light of unrelativized value, which is not itself a part of the world, on to the world. And it is right that we should do so. In illuminating the world like this, we are not merely viewing it in one way rather than another. We are viewing it *aright*. But we are doing so of our own volition.[10]

---

[9] The relevant material in Wittgenstein is *Tractatus Logico-Philosophicus*, 6.4 ff.
[10] Cf. again ibid.

There are two things that I want to note parenthetically about this. The first is the hint of a combined "empirical externalism" and "transcendental internalism", of a piece with the combined empirical realism and transcendental idealism that we are also shown. But it is no more than a hint. The externalism that we are shown is uncompromising. It requires, even at the transcendent level, unconditional inherent motivation ("We are viewing the world *aright*"). The second thing I want to note is that, as with other things that we are shown, this externalism may furnish us with a powerful regulative principle (see Chapter Ten, § 5): to proceed as if any value that depends on our aspiration to be infinite depends on nothing. Given how deep our aspiration is, and given how important it is to our identity, we may find that following such a principle is one good way of being true to ourselves.

6

Our aspiration to be infinite lies at the very roots of what is of value for us. How then is the aspiration itself to be evaluated? Is it a good thing or a bad thing?

There are many ways, obviously, of refining this question. But I think it is a legitimate question for all that. My attitude towards it may appear to be one of ambivalence. On the one hand I have repeatedly associated our aspiration with temptations to which we are subject and confusions to which we are prone. I seem to be castigating it as a bad thing. Indeed I did say at the end of Chapter Nine that it would have been better if we had not had the aspiration. On the other hand, by linking value with infinitude as I have done in this chapter, and by emphasizing the way in which impossible goals can serve as regulative ideals, I seem to be championing our aspiration as a good thing.

A third possibility, of course—a possibility to which my rooting of value in our aspiration might even be thought to commit me—is that in itself it is neither a good thing nor a bad thing, just some kind of brute datum. However, I want to dismiss this third possibility straight away. It is true that I have rooted value in our aspiration. But that does not prevent the aspiration itself from being good or bad, even in terms of the value so rooted. There is no reason whatsoever why evaluation should not be directed at its own source. An ambitious person may delight at the machinations whereby her very ambition contributes to its own fulfilment. An insomniac may despair at the way in which his longing for sleep keeps him wretchedly awake. I think our aspiration to be infinite *is* either good or bad.

But before I say which, I want to draw a distinction. Whenever I have referred to the third principle, I have done so in these terms: I have spoken of our aspiration to be infinite. At other times, for instance when I first alluded to these ideas in Chapter Two and several times recently, I have spoken of our craving for infinitude. I may have given the impression that I take these to be entirely equivalent. I do not. I take the former to be a corruption of the latter. (This is not to deny that our aspiration to be infinite *is* our craving for infinitude. I am quite happy to say that it is; but only in the sense in which the pile of ashes in the urn over there is Uncle George.) I have not drawn this distinction before now, because nothing I have said before now has turned on the fact that our aspiration is a corruption. But it is, and in so far as it has an incorrupt counterpart, either as a historical fact or merely as an idealization, then this distinction is crucial to the question that we are now considering. Our aspiration to be infinite is emphatically and primordially bad. Its incorrupt counterpart is (was? would be? would have been?) good.[11]

These are large claims. I cannot fully expound them now. But I can state briefly what I have in mind.[12] Infinitude, according to my earlier stipulation, includes ideals of representation, conation, and agency. These are regulative ideals involving unconditionedness. To satisfy them would mean thinking what is true, wanting what is right, and doing what is required. It would mean being perfectly rational. A craving for infinitude, in an incorrupt form, would be largely a craving for the instantiation of such ideals. This would make it something good, *by its own lights*. It is rational to want to be rational; or, more generally, to want rationality to be instantiated. But the aspiration to be infinite has a different focus. It includes the aspiration to be rational, but it includes it as a residue within the distorted aspiration to be (so to speak) rationality itself. Our crav-

---

[11] Cf. Charles Taylor, *Sources of the Self*, pp. 137 ff.; and Dorothy Emmett, *The Role of the Unrealisable*, pp. 74–5.

[12] At various points in what follows, cf. Spinoza, *Ethics*, Pts. IV and V.

ing for infinitude has a perspectival character corresponding to the
point of view from which alone we exist. (See the remarks on the
Engagement Principle in the first section of this chapter.) When the
craving is distorted, this perspectival character is turned in on itself
in such a way that the craving becomes an aspiration *that we alone
exist*—or, in its most distorted form, that the subject alone exists. It
becomes the aspiration to be a complete self-sufficient unconditioned whole, to be that which the craving for infinitude is a craving for. Whereas the incorrupt craving for infinitude would be
essentially expansive, leading the subject to try to situate itself within the infinite whole, the aspiration to be infinite is essentially inert,
leading the subject to try to situate the infinite whole within itself.
And, again by its own lights, it (the aspiration to be infinite) is bad.
There is an irrationality in wanting to be that which makes anything rational. It is a revolt, and an offence, against that which truly
makes anything rational: rationality itself.

Our aspiration to be infinite is bad, pervasive, and deep. Little
else, I suggest, has quite the same significance in shaping our lives.
Yet when I said at the end of Chapter Nine that it would have been
better if we had not had this aspiration, I did so rather pusillani-
mously. I immediately went on to say that the sense in which this
was true was a hollow sense having little purchase on us. Should I
not have been more forthright?

No. Regrettably no. Our aspiration is bad in much the same way
in which evil is bad. *That* it is bad has little purchase on us because
it has little or no empirical content. That it *exists* has huge empirical content. But we have hardly any more idea in the latter case
than we have in the former what the alternative would have been
like. We can scarcely so much as think about ourselves without this
aspiration. It is not as if, by means of some simple resolution, we
can stop aspiring to be infinite, any more than we can, by means of
some simple resolution, eliminate evil. Our aspiration is something
that we have to *come to terms with*.

This is part of our having to come to terms with our finitude.
And this in turn is part of our having to learn how to be finite. The
phrase 'learn how to be finite' sounds odd in connection with us,
given that finite is what we already inescapably are. But we can be
finite in different ways, some of which are better than others: our
aspiration to be infinite is itself a testament to this. Learning how
to be finite is learning how best to be finite. (The phrase 'learn how

to do *x*' is like the phrase 'know how to do *x*'. It is used against a background of presupposed goods: see Chapter Eight, § 1.) Of course, if what I have been saying in the latter part of this chapter is right, learning how to be finite is a continual process which we have no reason to suppose that we shall ever complete or even come close to completing.

Knowing how to be finite, the desired outcome of this process, is a paradigm of ineffable knowledge. It has nothing to answer to. It is knowledge of how to be finite *in accord with our craving for infinitude*. But there is no independent right or wrong about it. There is no intrinsic propriety about this way of being finite.

Reflective activation of this ineffable knowledge, in so far as we can achieve it, leads to our being shown that we are infinite. Our being shown that we are infinite is thus an aspect of our coming to terms with the fact that we are finite. It can help us to curb our aspiration *not* to be finite. This was one of the ironies that I mentioned when I first introduced these ideas in Chapter Nine, § 4.

Our being shown that we are infinite involves our being shown that the infinite exists. Our being shown that the infinite exists suggests that we might also be shown that God exists. (Our craving for infinitude is a craving for God.) I think we *are* shown that God exists. And I think our being shown that God exists can further help us in learning how to be finite. This has no implications, however, for whether God does exist. The phrase 'God exists' in the sentence 'We are shown that God exists' is a piece of nonsense. How this piece of nonsense is to be assessed in other contexts, and in particular what kind of sense we are to make of it—what kind of sense we *can* make of it—are the vast, perplexing questions that they have always been.

There are those, familiarly, who have thought that, on one way of making sense of the claim that God exists, it admits of an ontological proof: existence is a perfection that God cannot lack.[13] Others, not always intentionally, have suggested that, on that same way of making sense of the claim that God exists, it admits of an ontological *dis*proof: existence is an imperfection that God cannot have. As it were, there can be no such "thing" as God: God is too big for mere existence. Thus Wittgenstein writes in the *Tractatus*

---

[13] e.g. René Descartes, *Meditations on First Philosophy*, V.

that "God does not reveal himself *in* the world."[14] And Murdoch writes:

No existing thing could be what we have meant by God. Any existing God would be less than God. An existent God would be an idol or a demon... God does not and cannot exist.[15]

Murdoch's main point in this passage, however, is not this. Her main point comes in the next sentence: 'What led us to conceive him *does* exist . . .' I agree. I would link this to my claim that we are shown that God exists. And I would urge us, in the same way that Kant urged us, to adopt a regulative principle to proceed as if God exists.[16] This principle is a device which, like any other, indeed more than any other, is subject to abuse. But it answers in a way that nothing else answers to something deep within our finitude. It is a device which we would be free to abandon if ever we knew how to be finite. While we are still learning, however, it is our only way of sustaining *hope*: the hope that we *can* still know how to be finite; the hope that we have not, by ignoring what is true, by abhorring what is right, and by failing to do what we are required to do, irrevocably closed off the very possibilities of infinitude that we crave. To proceed as if God exists is to proceed as if these possibilities can never be closed off. It is to proceed as if what ultimately matters enjoys a kind of infinite resilience.

In so far as there is a distinction between believing *that God exists* and believing *in God*, adopting this regulative principle is a way of believing in God. Believing in God helps us to come to terms with our own finitude. It may also help us to come to terms with the finitude of everything else. That is, it may help us to come to terms with the fact that there is no such thing as God. If so, then we are left with a chilling paradox. Not only is there reason to believe in God even if God does not exist. There may be reason to believe in God *because* God does not exist.

---

[14] Wittgenstein, *Tractatus*, 6.432, his emphasis.
[15] Iris Murdoch, *Metaphysics as a Guide to Morals*, p. 508. In the quotation that follows, her emphasis.
[16] Immanuel Kant, *Critique of Practical Reason*, Pt. I, Bk. II, ch. 2, § v.

FURTHER READING

Much of this chapter is derived from my 'On There Being Nothing Else to Think, or Want, or Do', and *The Infinite*, ch. 15. I should like to thank the editors and publisher of *Essays for David Wiggins* for permission to re-use material from the article, and Routledge for permission to re-use material from the book.

Of general relevance to the chapter are: Albert Camus, *The Rebel*; James Edwards, *Ethics Without Philosophy*; Martin Heidegger, *Being and Time*; Luce Irigaray, *Elemental Passions*, especially §§ XI and XIV; Luce Irigaray, 'Divine Women'; Karl Jaspers, *The Perennial Scope of Philosophy*; Søren Kierkegaard, *The Sickness Unto Death*; Emmanuel Levinas, *Totality and Infinity*; Iris Murdoch, *The Sovereignty of Good*; Iris Murdoch, *Metaphysics as a Guide to Morals*; Thomas Nagel, *The View From Nowhere*, chs. 8–9; Jean-Paul Sartre, *Being and Nothingness*; Paul Standish, *Beyond the Self*; and David Wiggins, *Needs, Values, Truth*.

On the paradoxes associated with our self-conscious awareness of our own limitations, see Graham Priest, *Beyond the Limits of Thought*.

A kind of instrumentalism is espoused by David Hume in *A Treatise of Human Nature*, and in *Enquiry Concerning the Principles of Morals*. It is rejected both by Aristotle, in *Nicomachean Ethics*, and by Immanuel Kant, in *Groundwork of the Metaphysic of Morals*. For more modern contributions to this debate, see Martin Hollis, *The Cunning of Reason*; and Joseph Raz (ed.), *Practical Reasoning*.

For a defence of internalism, see Bernard Williams, 'Internal and External Reasons'. John McDowell comments on Williams's paper in 'Might There Be External Reasons?', to which Williams himself replies, in J. E. J. Altham and Ross Harrison (eds.), *World, Mind, and Ethics*, pp. 186–94. See also: Philippa Foot, 'Morality as a System of Hypothetical Imperatives', to which John McDowell replies in 'Are Moral Requirements Hypothetical Imperatives?'; Michael Smith, *The Moral Problem*; and Michael Smith, David Lewis, and Mark Johnston, 'Dispositional Theories of Value'.

GLOSSARY

Each definition is followed by the chapter and section in which it first occurs. 'Iff' abbreviates 'if and only if'.

An outlook is **Absolute** iff it does not exclude any other possible outlook (in a sense of exclusion discussed in Chapter Five). Equivalently, an outlook is Absolute iff the representations produced in accord with it may be absolute (Chapter Five, § 1).

A representation is **absolute** iff it is from no point of view (Chapter One, § 1). Equivalently, a representation is absolute iff it can be integrated by simple addition with any other possible representation (Chapter One, § 3). See Chapter Five, § 1 for discussion of how the Basic Argument itself further clarifies what an absolute representation is.

The **Basic Argument** is the argument given in Chapter Four for the possibility of absolute representations (Chapter Four, § 2).

The **Basic Assumption** is the assumption on which the Basic Argument rests, that representations are representations of what is there anyway (Chapter Four, § 4).

The **best** explanation of a representation is a true interpretative explanation of it which is superior to any other true interpretative explanation of it (Chapter Two, § 5).

A **conception** of something is a set of true representations concerning that thing (Chapter Four, § 3).

A representation is **conditioned** iff it is not unconditioned (Chapter Eleven, § 3). Parallel definitions are available of a conditioned conative state and a conditioned deed.

The **content** of a representation is how things must be if it is true (Chapter One, § 3).

A state of knowledge is **effable** iff it is a representation (Chapter Seven, § 3). 'Expressible' and 'representational' are used as synonyms for 'effable'.

Empirical idealism is idealism with the rider that the dependence involved is immanent (Chapter Six, § 1).

To **endorse** a representation is to produce another representation with the same content as it (Chapter One, § 3).

To **endorse** a representation **by simple repetition** is to endorse it by producing another representation of the same type as it (Chapter One, § 3).

The **Engagement Principle** is the principle that all the representations that directly engage us are perspectival (in a sense of direct engagement discussed in Chapter Eleven) (Chapter Two, § 2).

The **Fundamental Principle** is the principle that, given any pair of true representations, it is possible to produce a true representation that weakly entails each of them (Chapter Two, § 1).

Idealism is the view that some aspect of the form of that to which our representations answer depends on some aspect of the representations (Chapter Six, § 1).

Something is **immanent** iff it is in the domain of a quantifier that can appear in one of our representations (Chapter Five, § 8).

Two points of view are **incompatible** iff no representation can be produced from both of them (Chapter One, § 3).

Indirectly to endorse a representation is to produce another representation that weakly entails it (Chapter One, § 4).

Indirectly to integrate two representations is to produce a third representation that weakly entails each of them (Chapter One, § 4).

A state of knowledge is **ineffable** iff it is not a representation (Chapter Seven, § 3). 'Inexpressible' and 'non-representational' are used as synonyms for 'ineffable'.

A representation is **inherently perspectival** iff it is from a point of view such that there could not be a representation with the same content as it that was not also from that point of view (Chapter One, § 4).

To **integrate** two representations is to produce a third representation whose content is the product of theirs (Chapter One, § 3).

To **integrate** two representations **by simple addition** is to integrate them by producing a representation which is the conjunction of two representations of the same types as theirs (Chapter One, § 3).

An explanation of a representation (that is to say, an explanation of its occurrence) is **interpretative** iff it includes an explanation of why the producer of the representation accepts it (Chapter Two, § 5).

Nihilism is the rejection of the Basic Assumption (Chapter Five, § 7).

A representation is **objective** iff it is from no point of involvement (Chapter One, § 1). See the diagram at the end of this glossary for an illustration of the relationship between the objective/subjective distinction and the absolute/perspectival distinction.

The **Opposition Argument** is the argument given in Chapter Five for the impossibility of absolute representations (Chapter Five, § 1).

An **outlook** is a way of seeing the world (Chapter Five, § 1).

The **Outlook Assumption** is the assumption on which the Opposition Argument rests, that to represent the world in accord with an outlook is to represent it from a point of view (Chapter Five, § 1).

An outlook is **Perspectival** iff there is some other possible outlook that it excludes (in a sense of exclusion discussed in Chapter Five). Equivalently, an outlook is Perspectival iff the representations produced in accord with it must be perspectival (Chapter Five, § 1).

A representation is **perspectival** iff it is from a point of view (Chapter One, § 1). Equivalently, a representation is perspectival iff there is some other possible representation with which it cannot be integrated by simple addition (Chapter One, § 3).

A **point of involvement** is a point of view defined in terms of concerns, interests, or values (Chapter One, § 1).

A **point of view** is a location, in the broadest possible sense (Chapter One, § 1).

A state of knowledge is **practical** iff it is not propositional (Chapter Eight, § 1).

A **proposition** is just like a linguistic representation except that the question of whether it is true or false is left open (Chapter Ten, § 4).

A state of knowledge is **propositional** iff it is knowledge that something is the case and the canonical evidence for the knower's being in the state includes the knower's asserting that this thing is the case (Chapter Eight, § 1).

A representation is **radically perspectival** iff it is from a point of view such that there could not be another representation of the same type as it that was not also from that point of view (Chapter One, § 3).

A **range** of points of view is a maximal class of points of view any two of which are incompatible (where the maximality of the class means that no point of view outside the class is incompatible with each of those in it) (Chapter Four, § 3).

An explanation of a representation (that is to say, an explanation of its occurrence) is **reflexive** iff, according to it, the producer of the representation accepts the representation as a result of rational self-conscious reflection on that very explanation (Chapter Eleven, § 3).

A **regulative principle** is a rule for directing our behaviour in accord with the supposition that some concept, which cannot in fact be applied to reality, can be (Chapter Ten, § 5).

A **representation** is anything which has content and which, because of its content, is either true or false (Chapter One, § 2).

For *A* to be **shown** that *x* is for *A* to have ineffable knowledge and for *x* to be what results when an attempt is made to put this knowledge into words (Chapter Seven, § 3, reinforced in the Interlude between Chapters Nine and Ten).

A representation is **subjective** iff it is from a point of involvement (Chapter One, § 2). See the diagram at the end of this glossary for an illustration of the relationship between the objective/subjective distinction and the absolute/perspectival distinction.

One explanation is **superior to** another iff it better conforms to a paradigm involving maximum reflection and minimum perspective (Chapter Two, § 5).

To **supersede** a range of points of view is to produce a representation that is not from any point of view in the range (Chapter Four, § 3).

Something is **transcendent** iff it is not immanent (Chapter Five, § 8).

Transcendental idealism is idealism with the rider that the dependence involved is transcendent (Chapter Six, § 1).

The **type** of a representation is the role it must play in the psychology of its producer if it expresses a belief of its producer (Chapter One, § 3).

A representation is **unconditioned** iff its best explanation is reflexive (Chapter Eleven, § 3). Parallel definitions are available of an unconditioned conative state and an unconditioned deed.

We are all and only those beings who are finite, who are self-consciously finite, and who aspire to be infinite (Chapter Nine, § 4).

One representation **weakly entails** another iff the latter is a consequence of the former (in a sense of consequence that remains undefined: see the discussion immediately preceding the definition in Chapter One) (Chapter One, § 4).

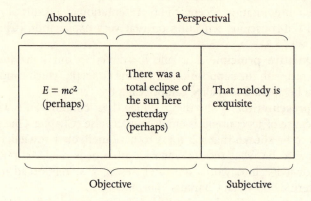

Diagram illustrating the relationship between the objective/
subjective distinction and the absolute/perspectival
distinction

BIBLIOGRAPHY

Allison, Henry E., *Kant's Transcendental Idealism: An Interpretation and Defense* (New Haven, Conn.: Yale University Press, 1983).

Alston, William P., 'Ineffability', *Philosophical Review* **65** (1956).

Anscombe, G. E. M., *An Introduction to Wittgenstein's Tractatus* (London: Hutchinson, 1959).

Aristotle, *Nicomachean Ethics*, trans. J. A. K. Thomson (Harmondsworth: Penguin, 1955).

Ayer, A. J., *The Problem of Knowledge* (Harmondsworth: Penguin, 1956).

Barwise, Jon, and Perry, John, *Situations and Attitudes* (Cambridge, Mass.: MIT Press, 1983).

Bell, David, 'The Art of Judgement', *Mind* **96** (1987).

Bernstein, Richard J., *Beyond Objectivism and Relativism: Science, Hermeneutics, and Praxis* (Oxford: Basil Blackwell, 1983).

Black, Max, *A Companion to Wittgenstein's 'Tractatus'* (Cambridge: Cambridge University Press, 1964).

Blackburn, Simon, 'Enchanting Views', in Peter Clark and Bob Hale (eds.), *Reading Putnam* (Oxford: Basil Blackwell, 1994).

Bolton, Derek, 'Life-form and Idealism', in Godfrey Vesey (ed.), *Idealism Past and Present* (Cambridge: Cambridge University Press, 1982).

Brandom, Robert, 'Points of View and Practical Reasoning', *Canadian Journal of Philosophy* **12** (1982).

Brewer, Bill, 'Compulsion by Reason', *Proceedings of the Aristotelian Society* Supp. Vol. **69** (1995).

Broad, C. D. 'Ostensible Temporality', reprinted in Richard M. Gale (ed.), *The Philosophy of Time: A Collection of Essays* (Brighton: Harvester Press, 1968).

Brueckner, Anthony, 'Brains in a Vat', *Journal of Philosophy* **83** (1986).

Campbell, John, *Past, Space, and Self* (Cambridge, Mass.: MIT Press, 1994).

Camus, Albert, *The Rebel*, trans. Anthony Bower (Harmondsworth: Penguin, 1971).

Cantor, Georg, *Gesammelte Abhandlungen Mathematischen und Philosophischen Inhalts*, ed. E. Zermelo (Berlin: Springer, 1932).

Carruthers, Peter, *The Metaphysics of the Tractatus* (Cambridge: Cambridge University Press, 1990).

Cassam, Quassim, 'Kant and Reductionism', *Review of Metaphysics* **43** (1989).

—— 'Reductionism and First-Person Thinking', in David Charles and Kathleen Lennon (eds.), *Reductionism, Explanation, and Realism* (Oxford: Oxford University Press, 1992).

Cavell, Stanley, 'The Availability of Wittgenstein's Philosophy', reprinted in *Must We Mean What We Say?* (Cambridge: Cambridge University Press, 1976).

Chang, Jung, *Wild Swans: Three Daughters of China* (London: Flamingo, 1993).

Charles, David, 'Supervenience, Composition, and Physicalism', in David Charles and Kathleen Lennon (eds.), *Reduction, Explanation, and Realism* (Oxford: Oxford University Press, 1992).

—— and Lennon, Kathleen (eds.), *Reduction, Explanation, and Realism* (Oxford: Oxford University Press, 1992).

Cooper, David E., 'Ineffability', *Proceedings of the Aristotelian Society* Supp. Vol. **65** (1991).

Craig, Edward, *Knowledge and the State of Nature: An Essay in Conceptual Synthesis* (Oxford: Oxford University Press, 1990).

—— 'Meaning, Use and Privacy', *Mind* **91** (1982).

—— 'The Practical Explication of Knowledge', *Proceedings of the Aristotelian Society* **87** (1986–7).

Crane, Tim and Mellor, D. H., 'There is No Question of Physicalism', *Mind* **99** (1990).

Crowther, Paul, *The Kantian Sublime: From Morality to Art* (Oxford: Oxford University Press, 1989).

D'Agostino, Fred, 'Transcendence and Conversation: Two Concepts of Objectivity', *American Philosophical Quarterly* **30** (1993).

Dancy, Jonathan, *Moral Reasons* (Oxford: Basil Blackwell, 1993).

Davidson, Donald, 'On Saying That', reprinted in *Inquiries Into Truth and Interpretation* (Oxford: Oxford University Press, 1984).

—— 'On the Very Idea of a Conceptual Scheme', reprinted in *Inquiries Into Truth and Interpretation* (Oxford: Oxford University Press, 1984).

—— 'Quotation', reprinted in *Inquiries Into Truth and Interpretation* (Oxford: Oxford University Press, 1984).

Davies, Martin, 'Tacit Knowledge and Subdoxastic States', in Alexander George (ed.), *Reflections on Chomsky* (Oxford: Basil Blackwell, 1989).

Deleuze, Gilles, *The Logic of Sense*, trans. Mark Lester and Charles Stivale and ed. Constantin V. Boundas (New York: Columbia University Press, 1990).

Dennett, Daniel, 'Styles of Mental Representation', *Proceedings of the Aristotelian Society* **83** (1982–3).

Derrida, Jacques, *Margins of Philosophy*, trans. Alan Bass (Brighton: Harvester Press, 1982).

Descartes, René, *Discourse on the Method*, in *The Philosophical Writings*, vol. i, trans. John Cottingham, Robert Stoothoff, and Dugald Murdoch (Cambridge: Cambridge University Press, 1985).

—— *Meditations on First Philosophy*, in *The Philosophical Writings*, vol. ii, trans. John Cottingham, Robert Stoothoff, and Dugald Murdoch (Cambridge: Cambridge University Press, 1984).

—— *Principles of Philosophy*, in *The Philosophical Writings*, vol. i, trans. John Cottingham, Robert Stoothoff, and Dugald Murdoch (Cambridge: Cambridge University Press, 1985).

Diamond, Cora, 'The Face of Necessity', reprinted in *The Realistic Spirit: Wittgenstein, Philosophy, and the Mind* (Cambridge, Mass.: MIT Press, 1991).

—— *The Realistic Spirit: Wittgenstein, Philosophy, and the Mind* (Cambridge, Mass.: MIT Press, 1991).

Dummett, Michael, *Elements of Intuitionism* (Oxford: Oxford University Press, 1977).

—— *Frege: Philosophy of Language*, 2nd edn. (London: Duckworth, 1980).

—— *The Logical Basis of Metaphysics* (London: Duckworth, 1991).

—— 'More About Thoughts', reprinted in *Frege and Other Philosophers* (Oxford: Oxford University Press, 1991).

—— 'The Philosophical Basis of Intuitionistic Logic', reprinted in *Truth and Other Enigmas* (London: Duckworth, 1978).

—— 'The Philosophical Significance of Gödel's Theorem', reprinted in *Truth and Other Enigmas* (London: Duckworth, 1978).

—— 'Realism and Anti-Realism', in *The Seas of Language* (Oxford: Oxford University Press, 1993).

—— 'The Reality of the Past', reprinted in *Truth and Other Enigmas* (London: Duckworth, 1978).

—— 'Reply to McGuiness', in Brian McGuiness and Gianluigi Oliveri (eds.), *The Philosophy of Michael Dummett* (Dordrecht: Kluwer Academic Publishers, 1994).

—— 'Reply to Wright', in Brian McGuiness and Gianluigi Oliveri (eds.), *The Philosophy of Michael Dummett* (Dordrecht: Kluwer Academic Publishers, 1994).

—— 'Truth', reprinted in *Truth and Other Enigmas* (London: Duckworth, 1978).

Dummett, Michael (*cont.*)

—— 'Wittgenstein on Necessity: Some Reflections', reprinted in *The Seas of Language* (Oxford: Oxford University Press, 1993).

—— 'Wittgenstein's Philosophy of Mathematics', reprinted in *Truth and Other Enigmas* (London: Duckworth, 1978).

Edwards, James, *Ethics Without Philosophy: Wittgenstein and the Moral Life* (Tampa, Fla.: University Press of Florida, 1982).

Einstein, Albert, *Relativity: The Special and General Theory*, trans. Robert W. Lawson (London: Methuen, 1960).

Emmett, Dorothy, *The Role of the Unrealisable: A Study in Regulative Ideals* (New York: St Martin's Press, 1994).

Engelmann, Paul, *Letters From Ludwig Wittgenstein, With a Memoir*, ed. B. F. McGuiness and trans. L. Furtmüller (Oxford: Basil Blackwell, 1967).

Evans, Gareth, *The Varieties of Reference*, ed. John McDowell (Oxford: Oxford University Press, 1982).

Feyerabend, Paul, *Against Method: Outline of an Anarchistic Theory of Knowledge* (London: Verso, 1978).

Fichte, J. G., *The Science of Knowledge*, ed. and trans. P. Heath and J. Lachs (New York: Appleton-Century-Crofts, 1970).

Foot, Philippa, 'Morality as a System of Hypothetical Imperatives', reprinted in *Virtues and Vices and Other Essays in Moral Philosophy* (Oxford: Basil Blackwell, 1978).

Forbes, Graeme, 'Realism and Skepticism: Brains in a Vat Revisited', *Journal of Philosophy* **92** (1995).

Franklin, R. L., 'Knowledge, Belief and Understanding', *Philosophical Quarterly* **31** (1981).

Frege, Gottlob, *The Foundations of Arithmetic: A Logico-Mathematical Inquiry Into the Concept of Number*, trans. J. L. Austin (Oxford: Basil Blackwell, 1980).

—— 'On Concept and Object', trans. P. T. Geach and reprinted in *Translations From the Philosophical Writings of Gottlob Frege*, eds. P. T. Geach and Max Black (Oxford: Basil Blackwell, 1952).

—— 'The Thought: A Logical Inquiry', trans. A. M. and Marcelle Quinton and reprinted in P. F. Strawson (ed.), *Philosophical Logic* (Oxford: Oxford University Press, 1967).

Fricker, Miranda, 'Perspectival Realism: Towards a Pluralist Theory of Knowledge', unpublished D.Phil. thesis, Oxford University, 1996.

Gadamer, H.-G., *Truth and Method*, trans. Joel Weinsheimer and Donald Marshall (New York: Crossroad, 1992).

Gale, Richard M. (ed.), *The Philosophy of Time: A Collection of Essays* (Brighton: Harvester Press, 1968).

Gatens, Moira, *Feminism and Philosophy: Perspectives on Difference and Equality* (Cambridge: Polity Press, 1991).

Glover, Jonathan, *I: The Philosophy and Psychology of Personal Identity* (Harmondsworth: Penguin, 1988).

Gödel, Kurt, 'On Formally Undecidable Propositions of *Principia Mathematica* and Related Systems I', trans. Jean van Heijenoort, in Jean van Heijenoort (ed.), *From Frege to Gödel: A Source Book in Mathematical Logic, 1879–1931* (Cambridge, Mass.: Harvard University Press, 1967).

Gombrich, E. H., *Art and Illusion: A Study in the Psychology of Pictorial Representation* (Oxford: Phaidon Press, 1960).

Goodman, Nelson, *Of Minds and Other Matters* (Cambridge, Mass.: Harvard University Press, 1984).

—— *Ways of Worldmaking* (Indianapolis, Ind.: Hackett Publishing Co., 1978).

Gregory, R. L., *The Intelligent Eye* (London: Weidenfeld & Nicolson, 1970).

Hacker, Peter, *Insight and Illusion: Themes in the Philosophy of Wittgenstein*, revised edn. (Oxford: Oxford University Press, 1986).

Harding, Sandra, *The Science Question in Feminism* (Milton Keynes: Open University Press, 1986).

—— *Whose Science? Whose Knowledge? Thinking From Women's Lives* (Milton Keynes: Open University Press, 1991).

Harman, Gilbert, 'Moral Relativism Defended', *Philosophical Review* **84** (1975).

Hautamäki, Antti, 'Points of View and their Logical Analysis', *Acta Philosophica Fennica* **41** (1986).

Heal, Jane, 'The Disinterested Search for Truth', *Proceedings of the Aristotelian Society* **88** (1987–8).

—— *Fact and Meaning: Quine and Wittgenstein on the Philosophy of Language* (Oxford: Basil Blackwell, 1989).

Hegel, G. W. F., *The Encyclopædia of the Philosophical Sciences*, Part I ('Logic'), trans. William Wallace (Oxford: Oxford University Press, 1975).

—— *Phenomenology of Spirit*, trans. A. V. Miller (Oxford: Oxford University Press, 1977).

Heidegger, Martin, *Being and Time*, trans. John Macquarrie and Edward Robinson (Oxford: Basil Blackwell, 1978).

Hollis, Martin, *The Cunning of Reason* (Cambridge: Cambridge University Press, 1987).

Hooker, Brad (ed.), *Truth in Ethics* (Oxford: Basil Blackwell, 1996).

Hookway, Christopher, 'Fallibilism and Objectivity: Science and Ethics', in J. E. J. Altham and Ross Harrison (eds.), *World, Mind, and Ethics: Essays on the Ethical Philosophy of Bernard Williams* (Cambridge: Cambridge University Press, 1995).

Hookway, Christopher, *Quine: Language, Experience and Reality* (Oxford: Polity Press, 1988).

—— *Scepticism* (London: Routledge, 1990).

Hopkins, James, 'Wittgenstein and Physicalism', *Proceedings of the Aristotelian Society* 75 (1974–5).

Horgby, Ingvar, 'The Double Awareness in Heidegger and Wittgenstein', *Inquiry* 2 (1959).

Hornsby, Jennifer, 'Agency and Causal Explanation', in John Heil and Alfred Mele (eds.), *Mental Causation* (Oxford: Oxford University Press, 1993).

Horwich, Paul, *Truth* (Oxford: Basil Blackwell, 1990).

Hossack, Keith G., 'A Problem about the Meaning of Intuitionistic Negation', *Mind* 99 (1990).

Hume, David, *Enquiry Concerning the Principles of Morals*, ed. L. A. Selby-Bigge, revised P. H. Nidditch (Oxford: Oxford University Press, 1975).

—— *A Treatise of Human Nature*, ed. L. A. Selby-Bigge, revised P. H. Nidditch (Oxford: Oxford University Press, 1978).

Husserl, Edmund, *Ideas: General Introduction to Pure Phenomenology*, trans. W. R. Boyce Gibson (London: Allen & Unwin, 1931).

Irigaray, Luce, 'Divine Women', in *Sexes and Genealogies*, trans. Gillian C. Gill (New York: Columbia University Press, 1993).

—— *Elemental Passions*, trans. Joanne Collie and Judith Still (London: Athlone Press, 1992).

—— 'An Ethics of Sexual Difference', in *An Ethics of Sexual Difference*, trans. Carolyn Burke and Gillian C. Gill (London: Athlone Press, 1993).

—— *This Sex Which is Not One*, trans. Catherine Porter and Carolyn Burke (Ithaca, NY: Cornell University Press, 1977).

Isaacson, Daniel, 'Arithmetical Truths and Hidden Higher-Order Concepts', reprinted in W. D. Hart (ed.), *The Philosophy of Mathematics* (Oxford: Oxford University Press, 1996).

Jackson, Frank, 'What Mary Didn't Know', *Journal of Philosophy* 83 (1986).

Janik, Allan, and Toulmin, Stephen, *Wittgenstein's Vienna* (New York: Touchstone, 1973).

Jardine, Nicholas, 'The Possibility of Absolutism', in D. H. Mellor (ed.),

Science, Belief, and Behaviour: Essays in Honour of R. B. Braithwaite (Cambridge: Cambridge University Press, 1980).

—— 'Science, Ethics, and Objectivity', in J. E. J. Altham and Ross Harrison (eds.), *World, Mind, and Ethics: Essays on the Ethical Philosophy of Bernard Williams* (Cambridge: Cambridge University Press, 1995).

Jaspers, Carl, *The Perennial Scope of Philosophy*, trans. Ralph Manheim (London: Routledge & Kegan Paul, 1950).

Jones, O. R., 'Can One Believe What One Knows?', *Philosophical Review* **84** (1975).

Kant, Immanuel, *Critique of Judgement*, trans. James Creed Meredith (Oxford: Oxford University Press, 1952).

—— *Critique of Practical Reason*, trans. Lewis White Beck (Indianapolis, Ind.: Bobbs-Merrill, 1956).

—— *Critique of Pure Reason*, trans. Norman Kemp Smith (London: Macmillan, 1933).

—— *Groundwork of the Metaphysic of Morals*, trans. H. J. Paton (New York: Harper & Row, 1964).

—— *Opus Postumum*, ed. Eckart Förster and trans. Eckart Förster and Michael Rosen (Cambridge: Cambridge University Press, 1993).

—— *Prolegomena to Any Future Metaphysics*, trans. Lewis White Beck (Indianapolis, Ind.: Bobbs-Merrill, 1950).

Katz, David, *Animals and Men: Studies in Comparative Psychology* (Harmondsworth: Penguin, 1953).

Kemal, Salim, *Kant and Fine Art: An Essay on Kant and the Philosophy of Fine Art and Culture* (Oxford: Oxford University Press, 1986).

Kierkegaard, Søren, *The Sickness Unto Death*, trans. Walter Lowrie (Princeton, NJ: Princeton University Press, 1954).

Klempner, Geoffrey V., *Naïve Metaphysics: A Theory of Subjective and Objective Worlds* (Aldershot: Avebury, 1994).

Kuhn, Thomas, 'Second Thoughts on Paradigms', in Frederick Suppe (ed.), *The Structure of Scientific Theories* (Chicago, Ill.: University of Illinois Press, 1977).

—— *The Structure of Scientific Revolutions* (Chicago, Ill.: University of Chicago Press, 1962).

Lear, Jonathan, 'The Disappearing "We"', *Proceedings of the Arisotelian Society* Supp. Vol. **58** (1984).

—— 'Leaving the World Alone', *Journal of Philosophy* **79** (1982).

—— 'Transcendental Anthropology', in Philip Pettit and John McDowell (eds.), *Subject, Thought, and Context* (Oxford: Oxford University Press, 1986).

Le Poidevin, Robin and MacBeath, Murray (eds.), *The Philosophy of Time* (Oxford: Oxford University Press, 1993).

Levinas, Emmanuel, *Totality and Infinity: An Essay on Exteriority*, trans. Alphonso Lingis (Dordrecht: Kluwer Academic Publishers, 1991).

Lewis, David, 'Attitudes *De Dicto* and *De Se*', reprinted in *Philosophical Papers*, vol. i (New York: Oxford University Press, 1983).

—— 'Mad Pain and Martian Pain', reprinted in *Philosophical Papers*, vol. i (New York: Oxford University Press, 1983).

—— 'Survival and Identity', reprinted in *Philosophical Papers*, vol. i (New York: Oxford University Press, 1983).

—— 'What Experience Teaches', in W. G. Lycan (ed.), *Mind and Cognition: A Reader* (Oxford: Basil Blackwell, 1990).

Lloyd, Genevieve, *Being in Time: Selves and Narrators in Philosophy and Literature* (London: Routledge, 1993).

—— *The Man of Reason: 'Male' and 'Female' in Western Philosophy* (London: Methuen, 1984).

Locke, John, *Essay Concerning Human Understanding*, ed. John Yolton (London: Dent, 1965).

Lucas, John, *Space, Time, and Causality: An Essay in Natural Philosophy* (Oxford: Oxford University Press, 1984).

Lyotard, Jean-François, *The Postmodern Condition: A Report on Knowledge*, trans. Geoffrey Bennington and Brian Massumi (Minneapolis, Minn.: Minnesota University Press, 1979).

McDowell, John, 'Are Moral Requirements Hypothetical Imperatives?', *Proceedings of the Aristotelian Society* Supp. Vol. **52** (1978).

—— 'Following a Rule', reprinted in A. W. Moore (ed.), *Meaning and Reference* (Oxford: Oxford University Press, 1993).

—— 'Mathematical Platonism and Dummettian Anti-Realism', *Dialectica* **43** (1989).

—— 'Might There Be External Reasons?', in J. E. J. Altham and Ross Harrison (eds.), *World, Mind, and Nature: Essays on the Ethical Philosophy of Bernard Williams* (Cambridge: Cambridge University Press, 1995).

—— *Mind and World* (Cambridge, Mass.: Harvard University Press, 1994).

—— 'Non-Cognitivism and Rule-Following', in S. H. Holtzmann and C. M. Leich (eds.), *Wittgenstein: To Follow a Rule* (London: Routledge & Kegan Paul, 1981).

—— 'On "The Reality of the Past"', in Christopher Hookway and Philip Pettit (eds.), *Action and Interpretation* (Cambridge: Cambridge University Press, 1977).

—— 'Quotation and Saying That', in Mark Platts (ed.), *Reference, Truth and Reality: Essays on the Philosophy of Language* (London: Routledge & Kegan Paul, 1980).

McGinn, Colin, *The Subjective View: Secondary Qualities and Indexical Thoughts* (Oxford: Oxford University Press, 1983).

McGuiness, Brian, 'The Mysticism in the *Tractatus*', *Philosophical Review* **75** (1966).

MacIntyre, Alisdair, *After Virtue: A Study in Moral Theory* (London: Duckworth, 1981).

McTaggart, J. M. E., *The Nature of Existence* (Cambridge: Cambridge University Press, vol. i, 1921; vol. ii, 1927).

Malcolm, Norman, 'Wittgenstein and Idealism', in Godfrey Vesey (ed.), *Idealism Past and Present* (Cambridge: Cambridge University Press, 1982).

Matthews, H. E., 'Strawson on Transcendental Idealism', reprinted in Ralph C. S. Walker (ed.), *Kant on Pure Reason* (Oxford: Oxford University Press, 1982).

Melia, Joseph, 'Anti-Realism Untouched', *Mind* **100** (1991).

Mellor, D. H., 'Analytic Philosophy and the Self', reprinted in *Matters of Metaphysics* (Cambridge: Cambridge University Press, 1991).

—— 'I and Now', reprinted in *Matters of Metaphysics* (Cambridge: Cambridge University Press, 1991).

—— 'Nothing Like Experience', *Proceedings of the Aristotelian Society* **93** (1992–3).

—— 'The Unreality of Tense', in Robin Le Poidevin and Murray MacBeath (eds.), *The Philosophy of Time* (Oxford: Oxford University Press, 1993).

Merleau-Ponty, M., *Phenomenology of Perception*, trans. Colin Smith (London: Routledge & Kegan Paul, 1962).

Moline, Jon, 'On Points of View', *American Philosophical Quarterly* **5** (1968).

Moore, A. W., 'Beauty in the Transcendental Idealism of Kant and Wittgenstein', *British Journal of Aesthetics* **27** (1987).

—— 'How Significant is the Use / Mention Distinction?', *Analysis* **46** (1986).

—— 'Human Finitude, Ineffability, Idealism, Contingency', *Noûs* **26** (1992).

—— 'Ineffability and Reflection: An Outline of the Concept of Knowledge', *European Journal of Philosophy* **1** (1993).

—— *The Infinite* (London: Routledge, 1990).

—— 'On Saying and Showing', *Philosophy* **62** (1987).

—— 'On There Being Nothing Else to Think, or Want, or Do', in Sabina Lovibond and S. G. Williams (eds.), *Essays for David Wiggins: Identity, Truth, and Value* (Oxford: Basil Blackwell, 1996).

Moore, A. W. (*cont.*)
—— 'Points of View', *Philosophical Quarterly* 37 (1987).
—— 'Solipsism and Subjectivity', *European Journal of Philosophy* 4 (1996).
—— 'Transcendental Idealism in Wittgenstein, and Theories of Meaning', *Philosophical Quarterly* 35 (1985).
Moravcsik, J. M., 'Understanding', *Dialectica* 33 (1979).
Murdoch, Iris, *Metaphysics as a Guide to Morals* (Harmondsworth: Penguin, 1993).
—— *The Sovereignty of Good* (London: Ark Paperbacks, 1985).
Nagel, Thomas, *Equality and Partiality* (New York: Oxford University Press, 1991).
—— *The Possibility of Altruism* (Princeton, NJ: Princeton University Press, 1978).
—— 'Subjective and Objective', reprinted in *Mortal Questions* (Cambridge: Cambridge University Press, 1979).
—— *The View From Nowhere* (New York: Oxford University Press, 1986).
—— 'What is it Like to be a Bat?', reprinted in *Mortal Questions* (Cambridge: Cambridge University Press, 1979).
Nehamas, Alexander, *Nietzsche: Life as Literature* (Cambridge, Mass.: Harvard University Press, 1985).
Nemirow, Laurence, 'Physicalism and the Cognitive Role of Acquaintance', in W. G. Lycan (ed.), *Mind and Cognition* (Oxford: Basil Blackwell, 1990).
—— 'Review of Thomas Nagel's *Mortal Questions*', *Philosophical Review* 89 (1980).
Newton, Isaac (1687) *Mathematical Principles of Natural Philosophy*, trans. Andrew Motte and Florian Cajori (Berkeley, Calif.: University of California Press, 1947).
Nietzsche, Friedrich, *Beyond Good and Evil*, trans. R. J. Hollingdale (Harmondsworth: Penguin, 1973).
—— *The Gay Science*, trans. Walter Kaufmann (New York: Random House, 1974).
—— *On the Genealogy of Morals*, trans. Walter Kaufmann and R. J. Hollingdale (New York: Random House, 1968).
—— 'On Truth and Lies in a Nonmoral Sense', in *Philosophy and Truth: Selections From Nietzsche's Notebooks of the Early 1870s*, trans. and ed. Daniel Breazeale (Brighton: Harvester Press, 1979).
—— *Thus Spoke Zarathustra*, trans. R. J. Hollingdale (Harmondsworth: Penguin, 1969).

—— *The Will to Power*, trans. Walter Kaufmann and R. J. Hollingdale and ed. Walter Kaufmann (New York: Random House, 1967).

Norris, Christopher, *Derrida* (London: Fontana, 1987).

Parfit, Derek, *The Metaphysics of the Self* (Oxford: Basil Blackwell, forthcoming).

—— 'Personal Identity', reprinted in Jonathan Glover (ed.), *The Philosophy of Mind* (Oxford: Oxford University Press, 1976).

—— *Reasons and Persons* (Oxford: Oxford University Press, 1984).

Parrett, Herman, 'Significance and Understanding', *Dialectica* 33 (1979).

Pears, David, *The False Prison: A Study in the Development of Wittgenstein's Philosophy* (Oxford: Oxford University Press, vol. i, 1987; vol. ii, 1988).

—— *What is Knowledge?* (London: Allen & Unwin, 1971).

—— *Wittgenstein*, 2nd edn. (London: Fontana, 1985).

Perry, John, *The Problem of the Essential Indexical and Other Essays* (New York: Oxford University Press, 1993).

Perry, John, and Blackburn, Simon, 'Thoughts without Representation', *Proceedings of the Aristotelian Society* Supp. Vol. **60** (1986).

Pettit, Philip and McDowell, John (eds.), *Subject, Thought, and Context* (Oxford: Oxford University Press, 1986).

Plato, *Letters*, trans. L. A. Post, in *The Collected Dialogues*, ed. Edith Hamilton and Huntington Cairns (Princeton, NJ: Princeton University Press, 1961).

Polanyi, Michael, *Personal Knowledge: Towards a Post-Critical Philosophy* (London: Routledge & Kegan Paul, 1962).

—— 'Tacit Knowing', in *The Tacit Dimension* (London: Routledge & Kegan Paul, 1967).

Popper, Karl R., *Conjectures and Refutations* (London: Routledge & Kegan Paul, 1965).

Priest, Graham, *Beyond the Limits of Thought* (Cambridge: Cambridge University Press, 1995).

Prior, Arthur N., 'Changes in Events and Changes in Things', reprinted in Robin Le Poidevin and Murray MacBeath (eds.), *The Philosophy of Time* (Oxford: Oxford University Press, 1993).

Proust, Marcel, *Remembrance of Things Past*, trans. C. K. Scott Moncrief, Terence Kilmartin, and Andreas Mayor, 3 vols. (Harmondsworth: Penguin, 1983).

Putnam, Hilary, 'Comments and Replies', in Peter Clark and Bob Hale (eds.), *Reading Putnam* (Oxford: Basil Blackwell, 1994).

Putnam, Hilary (*cont.*)

—— 'On Wittgenstein's Philosophy of Mathematics', *Proceedings of the Aristotelian Society* Supp. Vol. **70** (1996).

—— 'Pragmatism', *Proceedings of the Aristotelian Society* **95** (1994–5).

—— *Reason, Truth and History* (Cambridge: Cambridge University Press, 1981).

—— *Renewing Philosophy* (Cambridge, Mass.: Harvard University Press, 1992).

Quine, W. V., 'Goodman's *Ways of Worldmaking*', reprinted in *Theories and Things* (Cambridge, Mass.: Harvard University Press, 1981).

—— 'Facts of the Matter', in R. W. Shahan and K. R. Merrill (eds.), *American Philosophy From Edwards to Quine* (Norman, Okla.: University of Oklahoma Press, 1977).

—— 'Mind and Verbal Dispositions', reprinted in A. W. Moore (ed.), *Meaning and Reference* (Oxford: Oxford University Press, 1993).

—— 'On Empirically Equivalent Systems of the World', *Erkenntnis* **9** (1975).

—— *Pursuit of Truth* (Cambridge, Mass.: Harvard University Press, 1990).

—— 'Two Dogmas of Empiricism', reprinted in *From a Logical Point of View: Logico-Philosophical Essays* (New York: Harper & Row, 1961).

—— *Word and Object* (Cambridge, Mass.: MIT Press, 1960).

Rawls, John, *A Theory of Justice* (Cambridge, Mass.: Harvard University Press, 1972).

Raz, Joseph (ed.), *Practical Reasoning* (Oxford: Oxford University Press, 1978).

Ricoeur, Paul, *Oneself as Another*, trans. Kathleen Blamey (Chicago, Ill.: University of Chicago Press, 1992).

—— *Time and Narrative*, trans. Kathleen McLaughlin and David Pellauer (Chicago, Ill.: University of Chicago Press, vol. i, 1984; vol. ii, 1985; vol. iii, 1987).

Robinson, Howard, 'The Anti-Materialist Strategy and the "Knowledge Argument"', in Howard Robinson (ed.), *Objections to Physicalism* (Oxford: Oxford University Press, 1993).

—— (ed.), *Objections to Physicalism* (Oxford: Oxford University Press, 1993).

Rorty, Richard, *Philosophy and the Mirror of Nature* (Oxford: Basil Blackwell, 1980).

—— 'Putnam and the Relativisit Menace', *Journal of Philosophy* **90** (1993).

—— 'The World Well Lost', reprinted in *The Consequences of Pragmatism* (Brighton: Harvester Press, 1982).

Rosen, Gideon, 'Objectivity and Modern Idealism: What is the Question?', in Michaelis Michael and John O'Leary-Hawthorne (eds.), *Philosophy of Mind* (Dordrecht: Kluwer Academic Publishers, 1994).

Rucker, Rudy, *Infinity and the Mind: The Science and Philosophy of the Infinite* (Brighton: Harvester Press, 1982).

Ryle, Gilbert, *The Concept of Mind* (London: Hutchinson, 1949).

Sacks, Mark, 'Transcendental Features and Transcendental Constraints', *International Journal of Philosophical Studies* **5** (1997).

—— *The World We Found: The Limits of Ontological Talk* (London: Duckworth, 1989).

Sartre, Jean-Paul, *Being and Nothingness: An Essay in Phenomenological Ontology*, trans. H. E. Barnes (London: Methuen, 1957).

Saussure, Ferdinand de, *A Course in General Linguistics*, trans. Roy Harris (London: Duckworth, 1983).

Scheffler, Israel, *Conditions of Knowledge: An Introduction to Epistemology and Education* (Glenview, Ill.: Scott, Foreman & Co., 1965).

Schopenhauer, Arthur, *The World as Will and Idea*, trans. R. B. Haldane and J. Kemp (London: Routledge & Kegan Paul, 1950).

Sellars, Wilfrid, 'Empiricism and the Philosophy of Mind', reprinted in *Science, Perception and Reality* (London: Routledge & Kegan Paul, 1963).

Sen, Amartya, 'Positional Objectivity', *Philosophy and Public Affairs* **22** (1993).

Shoemaker, Sydney, 'Critical Notice of Parfit's *Reasons and Persons*', *Mind* **94** (1985).

Sidgwick, Henry, *The Methods of Ethics* (London: Macmillan, 1962).

Smith, Michael, *The Moral Problem* (Oxford: Basil Blackwell, 1994).

Smith, Michael, Lewis, David, and Johnston, Mark, 'Dispositional Theories of Value', *Proceedings of the Aristotelian Society* Supp. Vol. **63** (1989).

Snowdon, Paul, 'Knowing How and Knowing That: A Distinction and its Uses Reconsidered' (forthcoming).

Sosa, Ernest, 'Putnam's Pragmatic Realism', *Journal of Philosophy* **90** (1993).

Spinoza, Baruch, *Ethics*, trans. Andrew Boyle (London: Dent, 1959).

Standish, Paul, *Beyond the Self: Wittgenstein, Heidegger and the Limits of Language* (Aldershot: Avebury, 1992).

Stenius, Erik, *Wittgenstein's 'Tractatus': A Critical Exposition of its Main Lines of Thought* (Oxford: Basil Blackwell, 1964).

Strawson, Galen, *The Secret Connexion: Causation, Realism, and David Hume* (Oxford: Oxford University Press, 1989).

Strawson, P. F., *The Bounds of Sense: An Essay on Kant's 'Critique of Pure Reason'* (London: Methuen, 1966).

Stroud, Barry, *The Significance of Philosophical Scepticism* (Oxford: Oxford University Press, 1984).

Sullivan, Peter M., 'The '"Truth" in Solipsism and Wittgenstein's Rejection of the A Priori', *European Journal of Philosophy* 4 (1996).

Tanner, Michael, *Nietzsche* (Oxford: Oxford University Press, 1994).

Taylor, Charles, *Sources of the Self: The Making of Modern Identity* (Cambridge, Mass.: Harvard University Press, 1989).

Thomson, Garrett, 'Kant's Problem with Ugliness', *Journal of Aesthetics and Art Criticism* **50** (1992).

—— 'The Weak, the Strong and the Mild—Readings of Kant's Ontology', *Ratio* (NS) **5** (1992).

Vaihinger, Hans, *The Philosophy of 'As If': A System of the Theoretical, Practical and Religious Fictions of Mankind*, trans. C. K. Ogden (London: Routledge & Kegan Paul, 1935).

Vendler, Zeno, *Res Cogitans: An Essay in Rational Psychology* (Ithaca, NY: Cornell University Press, 1972).

Warnock, Mary, *Imagination and Time* (Oxford: Basil Blackwell, 1994).

White, A. R., *The Nature of Knowledge* (Totowa, NJ: Rowman & Littlefield, 1982).

Whorf, Benjamin Lee, 'An American Indian Model of the Universe', reprinted in *Language, Thought and Reality: Selected Writings of Benjamin Lee Whorf*, ed. J. B. Carroll (Cambridge, Mass.: MIT Press, 1956).

Wiggins, David, *Needs, Values, Truth: Essays in the Philosophy of Value* (Oxford: Basil Blackwell, 1987).

—— 'Truth, and Truth as Predicated of Moral Judgments', in *Needs, Values, Truth: Essays in the Philosophy of Value* (Oxford: Basil Blackwell, 1987).

—— 'Universalizability, Impartiality, Truth', in *Needs, Values, Truth: Essays in the Philosophy of Value* (Oxford: Basil Blackwell, 1987).

Williams, Bernard, 'Deciding to Believe', reprinted in *Problems of the Self* (Cambridge: Cambridge University Press, 1973).

—— *Descartes: The Project of Pure Enquiry* (Harmondsworth: Penguin, 1978).

—— *Ethics and the Limits of Philosophy* (London: Fontana, 1985).

—— 'Internal and External Reasons', reprinted in *Moral Luck* (Cambridge: Cambridge University Press, 1981).

—— *Morality: An Introduction to Ethics* (Cambridge: Cambridge University Press, 1972).

—— 'Persons, Character and Morality', reprinted in *Moral Luck* (Cambridge: Cambridge University Press, 1981).

—— *Problems of the Self* (Cambridge: Cambridge University Press, 1973).

—— 'Wittgenstein and Idealism', reprinted in *Moral Luck* (Cambridge: Cambridge University Press, 1981).

Williams, Michael, *Unnatural Doubts: Epistemological Realism and the Basis of Scepticism* (Oxford: Basil Blackwell, 1991).

Williamson, Timothy, 'Never Say Never', *Topoi* **13** (1994).

Wittgenstein, Ludwig, *Culture and Value*, ed. G. H. von Wright with Heikki Nyman and trans. Peter Winch (Oxford: Basil Blackwell, 1980).

—— *Notebooks: 1914–1916*, ed. G. H. von Wright and G. E. M. Anscombe and trans. G. E. M. Anscombe (Oxford: Basil Blackwell, 1979).

—— *On Certainty*, ed. G. E. M. Anscombe and G. H. von Wright and trans. Denis Paul and G. E. M. Anscombe (Oxford: Basil Blackwell, 1969).

—— *Philosophical Grammar*, ed. Rush Rhees and trans. Anthony Kenny (Oxford: Basil Blackwell, 1974).

—— *Philosophical Investigations*, trans. G. E. M. Anscombe, revised edn. (Oxford: Basil Blackwell, 1974).

—— *Philosophical Remarks*, ed. Rush Rhees and trans. Raymond Hargreaves and Roger White (Oxford: Basil Blackwell, 1975).

—— *Remarks on the Foundations of Mathematics*, ed. G. H. von Wright, Rush Rhees, and G. E. M. Anscombe and trans. G. E. M. Anscombe, 3rd edn. (Oxford: Basil Blackwell, 1978).

—— *Tractatus Logico-Philosophicus*, trans. D. F. Pears and B. F. McGuiness (London: Routledge & Kegan Paul, 1961).

—— *Zettel*, ed. G. E. M. Anscombe and G. H. von Wright and trans. G. E. M. Anscombe (Oxford: Basil Blackwell, 1967).

Wright, Crispin, 'About "The Philosophical Significance of Gödel's Theorem": Some Issues', in Brian McGuinness and Gianluigi Oliveri (eds.), *The Philosophy of Michael Dummett* (Dordrecht: Kluwer Academic Publishers, 1994).

—— 'Putnam's Proof that We are not Brains in a Vat', in Peter Clark and Bob Hale (eds.), *Reading Putnam* (Oxford: Basil Blackwell, 1994).

—— *Realism, Meaning and Truth* (Oxford: Basil Blackwell, 1987).

—— *Truth and Objectivity* (Cambridge, Mass.: Harvard University Press, 1992).

—— *Wittgenstein on the Foundations of Mathematics* (London: Duckworth, 1979).

Young, Julian, 'Wittgenstein, Kant, Schopenhauer, and Critical Philosophy', *Theoria* **50** (1984).

Ziff, Paul, *Epistemic Analysis: A Coherence Theory of Knowledge* (Dordrecht: Reidel, 1984).

INDEX

Note: An asterisk indicates something defined in the glossary.

truth (*cont.*)

partial realism; perspectival representations, how they are made true; realism; representations

*type of a representation 3, 9–17 *passim*,
22, 31–2, 36, 47–52 *passim*, 55, 63, 80,
85, 90, 98–9, 102, 123, 143–4

ultimate constituents of reality 232–3, 237,
250

*unconditionedness 80, 261–9 *passim*,
275–6

understanding 7, 11, 22–3, 26, 53–5, 76, 98,
108, 122–3, 130–1, 135, 139, 152,
159–64 *passim*, 166, 183–6, 187 n., 191,
203, 205–6, 213, 217, 220, 225, 239–50
passim, 259, 264–5, 267, 271, 273

as a species of knowledge xii, 161, 166,
183–6 *passim*, 189, 192, 196, 203, 225

sometimes has nothing to answer to xii,
162, 184–5, 189, 225, 273; *see also* concepts, cannot be right or wrong/have
nothing to answer to; ineffable knowledge, has nothing to answer to

see also communication; concepts; interpretation; language and languages;
misunderstanding; self-understanding

unity of reality *see under* reality

universal quantification and the universal
quantifier 110, 112, 119, 237–8, 244–5

see also Domain Dilemma

use/mention distinction 157 n., 250

values and evaluation x, xiii, 2, 4, 8, 12,
24–6, 51, 78, 80, 86–9, 100–7 *passim*,
113, 126, 129, 153, 225, 230–1, 237,
255, 263, 269–75, 278

aesthetic *see* aesthetics and aesthetic
evaluation

rationality as a value *see under* rationality

the incompatibility of values *see under*
incompatibility

their perspectival character and their relativity xiii, 26, 30, 33–4, 87, 129, 174,
253, 257, 262–3, 270–7 *passim*; *see also*
relativism

the value of our aspiration to be infi-
nite/craving for infinitude xiii, 253,
274–7

truth as a value *see under* truth

see also ethics and morality; showing and

being shown, our being shown that
the three limit notions are of value
tout court; three limit notions, the

Versatility (= the first mark of knowledge)
166, 176–8, 182–5 *passim*

vindication of a representation 35–7, 261,
266

*we

are conscious of ourselves as finite (=
the second principle) xiii, 115, 191,
195, 210, 212, 224, 232–6 *passim*, 243,
253–60 *passim*; *see also* Basic Assumption, our knowledge of it; self-
consciousness

are finite (= the first principle) x, xiii, 3,
158, 160, 190–1, 195, 205, 209–15 *passim*, 224, 232, 235, 237, 243–9 *passim*,
253–62 *passim*, 268, 270, 276–8; *see
also* Basic Assumption, its relation to
our finitude; death; knowledge, of
how to be finite; particularity of each
person's existence

aspire to be infinite/crave infinitude (=
the third principle) x, xi, xiii, 20, 37,
195, 205, 210–14, 220–1, 224, 232–5
passim, 253–78 *passim*; *see also* hubris;
values and evaluation, the value of
our aspiration to be infinite/craving
for infinitude

defined by the three principles 210, 220,
224, 232, 254, 256, 267, 269

exist only from our own point of view
9, 105, 224–8 *passim*, 232, 237, 254–6,
276; *see also* self-creation

the question who "we" are and the different ways of answering it 80, 99,
110–12, 115, 118, 123, 131–9 *passim*,
158, 198, 210; *see also* human beings;
persons

the various ways in which we carry
on/our various practices 36, 86, 89,
92–3, 128–36 *passim*, 160, 162–4, 207,
229, 231, 245, 248; *see also* forms of
life

*weak entailment 15–16, 21, 35, 43, 49, 76,
230

Whorf, Benjamin Lee 78, 92–5

Wiggins, David 16 n.

Williams, Bernard xi, 1, 36 nn., 38, 41, 61,
67, 130, 136, 175 n., 187–8, 269 n.

Wittgenstein, Ludwig 120, 126, 149, 164,
214, 259 n.